TEXTBOOKS AND SCHOOLING
IN THE UNITED STATES

TEXTBOOKS AND SCHOOLING
IN THE UNITED STATES

Eighty-ninth Yearbook of the
National Society for the Study of Education

PART I

Edited by
DAVID L. ELLIOTT AND ARTHUR WOODWARD

Editor for the Society
KENNETH J. REHAGE

19 NSSE 90

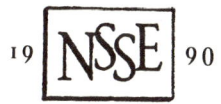

Distributed by THE UNIVERSITY OF CHICAGO PRESS ● CHICAGO, ILLINOIS

The National Society for the Study of Education

Founded in 1901 as successor to the National Herbart Society, the National Society for the Study of Education has provided a means by which the results of serious study of educational issues could become a basis for informed discussion of those issues. The Society's two-volume yearbooks, now in their eighty-ninth year of publication, reflect the thoughtful attention given to a wide range of educational problems during those years. In 1971 the Society inaugurated a series of substantial publications on Contemporary Educational Issues to supplement the yearbooks. Each year the Society's publications contain contributions to the literature of education from more than a hundred scholars and practitioners who are doing significant work in their respective fields.

An elected Board of Directors selects the subjects with which volumes in the yearbook series are to deal and appoints committees to oversee the preparation of manuscripts. A special committee created by the Board performs similar functions for the series on Contemporary Educational Issues.

The Society's publications are distributed each year without charge to members in the United States, Canada, and elsewhere throughout the world. The Society welcomes as members all individuals who desire to receive its publications. Information about current dues may be found in the back pages of this volume.

This volume, *Textbooks and Schooling in the United States,* is Part I of the Eighty-ninth Yearbook of the Society. Part II, which is published at the same time, is entitled *Educational Leadership and Changing Contexts of Families, Communities, and Schools.*

A listing of the Society's publications still available for purchase may be found in the back pages of this volume.

Library of Congress Catalog Number: 89-063573
ISSN: 0077-5762

Published 1990 by
THE NATIONAL SOCIETY FOR THE STUDY OF EDUCATION

5835 Kimbark Avenue, Chicago, Illinois 60637
© 1990 by the National Society for the Study of Education

First Printing, 5,000 Copies

Printed in the United States of America

v

Acknowledgment

As editors of this volume, David Elliott and Arthur Woodward have brought out a publication that effectively illuminates a wide range of issues surrounding the role of the textbook in elementary and secondary schools in the United States. They have assembled contributions from a distinguished set of authors, all of whom have been deeply involved in one way or another with problems relating to textbooks and instructional materials.

The National Society for the Study of Education is most grateful to the editors, to their advisory committee, and to each of the authors. Together they have produced a volume that will be a significant contribution to the Society's series of yearbooks.

Preface

In 1931 the National Society for the Study of Education published its Thirtieth Yearbook, *The Textbook in American Education*. Since then only a few benchmark publications have focused on the role of textbooks in school programs. One of these was *Text Materials in Modern Education: A Comprehensive Platform for Research*, edited by Lee J. Cronbach (Urbana, IL: University of Illinois Press, 1955). Another was *The Textbook in American Society*, edited by John Y. Cole and Thomas G. Sticht (Washington, DC: Library of Congress, 1981), which was based on a conference held at the Library of Congress in May, 1979. Each of these volumes dealt with the contemporary "state of the art" and with major issues involved in the content, production, selection and adoption, and use of elementary and secondary textbooks. However, if we use the results of a literature search as an indicator, interest in the school textbook as an object of study during the years intervening between these publications has at best been lukewarm. Indeed, in the process of preparing a recently published annotated bibliography of research and criticism on textbooks, we found relatively few titles issued between 1930 and 1970. Although there were brief flurries of interest during this forty-year period, and while a few topics such as the treatment of certain ethnic groups in textbooks have persisted as favorite dissertation topics, textbooks were not of much interest to educational researchers.

Since the late 1970s, however, interest has picked up markedly, energized in part by such influential reports as *A Nation at Risk*, which acknowledged the crucial part textbooks play in schooling (and also concluded that they needed improvement). So it is that research into the textbook and related issues has gained status as an acceptable field of scholarly endeavor. One indicator of this new status is the growth of the American Educational Research Association Special Interest Group on Textbooks, Textbook Publishing, Schooling, which has been sponsoring symposiums and paper sessions at annual meetings of AERA during most of this decade.

The Thirtieth NSSE Yearbook was published at a time of strong initiatives in school program reform spearheaded by advocates of progressive education. The current volume, the Society's Eighty-ninth Yearbook, comes just under sixty years later at a time when once more general interest in school reform is high. This time, however, evidence is mounting that the textbook has emerged from behind the scenes to become a major focus of the reform process, along with state and local school improvement efforts and a newly awakened interest in teacher professionalism and teacher education. Now more than ever before there is a realization that textbooks are an enduring and influential part of schooling, that they define much of what teachers teach and students learn, and that they are therefore worthy objects of discussion, debate, and research.

As the contributors to this volume indicate, textbooks are both an enduring feature and a present problem of great magnitude as we continue to think about improving the quality of education in this country. It is our hope that this yearbook will not only present a review of the issues of the present but also point directions for research and development in the future, and thus be another benchmark in scholarship on the textbook.

We would like to thank all the chapter authors for their contributions to this volume. We would like to thank also a number of people who have given us their help and encouragement. A. Harry Passow was an early advocate for this venture. In addition to writing chapters, Ian Westbury and Jeanne Chall were particularly helpful as we gave shape to the volume. We have also received much support from our friends and spouses. And, of course, Kenneth Rehage provided the now legendary encouragement and expertise that is taken for granted by the readers of NSSE yearbooks.

DAVID L. ELLIOTT
ARTHUR WOODWARD

Table of Contents

Section One
Instructional Materials in the Twentieth Century

Section Two
The Textbook Industry

PAGE

Section Three

Textbooks and Society

Section Four

Curriculum and Instructional Materials in the Future

Section One
INSTRUCTIONAL MATERIALS
IN THE TWENTIETH CENTURY

CHAPTER I

Textbooks, Textbook Publishers, and the Quality of Schooling

IAN WESTBURY

It is a truism that textbooks are the central tools and the central objects of attention in all modern forms of schooling. The implicit and explicit tasks that they prescribe define the core work of the school. As givens in particular situations, the textbooks that teachers have are the most significant resource for their teaching *and* often the most significant limiting force they face as they seek to accomplish their purposes. Educational development and curriculum development thus go hand in hand with textbook development and distribution. Yet, in spite of this centrality of the textbook to the school, and in spite of the persistent attention that has been given to *some* aspects of textbooks (e.g., design, readability, bias), the textbook seen holistically has been until quite recently a nearly invisible component of schooling, at least from the viewpoint of conventional educational research. The present volume, for example, is the first yearbook of the National Society for the Study of Education devoted to textbooks since the publication in 1931 of the Society's Thirtieth Yearbook, *The Textbook in American Education.*[1]

After this long period of neglect, however, there has been in recent years a torrent of writing and commentary about the textbooks and other materials used in American schools. The themes of this work have ranged far, as the chapters of this Yearbook suggest. Textbooks

1

are being criticized for their representation of content, their implicit assumptions about teachers, students, teaching and learning, and for their social and cultural biases. The industry that produces these textbooks has been charged with shoddy workmanship. However, research seeking guidelines for the improvement of all aspects of school textbooks has also burgeoned and, for some, this new interest in the textbook holds the promise that new kinds of books, and perhaps renewed approaches to teaching and learning, are possible.

The Role of the Textbook in the School

What role does the textbook play in modern systems of schooling? In all modern school systems the textbook has long served not only to support instruction but also to symbolize that instruction—in other words, the textbook defines the curriculum. In the American school system, however, this latter function of the textbook assumes a special force because of the absence of effective national regulation of the curriculum or of textbooks by way of official syllabi or external examinations. The textbooks a school, a district, or a state approves or uses are often the *only* symbols of what schools at large do. As a result, almost all concern about the curriculum finds its focus in concern about the textbooks used and this, in turn, leads to discussion of the developers and distributors of those texts—authors and publishers. But one often unnoticed by-product of this form of argument is the assumption that the source of control of what schools do is not in the hands of teachers and communities but, rather, in the hands of an industry which, as I will emphasize here, is profit-seeking. However, as I will argue, while it *is* the case that textbook publishers are in practice the only "national" agency with a presence as large-scale, nationally directed curriculum developers, it is not clear that these publishers have either an *effective* capability for this work or the authority they would need to do it effectively. Likewise, it is not clear that the seeming responsibility of publishers for textbook development can or should be separated analytically from the responsibilities of the users of these books or the regulators of the curriculum.

However, although textbooks, and textbook publishers, have a special place in schools in the United States, it must be recognized that the role the textbook has assumed in the American school only modulates a pattern found in *all* modern school systems. Teaching which has the textbook at its necessary heart is the sine qua non of all modern forms of teaching—and, with all of its obvious faults, such teaching is much more effective than most of us realize. It is only in the school systems of less-developed nations, where the availability of textbooks can be uneven, that we can see how important textbooks are in the delivery of schooling. For example, in their evaluation of the impact on achievement of textbook *availability* in the schools of developing nations, Heyneman, Farrell, and Sepulveda-Stuardo note that in the eighteen studies they reviewed which report relationships between textbooks and achievement, fifteen showed positive relationships. As they write:

> This does not mean that we know all that we need to know. What it does mean is that compared to other commonly measured potential correlates of school achievement, such as teacher training, class size, teacher salaries, boarding facilities, grade repetition, etc., the availability of books appears so consistently associated with higher achievement levels that it is worthy of more experimentation and close scrutiny as an instrument for affecting learning.[2]

As these authors observe, in developing nations textbook availability appears to be more firmly associated with achievement than even teacher training.

These findings have profound implications for the ways in which we see the place of textbooks in *all* school systems. But how do textbooks affect teaching and learning in the significant ways they seem to? Again this is a question that can be most readily explored in developing countries. One such study, using the Thai data from the Second International Mathematics Study, conducted under the auspices of the International Association for the Evaluation of Educational Achievement (IEA), concluded that textbook availability is associated with a more comprehensive curriculum, with more content-oriented (as opposed to student-oriented) forms of teaching, and with more efficient use of classroom time.[3]

These are significant claims, but I believe they only scratch the surface of recognition of what textbooks are in the culture of schooling and of the role they play in the school. The textbook is, in fact, at the heart of the school and without the ubiquitous text there would be no schools, at least as we know them. This fact is central to all discussions of both textbooks and textbook publishing.

The Textbook: A Brief History

The history of the institution of the school in the western educational tradition is intimately associated with the history of printing and with the capacity that technology gave for the mechanical reproduction of text, and therefore the possibility that an instructing text, i.e., a textbook, could be put into the hands of many students. Two periods in the history of the book in the school can be identified. One is associated with Europe's sixteenth and seventeenth centuries when the technology of the printed textbook emerged. The second is associated with the nineteenth century when the textbook became a basic instrument for the organization of curricula and teaching in national school *systems.*

With the invention of the printed book the tasks of thought could be separated from the immediate problem of preserving tradition. Likewise, schooling was freed from the constraints of completely oral instruction and the training of memory and could entertain such new agendas as teaching a reasoning which used the information stored in books as its basic resource. It was in the sixteenth and early seventeenth centuries that this potential was first realized and that the idea of teaching a systematic curriculum stored within a book emerged, along with the related possibility of a system of schools directed by ordered and orderly curricula. In this period pedagogues such as John Amos Comenius (1592-1670) worked within the framework of these then new understandings to invent textbooks in the modern sense, using pictures and carefully developed layouts to support equally carefully developed, vocabulary-controlled text. The most significant concrete outcome of Comenius's inventive work, his *Orbis sensualium pictus* (1658), a text for elementary Latin, remained in print for more than 200 years as a "basal" text. The format of this pioneering text is still in use today, not only in his area of Latin but also in basal readers, elementary arithmetic texts, and the like.[4]

But while similar in form to many modern texts, textbooks like Comenius's *Orbis sensualium pictus* were fundamentally different from modern textbooks in their patterns of use and, therefore, their *meaning.* Thus, prior to the nineteenth century, schools were rarely organized in ways we would recognize: teachers worked with individuals or small groups with little in the way of formal structure. Despite the ambitions of prophets like Comenius for a system of schools built around a curriculum and a textbook, no curricula-and-texts emerged in the sense of an organized and ordered body of understandings about what might be taught across a system of schools. Schools in this period would have small collections of texts, or their students would have the books they brought with them to school; teachers would use these books adventitiously to organize programs of instruction for individual students. As Perkinson notes, for example, in the United States at the turn of the nineteeth century, one student in a school might work on Noah Webster's *Spelling Book* (1783), while others might use other spellers, such as Dilworth's (published first in England in 1740), Fleming's (English, 1754), or Perry's (Scottish, 1777).[5] Each such text provided its own method of instruction and curriculum; each student learned what was in his or her text and teachers heard them recite their exercises individually or in small groups.

The emergence of national systems of education in the eighteenth and nineteenth centuries resulted in the replacement of this eclectic nonsystem by "systems" of schools in which what were to become national curricula were presented in textbooks that were explicitly written to be used across the systems. In England, for example, Kennedy's *Elementary Latin Grammar* (first published in 1843) was revised in 1866 and retitled *The Public School Latin Primer* when "the public school headmasters decided on the desirability of a common textbook."[6] Textbooks like Kennedy's *Primer* became *the* dominant influences on their subjects and the treatment of subject matters, and the approaches to teaching embedded in such texts came to define both the subjects of the new school systems, methods of instruction, and, sometimes implicitly but often explicitly, the standards that schools were expected to achieve. Many of these nineteenth-century textbooks remained in print for many years, a longevity that was both a cause and a consequence of their influence. Thus, to take two examples of texts that I used in both school and college, Mountford's revision of Bradley's revision of Arnold's *Latin Prose Composition* (first published in 1839) and Kennedy's *Latin Primer* were still widely used in the English world until the collapse of Latin as a subject in the 1950s and 1960s. Together these two books defined, and symbolized, Latin grammar and composition for teachers and students for more than a hundred years.

But while texts like Bradley's revision of Arnold's *Latin Prose Composition* were very significant in the history of both schooling and textbooks, it was the new popular elementary school of the nineteenth century that was to be the decisive influence in the emergence of the modern school—and the most decisive arena in which the modern technological, social, and cultural meaning of the textbook was to emerge. The mass provision of elementary education that emerged in the middle years of the nineteenth century required new methods of teaching to replace the individualized or small-group patterns of earlier centuries. The key social invention that lay behind this new kind of school was the discovery that a "trained," but often poorly trained, adult could teach large numbers of students simultaneously in classrooms.[7] But, to be effective, such simultaneous class teaching had to be organized around a center of attention that was common to all students in the classroom. That center was the teacher, but that teacher needed a structure of "grades" to narrow the range of achievement she had to deal with and a method which involved all the students in a room. This was offered by way of a text that was in the hands of all pupils in a classroom.

As such simultaneous methods of teaching spread beyond single schools and became the pattern for systems of schools, far-reaching implications emerged for the notion of a textbook. Standardized graded series of readers and the like became necessary resources for such systems of schools. The emergence of such systems, in turn, gave new form to the seventeenth-century vision of a curriculum-and-text-book as a systematically organized vehicle for mass education. The "pedagogical juggernaut" that emerged, to use David Hamilton's metaphor,[8] came to define understandings of schooling and, *pari passu*, modern understandings of schooled culture. The "educated" knew, and appreciated, the content of the school's curriculum—the poems, the stories, the history, and the like which were the grist of national school systems' elementary school readers and other texts.[9]

The history of the schools in America's nineteenth century conforms to this general pattern and can be symbolized by the emergence of the McGuffey *Eclectic Readers*. McGuffey's readers first appeared in 1836. Between 1836 and 1850, seven million copies were sold; from 1850 to 1890, sales averaged ten million per decade and another fifteen million copies were sold between 1890 and 1920. A companion text, Ray's *Eclectic Arithmetic* (1837), was equally successful with annual sales of over a quarter of a million copies as late as 1913. As in other countries, the McGuffey *Readers* and Ray's *Arithmetic* came to define "reading" and "arithmetic" for Americans, the result of an interaction between professional and community expectations and the individual initiative of a publisher responding to a new kind of market for textbooks. As Perkinson puts it, W. B. Smith of Cincinnati, the publisher of McGuffey's *Readers* and Ray's *Arithmetic*, realized that while "each community could create the kinds of schools it wanted, . . . what each community wanted was, it seemed, less anarchy and more uniformity."[10]

In other words, a national curriculum for American schools

emerged as a result of an interaction between the aspirations of communities and the work of commercial publishers, with the state or the schools as organized institutions having little or no role in what occurred. It was this development that created America's nineteenth-century curriculum and this curriculum became, in turn, a cultural form that defined "school." But the context in which this occurred in the United States added nuances to the American story that were somewhat different from the nuances we see in many other nineteenth-century school systems. In the absence of effective constraints on local decision making imposed by the state, a church, or "established" institutions like colleges and universities, there were few controls limiting what publishers could entertain and schools could accept. Thus, as publishers sought adoptions in America's unregulated, competitive marketplace, textbooks, and with them the curriculum, changed—and changed more rapidly than they did elsewhere. Texts became easier to read, larger in size, smaller in terms of the number of pages, and increasingly included illustrations. Their content became more "practical" and less formal and their style of presentation more interesting.[11]

This mid-nineteenth-century emergence of curricular uniformity by way of the increasingly widespread use of a small number of textbooks was, of course, also the result of, and was accelerated by, fundamental technological developments affecting both the culture and forms of social organization. After the Civil War, railroads increasingly unified the nation. In publishing, as in many industries, national firms were able to dominate smaller regional or local firms as marketing became feasible across the nation, with the consequence that, by the decade after the Civil War, textbook publication was increasingly dominated by a small number of national publishers. And, in textbook publishing as in other areas, these developments produced populist reactions which, in the case of textbooks, focused on price. Publishers began to be seen as responsible for rising textbook prices. Demands arose both for free textbooks and for regulation of their prices. In 1882, Massachusetts became the first state to require all communities to provide free textbooks for their students. This notion of free textbooks provided by the school, and the related "adoption" or "approval" of these texts became American institutions and, in their turn, created a need for a structure of regulation of the pricing and physical quality of textbooks, *but not of the curriculum which those textbooks define*, which has survived to the present.[12]

The Textbook Industry and the Curriculum

In the balance of this chapter I will explore some of the consequences in the present of both the role of the textbook in the modern school system and the historically embedded structures and practices associated with the provision and regulation of this core of the school. In the United States, the most significant of these structures and practices for our purposes is the lack of an effective national system of control of the curriculum of the kind found in most other countries. As I suggested earlier, this absence of a mechanism of curriculum control, with the attendant apparatus symbolizing the work that the schools should be doing, has inevitably thrown a peculiar and paradoxical burden onto the textbook publishing industry: publishers not only provide textbooks but they provide (and create) the curriculum by embodying the curriculum in their texts. Even in states that have histories of aggressive regulation of textbooks, publishers propose while the regulators dispose. While such states can develop guidelines that specify the curricula that should be taught in their schools, the state's effective control is limited to an influence over publishers who develop their books for an unregulated national market. *Thus while these states can direct some of what publishers do, they do not have an effective capability to control the work of their own schools (the real marketplace which determines the character of the curriculum) and they have no capability to direct the national marketplace or the national curriculum.*[13] The effect of this structure has been to give enormous responsibility and enormous problems to the publishing industry: it must define the nature of the curriculum, both as a fact and a symbol, and develop appropriate materials to support that curriculum.

How well has the industry coped with the tasks that it has been given, if only by default—the provision not only of textbooks but also curricula for the schools? The thrust of the recent critical preoccupation with textbooks and textbook publishers suggests that they have not performed well. *But does a profit-seeking industry in the kind of context that I have been describing have the capability that is needed to function both as a national curriculum authority and as an effective developer and distributor of school books?* This is the question which lies at the heart of this Yearbook. Of course, all I can do in this introductory chapter is sketch my answer to the question, leaving it to other chapters to supply more details and to provide alternative answers.

I assume all would agree about some of the basic issues that any answer to my question must address. But, first, it must be emphasized that the publishing industry and the schools together have developed mechanisms which *do* provide textbooks to all schools. And, together, the schools and publishers have created a national curriculum which is taught from Bangor, Maine to San Diego, California. While these "accomplishments" may be so commonplace as to seem not worth mentioning, they are nevertheless real when seen from the perspectives of some other public services or of low-income societies. It is from *within* this context that we must consider what seem to be the problems associated with both the curriculum and textbooks.

Because textbooks have long been ubiquitous in American schools, their presence has long been taken for granted and public concern has centered for many years on their "quality" and the curriculum they carry. This concern for the quality of textbooks has been a persistent feature of American education and is, of course, most visible in discussions of the values that are embedded in the schools. But while important to students of culture, debates about the "values" that the school should reflect do not produce a clean database that can be used to answer my question about the capacity of the publishing industry to lead curriculum development for American schools. Another, albeit parallel, set of tensions and conflicts at the intersection of publishing and schooling is sharper and potentially very significant in its implications for any evaluation of the textbook publishing industry and the American pattern of curriculum control. I refer to the curriculum reform movement of the 1950s and 1960s.

An axiom of that curriculum reform movement was that the task of curricular renewal deemed necessary after a period of twenty or more years (during which there had been little or no investment in the academic curriculum) centered on textbooks and the curricula they both symbolize and structure. The activity of that period and the new curricula that resulted both reflected and responded to courses which were seen by elites as out of date in "content" and inappropriate to the "new" role of the schools to prepare large numbers of students for mass higher education. New texts were needed to symbolize what was needed by this new role, and to direct teachers in curriculum revision and in the development of the new modes of teaching appropriate to the new role. PSSC *Physics* and the like became the dominating symbols of the curriculum development of that period.[14] But texts and curricula like PSSC *Physics* were developed outside both the school and commercial publishing systems with government funds as the source of the necessary capital, although the necessity that this seemed to reflect was seen as a commentary on the schools rather than on the publishing industry as such. And although the capabilities of the industry were drawn on for the design, manufacturing, and physical distribution of the new texts, much, if not most, of the actual marketing of the new courses and texts was also undertaken using government funds and university personnel and facilities. (Twenty or so years afterward we know that much of this effort was comparatively unsuccessful. Some, but by no means all, of the new courses were widely used for a short while and some of the new material was incorporated into existing and new conventional textbooks, but most of this effort eventually faded from sight.[15])

The concerns of the late 1970s and 1980s have been different from those of the 1950s and 1960s. The issue has been not so much the content of textbooks but their instructional quality. A stream of books and papers has analyzed textbooks and found them wanting in their instructing rhetorics, organization, and design. It is commonly argued that, while textbooks have become larger, better illustrated, and seemingly more appropriate to students and teachers, and while publisher-developed packages of textbooks and associated materials have become more expansive, much of what is provided is poor.[16]

And at the same time as such critiques of textbooks are being offered, there is a parallel body of work that has sought to articulate new design principles for textbook authors and publishers.[17] Increasingly, this literature suggests, a new era could be around the corner, one in which better designed, better written, and better organized textbooks—and by implication teaching practices—are possible. But we must ask how likely it is that the textbook developers (authors, editors, publishers) can and will respond to these new principles. The critique and proposals of these lines of research and development, and the possibility of improvement of the kind being suggested, presume that the textbook publishing industry has a capability to undertake fundamental curriculum design and development *and* the consequent materials design and development that such a program implies. *This was not the presumption of the postwar period of curriculum reform. Is it a reasonable presumption for the present?*

TEXTBOOK PUBLISHERS AS CURRICULUM MAKERS

Most of the discussion of both the past and the present that has sought to understand what happens behind publishers' doors argues quite directly that the publishing industry *does not* have the capability to undertake fundamental curriculum and materials development that might impact on schools in significant ways. Thus, as I have emphasized, textbook publishing is a commercial, nationally unregulated, profit-seeking industry. It is not an industry whose work is directed (as is the case in many other countries) by governmental curriculum development agencies with the power to command conformity to their expectations prior to approval. Likewise, the curriculum of American schools is not, in the main, directed by the pressures associated with examining (as distinct from testing) authorities. A complex set of formal and informal influences determines the curriculum of the American school. Among all these forces, the *marketplace* represented by the school *system* is necessarily the major force influencing what the textbook publishing industry develops in its role as the principal national curriculum development agent, and how development is undertaken. The way the industry sees that market determines the practices of the industry.

What do we know about the textbook marketplace and the practices of publishers as they approach that market? Do the practices of the industry emerge from the character of the marketplace for elementary and high school textbooks? Squire and Morgan offer a description of that marketplace and, while there are some broad trends, the overwhelming pattern outside the area of elementary reading is fragmentation. But while the American textbook market is marked by many different specialized segments and niches, it is, at the same time, dominated by a small number of major firms. The products of these firms determine what is published and what, therefore, is available for the schools. How can we account for the domination of so few firms in a context that is, on its face, open to many potential entrepreneurs, whether publishers or authors, with ideas about what *their* textbook might be like?[18]

In order to answer this question, we need to consider first the scale of the tasks the publishing industry undertakes as it develops its core products, i.e., the basal reading and mathematics series used in elementary schools or the basic texts of the secondary school. For example, the development of any basal series is a complex undertaking requiring writing, design, and art, and the like for six or more graded readers, six or more workbooks, sets of supplementary materials, tests, perhaps diagnostic and recording systems, overlays, duplicating masters, and, always, six teacher's guides.[19] Inevitably, this requires both considerable organization and writing and, as a result, the investment that a publisher must make to bring an idea for any such series to the national market is substantial. But, as Goldstein has observed, no matter how novel or effective the work done on a given text or series might be, publishers have no mechanism for protecting their investment in writing or development. In contrast, for example, to industrial firms developing new products where the protection of a patent is available, the legal framework governing the protection of a publisher's or author's investment in his or her "intellectual property" (copyright) does not protect the underlying ideas or approaches embedded in any book, *only the actual text*. The result is a context in which the ideas underlying a successful development may be immediately exploited by competitors, with the omnipresent danger that any resulting enhancement may well be better in significant ways than the original. Expensive, novel, or creative development can therefore be a foolhardy investment for a textbook publisher.[20]

After the writing of any textbook or series is complete, textbooks must be manufactured and warehoused for distribution in a concentrated period in the summer of each year. Text publishers must carry large inventories to support their seasonal sales, with the implication that large amounts of capital, in addition to that which is required for development, must be tied up in inventory. Furthermore, product cycles are short. States and districts adopt texts on comparatively rigid five- or six-year cycles, with the implication that publishers' investments in both development and inventory must be recovered (and profits made!) during brief windows of opportunity in the first two or three years of an adoption cycle. Because many school districts and states insist on using up-to-date materials, a demand that has been increasingly reinforced in recent years by cultural forces, each adoption period requires its own new products[21] appropriate to the new demands that might be articulated by adoption committees.

With so much invested, and so much at stake in each adoption cycle, text publishers have sought for over a hundred years to gain control over the fate of their wares by way of a vertical integration that would give them close and direct access to, and information about, their markets. Thus, textbook publishers are not only the editors and designers of their books but also direct marketers and distributors. But, while eminently logical, such vertical integration has produced its own special problems for textbook publishers. The school market is organizationally fragmented and requires substantial effort before an effective national presence can be achieved. When a publisher aspires to significant national sales, effective marketing presences must be in place to service (and secure feedback from) the multitude of decision-making jurisdictions that are the hallmark of the United States school system. This requires marketing analysts and survey research, mailing lists and copywriters, and also sales forces that can not only meet the heavy demands made by adoption states and large districts but also establish a personal presence near the schools in publishers' "open territory." These overheads, in turn, put a premium on the development of "lists" to enhance the cost-effectiveness and efficiency of marketing. But all of this makes heavy demands on firms for developmental capital and for cash flow and tilts cost-effectiveness within the industry toward larger enterprises, the discovery that W. B. Smith made in the middle years of the nineteenth century.

The marketplace for textbooks is not, of course, populated by the student users of texts but by teachers, and more specifically by the decision-making teachers, supervisors, and publics who determine which textbooks will be used in a district or state. Jurisdictions vary widely in the ways in which they select textbooks but there is a fundamental distinction between two kinds of adopters. Twenty-two states determine which textbooks will be used in their schools by providing reimbursement for district textbook expenditures only if the books used are drawn from a state-approved list. The remaining twenty-eight states leave adoption to local school districts, which, of course, vary enormously in size and sophistication.[22] The set of "adoption states" includes California and Texas, two major jurisdictions, and the rejection of a text or series by either of these states can complicate, if not end, the possibility of profitability of a textbook or series. But although these states have a special significance in the minds of publishers (and for this reason can determine how a book is written or presented), there is a sense in which practices of even these states merely highlight the forces that are associated with textbook purchase everywhere. And, of course, these forces define the character of the marketplace in which publishers work.

A decision to adopt one or another textbook is, typically, a decision for many teachers, many classrooms, and many students; every adoption decision must acknowledge this diversity. Moreover, adoption decisions can have significant consequences for school boards and curriculum leaders as feedback is received from teachers and from publics. The professional and lay constituencies that surround a text adoption committee properly demand quality materials *and* social and cultural responsiveness on the part of both textbooks and adoption committees.

The issues that are of concern to the schools' constituencies ebb and flow and may surface in either conservative or progressive guises, but they appear most characteristically as concerns about the appropriateness of the cultural and educational values found in texts. Public debate about the values that should be reflected in texts and the curriculum has a long history as a political problem for schools and publishers, *but such debates also have significant and immediate regulatory and bureaucratic aspects.* Decision makers about textbooks must both define their educational and cultural values and find ways of operationalizing their points of view so that they can have starting points for evaluating prospective textbooks, all within both political and regulatory contexts. Lacking any tools of sophisticated analysis of textbook quality, regulators have had to go at the problem mechanically.

Such mechanical resolutions of the problem of regulating the evaluation of textbooks takes on many forms. Textbooks must contain relevant and appropriate content, so the results of tests evaluating the appropriateness of their content must be available. Textbooks should be readable by average students, so readability formulas should be used to evaluate their appropriateness. Texts must "correlate" with the curriculum (although, in practice, they define the curriculum), so elaborate "correlational analyses" of scope and sequence are demanded by adoption committees. Texts should be up-to-date in "content" or "values," so new editions and recent copyright dates are required to ensure that new understandings of subject matter and teaching processes are incorporated. Texts must be of maximal assistance to teachers, so teacher's manuals, duplicating masters, tests, and classroom management systems are desirable, if not necessary, additions to the basic package of student materials. These items can become easily defined components of a checklist, with the implication that their availability in a comprehensive textbook package can tilt the balance in favor of a publisher's product.[23] But, since little time or expertise is typically available to adoption committees to do their work[24] and since decisions must often take place *before* the text has become available for use and review, criteria are often invoked in highly formal ways and actual decisions to adopt are all too often made using what are, at bottom, superficial criteria.

Using both editorial and marketing strategies, publishers seek the predictability needed to develop competitive products for this complex marketplace. They seek to ensure that their texts conform to current and emerging professional, and lay, expectations about what appropriate texts should contain. They draw attention to the "history" of their texts to appeal to brand loyalty; they emphasize the needs that their texts, but not others, address. A firm's capacity to secure the information that is needed to monitor the ever-changing and fragmented market and its ability to address trends in that market are much more important for the welfare of its titles than is the quality of any book's content.

The problems and difficulties that the overall adoption process always poses to publishers are exacerbated by the new demands that can surface in each iteration of the process. As I have already noted, such demands create an insistent requirement of continuing adaptation and revision of the materials in any list to meet the demands of each new adoption cycle. To meet this requirement, book and series development and production must become routinized within firms, and for complex and large-scale series this involves the work of large teams made up of specialists in all aspects of the publishers' craft. Inputs from editors, authors, in-house and free-lance writers, consultants and experts, artists and designers, photo researchers, production personnel, and marketing and sales personnel carrying feedback from the marketplace must somehow be incorporated within the development and redevelopment cycle. For series, such projects are necessarily coordinated, but by editor-managers who are inevitably distant from the actual work of development or writing. (It has often been noted that the writing of a series by a single author, or even a small group of authors, is almost impossible in these circumstances.) Even when single authors or small groups of authors develop a first version of what becomes a successful text or series, the need for continuing and continual updating creates an inevitable routinization of what they do. As a result, more often than not the task becomes not rewriting but cut-and-paste revision, undertaken or directed by an author-manager or, more often in the case of a series, an editor-manager. The content of such texts is all too often the one that Damerow discerned in his examination of mathematics textbooks in Germany, where authorship has been clearer than it has been in many recent American series.[25] Instead of presenting a coherent, evolving curriculum, "the curriculum of the textbooks is an accumulating curriculum": greater and greater quantities of information and new fads are incorporated, with little attention to the overall conceptual unity of what emerges. In Woodward's words:

Below the surface of the glossy, coffee-table books that emerge from the current textbook industry are: lessons that students find superficial and meaningless; end-of-chapter exercises that emphasize factual recall; photographs that do nothing to enhance the content of text; and skill lessons that avoid teaching higher-order teaching skills.[26]

Consequences

I began my discussion of the contemporary textbook industry by asking whether it was performing at all well the two-fold task that the governance structures of American education have assigned it—leadership and control over the curriculum *and* the production of quality textbooks to support that curriculum in the schools. I have suggested that many believe that the industry has not performed as it might with either of these tasks. But given the peculiar, culturally enveloped interaction between a structurally autonomous, profit-driven industry that functions as both a developer and deliverer of instructional materials and a diffusely organized school system that both directs (via the market) and depends on these instructional materials, could (and should) we expect more than we have gotten?

The symbiosis of publishers and school systems in the matrix offered by the structures and cultures of the American school system massively complicates any discussion of the accountability of publishers for the materials they produce for the schools. Let us return for a moment to the hoary issues of the values embedded in textbooks. If, for example, a region (e.g., the South) or a stratum of schools demands materials of a particular kind, and is able to enforce that demand through its approval and adoption processes, can, and should, we expect publishers to forego sales (and the profits needed to sustain the industry) by refusing to provide those materials?

In many critical discussions of the textbook industry, questions of this kind are posed in terms of the continuing problems associated with issues like Darwinian evolution, and are answered by invoking the responsibility of publishers to, for example, scholarship as a basis for the assessment of the ambiguities that often mark textbook treatments of such topics. But this answer locates a responsibility with *one* of the actors in an overall national system and neglects the responsibility of other actors in that system who approve or adopt textbooks (like the state or district authorities in communities that do not share the values being criticized). Such agencies have rarely intervened in any effective way to control either the curriculum or textbooks, and their quality. In the case of the long-contentious issue of evolution, some publishers could be judged as more responsible than many or most adoption committees and state departments of education.[27] In the same vein, the failure of the school system to develop widely used, timely, and effective media for reviewing textbooks would seem to raise its own questions. But they are questions that raise issues about the overall school system's perception of its need for rigorous appraisal of textbooks rather than issues about the capabilities of the textbook publishing industry as such.

We are left, therefore, with a paradox that has been noted many times in many other areas within education. The critics of textbooks and of the publishing industry and its practices are elites of one kind or another who want the school system to accept their judgments about what should be done. But, in textbook assessment, like in so many other areas of education, they have not developed effective mechanisms for institutionalizing their values in the system, apart from the institutionalization of advocacy and critique. And the schools have not been responsive to such elite advocacy and criticism of what they do and how they do it. Schrag, for example, begins his account of the teaching of thinking in schools with a comment by W. T. Harris made in 1898:

It is believed that the arrested development of the higher mental and moral faculties is caused in many cases by the school. The habit of teaching with too much thoroughness and too-long continued drill, the semimechanical branches of study, such as arithmetic, spelling . . . and even the distinctions for formal grammar, often leaves the pupil fixed in lower stages of growth and unable to exercise the higher functions of thought.

But, as Schrag goes on to note,

Once we realize that this particular criticism of schooling is at least a century old, the fact that we are presently no better at responding to it than we were, suggests that the issue is perhaps more complex than most educational researchers have been ready to believe.[28]

Comments of the kind offered by Schrag can be multiplied readily and applied to many areas of the school and its curriculum. At bottom, the answers to the seeming paradoxes that they represent come back to one or two factors: more often than not the persistence of this or that practice within the schools is a response either to the actual conditions within which teachers work or to the cultural contexts that define teaching. These contexts and conditions have not changed in ways that would support the alternative methods that the critics of the old and advocates of the new, and their elite constituencies, would prefer.[29]

One can only speculate at this time about whether the kind of criticism of textbooks found in many chapters of this Yearbook will meet the same fate. Publishers work within a highly visible, highly practical, and highly politicized context and cannot ignore their critics in ways that teachers can when they close the classroom door. But while deferring both to their vociferous public critics and to advocates of better ways, publishers must serve their markets and, for many teachers and schools, the textbooks they have seem quite satisfactory, both educationally and culturally. From the perspective of the publishing industry, which services markets, the differing needs of varying markets can be quite adequately met by segmentation of product, of both particular books or series, and even of individual firms themselves.

This has been the practice of the industry. As Woodward and Elliott have noted in their discussion of the industry's responses to the demands of the evolution problem:

Some publishers will take the "high road," confident that their textbooks will meet the needs of a significant portion of the market; others will pursue the market segment that demands compliance to a political or religious credo; and still others will attempt to satisfy as many segments as possible through carefully orchestrated compromise.[30]

All of the texts that Woodward and Elliott analyzed in their study have markets of one kind or another. Such market segments rarely engage each other in explicit dialogue about what they are doing, and so do not need to adjudicate their differences. The result is that the publishers and textbooks which serve these markets do not need to find any common meeting ground in which they might listen to their critics. There is nothing in the overall system that requires either sustained dialogue about the curriculum or accountability of publishers to the system for the quality of what they do. And, of course, all suggestions that such mechanisms might be developed have been rejected by the overall system.

In other words, and this is the argument that I have tried to develop in this essay, the textbook industry and its products are totally intertwined with both the structures and the cultures of the school system. The industry is a faithful reflection of the system, i.e., the markets that it serves and the larger contexts in which it works.

The books the industry produces are essential to the work of the entire school system, but are produced in a context of profound constraints on what they might be like and on the ways in which they might be improved. There are problems in the legal framework that supports the research and development publishers are assumed to undertake, and might undertake, in the availability of capital for investment in development, in the development process itself, and in the signals that the marketplace gives an industry whose direction is set by that market. There are constraints set within the schools themselves in the ways that they make decisions, in the ways that they respond to constituencies, and in the ways in which they provision classes with materials. There are constraints in the ways research, whether on textbooks or anything else, is related to practice. In these multiple contexts, the textbook publishing industry leads by following, and in so doing faithfully reflects the realities of and demands within the American school system.

The problems which follow are not unique to the textbook industry and cannot be solved by the industry alone, by the elites who criticize its products or practices, or by a focus on this one piece of the system. In his discussion of thinking in the school, Schrag claims that "if we are to discuss the teaching of thinking, we must have a clearer understanding of what thinking is" and how our conceptions of thinking relate to the set of contexts in which our conceptions might be nested.[31] This is as true of textbooks. I have suggested here that textbooks are at the core of the whole institution of the school as we know it and that it is this whole that determines the character of the part represented by the texts we see and use. As we face the issue of the quality of textbooks and of the capability of publishers to provide appropriate and satisfactory materials for that system, we must face the problems of the school system at large. *It is the school system as a whole that has not found ways of defining effective leadership which can deliver sustained direction to the day-to-day work of the schools.* It is the school system that does not have the capabilities for curriculum leadership and direction setting. To charge one part of the system with lacking something that the system as a whole lacks is an unwarranted projection of the problems of the whole onto that part.

Footnotes

1. Guy M. Whipple, ed., *The Textbook in American Education*, Thirtieth Yearbook of the National Society for the Study of Education, Part II (Bloomington, IL: Public School Publishing Co., 1931). James R. Squire, former senior vice-president of Ginn &

Co., recently wrote that "American textbook publishers who have long felt that they suffered from too little attention from the educational community may now feel they are suffering from too much attention." See James R. Squire, "Textbooks to the Forefront," *Book Research Quarterly* 1 (Summer 1985): 12.

2. Stephen P. Heyneman, J. P. Farrell, and M. A. Sepulveda-Stuardo, "Textbooks and Achievement in Developing Countries," *Journal of Curriculum Studies* 13 (July-September 1981): 227.

3. Marlaine E. Lockheed, Stephen C. Vail, and Bruce Fuller, "How Textbooks Affect Achievement in Developing Countries: Evidence from Thailand," *Educational Evaluation and Policy Analysis* 8 (Winter 1986): 390.

4. See, for example, Walter J. Ong, S. J., *Ramus, Method, and the Decay of Dialogue* (Cambridge, MA: Harvard University Press, 1958). See also, David Hamilton, "The Pedagogical Juggernaut," *British Journal of Educational Studies* 35 (February 1987): 18-29, and idem, *Towards a Theory of Schooling* (London and Philadelphia: Falmer, 1989).

5. Henry J. Perkinson, "American Textbooks and Educational Change," in *Early American Textbooks 1775-1900: A Catalog of Titles Held by the Educational Research Library* (Washington, DC: U.S. Department of Education, 1985), p. x. For a discussion of teaching in English schools before ca. 1870, see Malcolm Seaborne, *The English School: Its Architecture and Organization, 1370-1870* (London: Routledge and Kegan Paul, 1971).

6. See William A. Reid, "Curriculum Change and the Evolution of Educational Constituencies: The English Sixth Form in the Nineteenth Century," in *Social Histories of the Secondary Curriculum: Subjects for Study*, ed. Ivor F. Goodson (London and Philadelphia: Falmer 1985), p. 300.

7. For discussions of "simultaneous instruction," see David Hamilton, "Adam Smith and the Moral Economy of the Classroom System," *Journal of Curriculum Studies* 12 (October-December 1980): 281-99, and idem, "Classroom Research and the Evolution of the Classroom System" (Unpublished manuscript, Department of Education, University of Glasgow, 1977). See also, Ian Westbury, "Research into Classroom Processes: A Review of Ten Years' Work," *Journal of Curriculum Studies* 10 (October-December 1978): 283-308.

8. Hamilton, "The Pedagogical Juggernaut."

9. D. Shayer, *The Teaching of English in Schools 1900-1970* (London: Routledge and Kegan Paul, 1972). Shayer reported, for example, that the contents of English school anthologies between 1900 and 1930 could be predicted with complete accuracy and would include Wordsworth's *Daffodils*, Blake's *The Tiger*, and so on. He points out that in the 1960s many English pupils regarded these canonical poems as *the* most important poems. I read these poems in the course of my schooling in Australia in the 1950s. See Ian Westbury, "The Curriculum: What Is It and How Should We Think about It?" in *The Challenge of Educational Change*, ed. M. Bloomer and K. E. Shaw (Oxford: Pergamon Press, 1979).

10. Perkinson, "American Textbooks and Educational Change," p. x.

11. Ibid., p. xi.

12. Ibid., pp. xiv-xv.

13. "Because of the publicity generated by large southeastern and western state adoptions, critics of such large adoptions frequently feel that some states unduly influence the content of instructional materials. That they serve to identify (and publicize) objections to textbooks is true. . . . However [publishers] are not likely to make changes demanded by a Texas or California alone, even less a Louisiana or Oregon, unless there is substantial support for such change across the nation." Squire, "Textbooks to the Forefront," p. 16.

14. For this argument, see Ian Westbury, "Who Can Be Taught What? General Education in the Secondary School," in *Cultural Literacy and the Idea of General Education*, ed. Ian Westbury and Alan C. Purves, Eighty-seventh Yearbook of the National Society for the Study of Education, Part II (Chicago: University of Chicago Press, 1988), pp. 184-90.

15. See, for example, J. D. Hess, *The Era of the New Social Studies* (Boulder, CO: ERIC Clearinghouse for Social Studies Education and Social Science Education Consortium, 1977). ERIC ED 141-191.

16. For a sample of the critical literature, see Bonnie B. Armbruster and Thomas H. Anderson, "Structures of Explanation in History Textbooks, or So What If Governor Stanford Missed the Spike and Hit the Rail," *Journal of Curriculum Studies* 16 (April-June 1984): 181-94; Avon Crismore, "The Rhetoric of Textbooks," *Journal of Curriculum Studies* 16 (July-September 1984): 279-96; Arthur Woodward, "Textbooks: Less Than Meets the Eye," *Journal of Curriculum Studies* 19 (November-December 1987): 511-27; Richard C. Anderson, Jean Osborn, and Robert J. Tierney, eds., *Learning to Read in American Schools* (Hillsdale, NJ: Erlbaum, 1984); Michael W. Apple, "The Political Economy of Text Publishing," *Educational Theory* 34 (Fall 1984): 307-319; idem, "The Culture and Commerce of the Textbook," *Journal of Curriculum Studies* 17 (April-June 1985): 147-62.

17. See, for example, Bonnie B. Armbruster and Thomas H. Anderson, "Producing 'Considerate' Expository Text: or Easy Reading Is Damned Hard Writing," *Journal of Curriculum Studies* 17 (July-September 1985): 247-74; Michael MacDonald-Ross, "Graphics in Text," *Review of Research in Education* 5, ed. Lee S. Shulman (Itasca, IL: F. E. Peacock, 1978), pp. 49-58; idem, "Language in Texts," *Review of Research in Education* 6, ed. Lee S. Shulman (Itasca, IL: F. E. Peacock, 1979), pp. 229-75; Thomas M. Duffy and Robert Waller, eds., *Designing Usable Texts* (Orlando, FL: Academic Press, 1985).

18. See James R. Squire and Richard T. Morgan, "The Elementary and High School Textbook Market Today," chapter 8 in this volume. The eight largest companies in the industry account for 76 percent of the elementary-high school and college textbook sales. See U. S. Department of Commerce, Bureau of the Census, *1982 Census of Manufactures: Concentration Ratios in Manufacturing* (Washington, DC: Bureau of the Census, U. S. Department of Commerce, 1986), pp. 7-74. However, the patterns of concentration in the elementary-high school market can look different when seen from the perspective of particular market niches. In 1981-1982, Scott Foresman's *Mathematics Around Us*, Holt's *School Mathematics*, and Houghton-Mifflin's *Modern School Mathematics* were used in 39 percent of traditional grade eight mathematics classes. No other text was used in more than 1 to 2 percent of classes. In grade eight remedial mathematics, the two dominant texts were used in only 16 percent of classes. These findings come from my analysis of teacher responses to a question from the IEA Second International Mathematics Study asking for information about textbooks used in the Study's target classes. For a discussion of the problems of a small publisher, see M. Blouke Carus, "The Small Publisher in a National Market," chapter 6 in this volume.

19. For my discussion of the textbook publishing industry, I have drawn on Eric Broudy, "The Trouble with Textbooks," *Teachers College Record* 77 (September 1975): 13-34. Wilbur Schramm, "The Publishing Process," in *Text Materials in Modern Education: A Comprehensive Platform for Research*, ed. Lee J. Cronbach (Urbana: University of Illinois Press, 1955), pp. 129-65, is still provocative.

20. For this argument, see Paul Goldstein, *Changing the American Schoolbook: Law, Politics, and Technology* (Lexington, MA: D. C. Heath and Co., 1978).

21. In 1985, California's adoption contracts were worth $134 million. A successful book or series has a significant effect on a publisher's bottom line and both the schedules

for states like California and Texas, and the likely success of one or another publisher's series, are subjects of discussion in the business press, e.g., *Value Line*.

22. For an extensive discussion of the adoption process, see the special feature on school adoptions and textbook quality in *Book Research Quarterly* 1 (Summer, Fall 1985). Squire suggests that too much may have been made of the significance of the state adoption process. Although adoption states account for about 50 percent of publishers' sales (a percentage that has increased over the last decade), most large cities in publishers' open territory "have established systematic procedures for reviewing textbooks on a rotating sequence." Squire also notes that "many adoptions in cities such as Detroit are larger than comparable state listings in Mississippi." He estimates that not more than 20 percent of school districts now lack an organized multiyear adoption program. Squire, "Textbooks to the Forefront," p. 13.

23. Squire offers a sample of the kinds of issues that surface in the adoption process: "If Florida insists on testing children's knowledge of the basic words on Dolch's decades-old word list, Florida will find instruction on these words included in submitted programs. . . . Today's selection committees require multiethnic, nonsexist materials that also avoid discrimination against the elderly or the handicapped. . . . Some states . . . will often specify the way in which they require topics like evolution and creationism, free enterprise, or nutrition and junk foods to be handled." Squire also notes that publishers regularly survey national mores "to assure that instructional materials meet local and state standards." Squire, "Textbooks to the Forefront," p. 15.

The teacher's guide in Houghton Mifflin's basal reading series includes eleven professional papers, covering thirty-five pages, written by the authors of the series on topics such as decoding, teaching comprehension, study skills, content reading, readability, developing literary appreciation, and so forth. One hundred professional references are provided for further reading. The series includes a research bulletin and a series of monographs and videotapes designed for in-service use. The materials include a three-leveled teacher's guide to accommodate the needs of students in three or four reading groups. John T. Ridley, "Counterpoint 1," *Book Research Quarterly* 2 (Spring 1986): 74-75.

24. Ibid, p. 75. Ridley, editor-in-chief of the School Division of Houghton Mifflin, notes that when his firm dropped answers to the suggested questions in a guide published in the mid-1970s, "the resulting clamor caused the answers to be reinstated."

25. P. Damerow, "Concepts of Geometry in German Textbooks," in *Comparative Studies of Mathematics Curricula: Change and Stability, 1960-1980*, Materialen und Studien Band 19 (Bielefeld: Institut für Didaktik der Mathematik der Universität Bielefeld, 1980), pp. 281-303.

26. Arthur Woodward, "Political Issues Obscure Questions of Pedagogy," *Education Week*, 21 January 1987, p. 28.

27. For a discussion of the treatment of Darwinian evolution, see Arthur Woodward and David L. Elliott, "Evolution and Creationism in High School Textbooks," *American Biology Teacher* 49 (March 1987): 164-70.

28. Francis Schrag, *Thinking in School and Society* (London and New York: Routledge, 1988), p. 2.

29. See, for example, Larry Cuban, *How Teachers Taught: Constancy and Change in American Classrooms 1890-1980* (New York and London: Longman, 1984). I owe this observation to W. A. Reid of the Institute of Education, University of London.

30. See, for example, Woodward and Elliott, "Evolution and Creationism in High School Textbooks," p. 170.

31. Schrag, *Thinking in School and Society*, p. 2.

CHAPTER II

Textbooks and the Curriculum during the Progressive Era: 1930-1950

ARTHUR W. FOSHAY

To understand how the materials of instruction, and especially the textbook, evolved during the 1930s and 1940s, it is necessary to understand the context of educational theory out of which they emerged. The textbooks and other materials used in the classroom during this period were profoundly influenced by the Progressive movement in education, which had taken on that name at the beginning of the century.

The Progressive Movement

The history of the Progressive movement is usually thought of as beginning during the eighteenth century with the publication of Rousseau's *Emile*, which itself emerged from an intellectual climate that placed faith in untrammelled nature, as epitomized by Pope's line from the *Essay On Man* ("where every prospect pleases, and only Man is vile"), and in the notion of the Noble Savage, as expressed by Chateaubriand and James Fenimore Cooper, and, later, in Nature as celebrated by the English Romantic poets. The movement had strong roots in theology, and was in some degree a revolt against the prevailing rationalism of the time.

Its main implication for education was to place the growing child in direct contact with Nature (read *God*) and to rely on his essentially divine nature to guide his development. Rousseau, Pestalozzi, and Froebel, among others, gave expression to this movement in education. Others expressed it in the arts and in limited degree in philosophy.

It is useful to remember that almost all reforms in education have been rebellions against either a perceived sterility and formalism, or against a perceived laxity. The nineteenth-century reform of the European and American university was against a perceived laxity, as is the reform now under way in American public schools. The Progressive movement derived much of its appeal among educators as a rebellion against the perceived sterility and rigidity of the nineteenth-century schools. Rigidity and formalism had been ridiculed by writers since the seventeenth century, from Overbury's "Pedant," to Pope (in *The Dunciad*), to Dickens (in *Hard Times*), to Mark Twain (in *Tom Sawyer*).

In the United States, the revolt against formalism began most notably with Francis Parker, shortly after the Civil War. At first, the revolt was defined negatively—by what it was *not*. Later, beginning especially with Dewey's *Child and the Curriculum*,[1] it began to achieve affirmative definition. By 1941, Tyler summarized the movement under the following eight trends in modern education:

1. "the acceptance of a wider range of educational objectives."
2. ". . . the emphasis on greater integration or unification of the educational program."
3. ". . . the use of varied media of learning and of expression."
4. ". . . greater sequence and continuity in the educational program."
5. ". . . increasing emphasis being given to the development of skills in study rather than to the memorization of specific facts appearing in the textbook."
6. ". . . varied organizations of the learning experiences of students. . . . It is important for the learner to be able to organize and reorganize material in various contexts and for various purposes."
7. ". . . greater attention to local community needs and resources."
8. ". . . instruction dealing with the so-called personal-social needs of students."[2]

It follows, according to Tyler, that the place of the textbook has changed.[3] No longer is the textbook the sole source of information. The school should "train the students in using a variety of sources" and "consider organization as a major function of textbooks." There is a need for "careful planning of sequential development within the same textbook and from the textbook of one year to that of the next;" "textbooks should include new materials such as those relating to the personal-social problems of students;" textbooks should take into account the "wide individual differences among learners."

As the twentieth century unfolded, four technical developments came to have a substantial effect on the new Progressive movement. They were:

1. the emergence of learning theory and the downfall of faculty psychology,
2. the emergence of child growth and development as a distinct field in psychology,
3. the emergence of a psychology of education, and
4. the development of systematic measurement of intellectual functioning.

All these developments had consequences for the making of instructional materials, and especially for textbooks. The high rate of failure in the eight-grade elementary school—the "people's college"—made evident with the first attempts at systematic achievement testing, led to a reexamination of McGuffey's readers, and this reexamination led to further developments: (a) the replacement of the McGuffey moralistic tales with fantasies and nursery tales, these being thought to be more "childlike"; and (b) modification of the texts of readers to replace the heavy emphasis on phonics with more "meaningful" material, and to make the texts more available to beginners by starting more slowly.

During the 1920s and 1930s, attempts were made to base readers on the systematic study of vocabulary development, and later on what came to be called "readability." The student was to learn to use all the available cues to extract meaning from the page—immediate recognition of words, cues from the context, cues from illustrations, and, finally, phonetic analysis. Teachers were informed that the average child required fifty-seven exposures to a word before recognizing it on sight. Hence, "Look, look. See, see."

As Chall points out, these developments led to a tension between technique and substance.[4] Teachers had learned to use direct experience, "active methods," and "direct involvement," so they invented "experience charts," made up of children's actual experience. The charts were dictated by the children, written on large pieces of newsprint by the teacher, and read by the children from the charts. The substance was thus made immediately "meaningful," a term that became a catchword of the period.

It was widely believed that teachers relied on textbooks too much and that children were generally required only to memorize and give back what the text contained. Bagley disputed this in the Thirtieth Yearbook of the National Society for the Study of Education.[5] He caused 539 class exercises to be viewed in classes all over the United

States, and concluded that "one or another form of the socialized-recitation and project methods appeared approximately as frequently in these lessons as did the 'straight' recitation from a single textbook" (p. 24). The amount of "straight" recitation increased from about 33 percent in the elementary schools to 42.8 percent in the high schools.

As the 1930s moved along, the textbook gradually lost its place as the center of a child's school experience. It was replaced by experience charts, by projects, by home-made skits, and by much, much talk. The book did not disappear, of course. Far from it; more books than ever were being used in the "progressive" elementary school classes, but the single, basal textbook series was challenged. It was no longer the main event, or the whole show. At least, that was the way the educational spokesmen of the time talked. However, close observers of classroom practice, such as elementary school principals (I was one), noticed that most teachers continued to teach from the textbook, much as they and their predecessors always had.

The readers of the day, however, reflected the tension between technique and substance, or meaning. The Elson readers of the late 1920s were "meaningful" in that, like the upper-grade McGuffey readers, they emphasized literary value. Later, when they became the Elson-Gray readers, they took full advantage of the research of the 1920s on vocabulary development, and sacrificed some aspects of meaning for technique, especially in the primers. Still later, during the late 1940s, the readers became less challenging, in the interest of accommodating the children who seemed to need to start more slowly. Chall points out that this seems to have had a depressing effect on the SAT scores of college-bound students ten years later.[6]

Let us examine some selections from the *New England Primer, The McGuffey Readers,* and *The Elson Readers* of 1927. We will notice the continuing moral (though not religious) emphasis. First, from the well-known alphabet couplets in the *New England Primer* (c. 1790):[7]

> In Adam's Fall
> We sinned All [The child begins with Original Sin]
>
> Young Obadias,
> David, Josias,
> All were pious
>
> Whales in the Sea,
> GOD's voice obey.

Next, from *McGuffey's Eclectic Primer,* lesson XVIII:[8]

This is a pet bird.
It lives in a new cage.
It will stand on Sue's hand, and sing.
Sue loves her pet bird.
So do I love it.

This, from the *Elson Readers Primer* (1927) is considerably longer:[9]

Alice and the Bird, by Emily Rose Burt
Alice was fast asleep.
A bird saw her.
"Wake up! Wake up!" sang the bird.
"Wake up, Little Girl!" it sang.
Alice waked up!
She jumped out of bed.
She saw the bird in the tree.

The story continues for four pages, ending:

How happy the bird was!
It had helped Alice all the day.

There were many other reading series, of course. They varied considerably in approach, from a heavy emphasis on word analysis at one extreme to a seeming absence of such technical matters in favor of "meaningful" content at the other. The teachers at the school where I was principal preferred the Gates readers over the others because they introduced some elements of humor, and the teachers liked to see the children chuckle over the stories. However, it is significant that neither the Elson-Gray nor the Gates readers listed the authors of the stories in the books by 1940. The readers stressed technique over substance. The teacher's manual proclaimed that the readers were based on extensive research (carried out during the 1920s) into vocabulary development and word recognition. Therefore, the number of new words introduced decreased sharply. Most of the teacher's manual stressed techniques of word recognition—phonics, visual cues (such as double letters as in "look" and "see"), cues from verbal context, and illustrations.

At the same time, some short-lived excesses appeared in a few elementary school classrooms. One of these, based in part on the Romantic faith in the importance of the child's unguided "natural" growth, was called the "child-centered" classroom, in which an attempt was made to have the children determine the content, the learning methods, and the evaluation of the school experience, and the classroom climate was "democratic" in the sense that there were no limits on what the children might do. All of this was in a context that placed primary emphasis on the social development of the children. Many of these classrooms quickly became so chaotic that in a short time teachers abandoned this version of "child-centeredness." The flaw in this approach was that it ignored the other intent of "child centeredness"—that if learners are drawn in to the design of their learning, it will appear reasonable to them, and they will pursue it with greater commitment. Such an approach did not imply that there should be no limits or framework provided by the teacher.

Another excess that attracted much attention was based on the idea that there is no such thing as completely passive learning. This idea was a corruption of the belief in firsthand experience and of Dewey's principle of learning by doing. Some teachers interpreted this principle to mean that if a child was not overtly active, he was not learning. Sitting still and reading or writing, or thinking, was suspect. Better to build a physical object, or make an art work, or carry on an activity that required cooperative group work. Carried to an extreme, as it was in a few classrooms, this led to a caricature of systematic education. Because of this, the idea of "activity units" became suspect. The notion of "active methods," interpreted in various ways, did take hold somewhat, however. In France, for example, "active methods" was interpreted at the *Lycée Pilote* at Sèvres to mean working with one's hands, as in making bookends, when I visited there in 1958. (The Director explained to me that such activity had the additional advantage of exposing the *élite* [i.e., selected] students at the school to the dignity of manual work, thus increasing their understanding of ordinary people.) Dewey's concept of experience, which underlies all this, remains an area of confusion in actual school practice to this day.

Two Other Themes of the 1930s

As the Great Depression and the threat of world war deepened during the 1930s, two other themes developed in education: the importance of the school as a social force, and the related concern for "democracy in the classroom."

THE SCHOOL AS A SOCIAL FORCE

The first of these, the school as a social force, was given impetus by the title of a publication by George Counts, *Dare the School Build a New Social Order?*[10] This publication appeared at the height of the new Social Frontier movement, itself an outgrowth of the self-consciously liberal political and economic movements that had appeared early in the century. The depression had frightened many thoughtful people, who feared that political chaos would follow the economic disaster of the time. These fears led to some changes in the textbooks and other professional publications, notably in the social studies, and to a lesser extent in science and mathematics.

The social studies texts of Harold Rugg were the most generally discussed, and Paul Hanna's social studies series was widely used. Hanna once told me that the grand purpose of his series, based on the well-known "expanding environments" concept, was to bring students to a realization (by grade eight) of the necessity of world government. Hanna and Rugg were colleagues at Teachers College, Columbia University, during the 1930s, and both were active participants in the Social Frontier movement.

Rugg's social studies books were attacked by the conservative press of the time, and gradually lost whatever favor they had achieved. By 1950, Rugg himself had withdrawn from that field to pursue other interests. It is difficult now to see what the problem was with the textbooks, except for Rugg's emphasis on the social, as well as the political, aspects of U.S. History.

An examination of three of the Rugg texts reveals only one reference by him to the social and economic difficulties now widely discussed. In the closing pages of his *A History of American Government and Culture* (1931), we find a brief section called "Difficult Problems of Economic Life."[11] No doubt reflecting the anxieties of the growing Depression, these "difficulties" are the following:

1. *The increasing difficulties in finding work* (italics in original). Today, in the industrial nations of the world, not less than 12,000,000 workers are out of work; the lives of not less than 50,000,000 people are thereby affected. The invention of new machines and the lack of careful planning in production of goods and food are throwing people out of work more rapidly than new jobs can be created for them.

2. *The rapid multiplication of human wants* . . .

3. *The unequal division of the national income among the people.* We have learned of the low standard of living of the masses compared with the wasteful and extravagant mode of living of a small wealthy class . . .

4. *The difficulty of the farmers in their efforts to secure a fair share of the national income . . .* (p. 294).

This passage contains terms like "masses" and "planning" which are still part of the Communist jargon, though that fact was not widely recognized in 1931. But the threat to the wealthy was recognized by the conservative press of the time, and Rugg was attacked for it. So were the other leaders of the Social Frontier movement. The Hearst newspaper in New York, I was once told, used to publish lists of "enemies of the country." These lists ordinarily included the names of the Social Frontier leaders at Teachers College, Columbia University—Rugg, Counts, Dewey, and the others. Once the list was published without Counts's name. Counts, a wit, told his friends he would sue.

It is interesting to compare this passage from Rugg (the only one I could find of this type) with a passage from Frank Abbott Magruder's *American Government* of 1930.[12] Magruder's book, which went through many editions, was by far the most widely used text in the country in the high school civics course. In the first chapter, "The Importance of Government," Magruder gives his reason number 6 for the importance of government:

Government Performs Functions in the Interest of the Community without Profit Which as Private Ventures Would Have to Be Performed for Profit. If the National government had not built the Panama Canal it would probably have been built as a private venture. Much of the western land irrigated by the National government would have been irrigated by private companies. If the National government had not built the Alaskan railroad, private capital might have; and if the United States had not established a postal system, private capital certainly would have organized such a system (p. 18).

One might ask who would offend the conservatives of the time more, Rugg or the widely accepted Magruder? Working for profit, to Magruder, was obviously somehow in conflict with working "in the interest of the community."

The interest in social matters, to contemporary eyes so mildly expressed in their textbooks by the likes of Rugg and Magruder, was also expressed a little in mathematics and science. In arithmetic, it was offered as a part of the social utility theme of the Progressives. George D. Strayer and Clifford B. Upton called their series *Social Utility Arithmetics: Think and Do Series*, thus being up to date. Book Four, in addition to conventional sections on whole numbers, fractions, decimals, and percentage, includes applications of arithmetic to practical problems. At the close of the chapter on decimals, for example, we find a section called "Measuring Valuable Land."

A surveyor near our house measured three valuable lots that were side by side. The first lot measured 35.78 ft. in width; the second measured exactly 25 ft.; and the third measured exactly 25.3 ft. How wide were the three lots together? Since the land was *valuable*, each lot was measured to the *nearest hundredth* of a foot.

In *Modern School Arithmetic*, by John R. Clark, Arthur S. Otis, Caroline Hatton, and Raleigh Schorling, at the eighth-grade level, the approach is a bit more explicit.[13] The last four chapters are called: "Interest and Banking," "Insurance and Taxes," "Investments and Budgets," and a review that includes sections on "The Cost of Running a School" and "The Best Investment You Can Make." No social commentary is implied, though John Clark was at that time in the Mathematics Department of Teachers College, and must have heard much from the Social Frontier.

A rationale for the reform of secondary school science was published in 1938 in *Science in General Education*, which was the report of a committee of the Progressive Education Association.[14] The book was widely read by teachers in training, and was somewhat influential on the materials of instruction of the time and on the making of curricula. The report cited at some length (p. 13) a study by Wilbur L. Beauchamp, who described the mixture of purposes—the confusion—in science education. Beauchamp was the author of one of the more widely used texts for junior high school science. In the face of this confusion, the committee sought to bring science into line with the thinking of the time: "The purpose of general education is to meet the needs of individuals in the basic aspects of living in such a way as to promote the fullest possible realization of personal potentialities and the most effective participation in a democratic society" (p. 23). In line with this, the committee attacked the emphasis in science on specific information for its own sake, cautioned against taking only the immediate felt needs of young people as a sufficient guide for the selection of learning experiences, and warned that it would be necessary to eliminate some material usually included in the science offering. It suggests that teachers answer the following questions in the course of selecting content: "What are the needs of the adolescent in X community? And what is revealed as one looks at the adolescent in his personal living, in his relationship to the social-civic and economic life of X community in particular?" (p. 446). The committee offers several illustrations of how the principles it suggests were applied in the design of secondary school science courses. The work of the year in "A Course in Functional Chemistry" is organized into six sections, as follows: Why Study Chemistry? Importance of Chemistry in Modern Life, The Fundamentals of Chemistry, Chemistry of the Individual, Chemistry of the Home, and Chemistry of the Community and Nation. The authors explain that the first three sections (which include, it will be noted, the "Fundamentals of Chemistry") occupy only one-third of the time given to the course. Two-thirds of the time is devoted to the individual, the home, and the community. However, the committee points out that such courses are the first year of a two-year sequence for the college-bound students. During the second year, these students receive a semester each of chemistry and physics, and end with an adequate knowledge in both fields. The "functional" courses, required of all students at grade eleven, are introductory for the college-bound.

The effect of the science recommendations was, of course, greatly diluted by the onset of World War II, and such courses did not, therefore, result in the production of specially designed instructional materials. Attention to the science proposals is included here to illustrate further the trend of thinking in the 1930s.

DEMOCRACY IN THE CLASSROOM

The other theme, democracy in the classroom, gained some of its appeal from the earlier Progressive principle that the child should be respected. The theme was greatly strengthened by a classic research study of 1940, Lewin and Lippitt's study of classroom atmosphere.[15] Lewin, a refugee from Hitler's Germany, found the American classroom to be an analogous authoritarian dictatorship. With Ronald Lippitt, Lewin designed an ingenious experiment that demonstrated that the authoritarian atmosphere produced behavior like that of the subjects of a dictatorship—the children destroyed their own work, and competed for the teacher's approval. The Lewin and Lippitt study was arguably the single most influential research study in education since Thorndike's studies early in the century that resulted in reinforcement theory.

Many people reported the results of the study in workshops and conferences. The classroom was not only to be a pleasant, kindly place; it was to be "democratic," i.e., the students were to take an important part in the decisions that would govern them. Hilda Taba, then of the University of Chicago, was supported by B'nai B'rith to carry the word of this finding, and also the other findings about racial and religious prejudice, to the teachers of the nation through conferences and workshops. She and others found a ready audience during the times of crisis of the late 1930s and early 1940s. The exhortation to develop a "democratic" classroom climate achieved widespread acceptance.

One consequence of this confluence of educational doctrines was to call into question the nature of the teacher's authority, and by extension the authority of the textbook. In the minority of classrooms (some estimated that it never exceeded 5 percent) that were self-consciously "progressive," the use of a single basic textbook series was abandoned in favor of a variety of reference materials and tangible objects, often in school libraries.[16] Many school libraries were established, or greatly increased in size. It was recommended by the American Library Association and some educational authorities that high school libraries have collections of at least 10,000 titles, and classroom library collections became increasingly common in elementary schools.

This brief account of the evolution of school textbooks during the early part of this century has been placed in the context of the Progressive education movement. It should also be placed in the context of the history of the use of textbooks since the emergence of schools for the common people during the eighteenth century, and indeed since the beginning of formal instruction in much earlier times. This history lives in the present.

The text as an educational resource begins with the reliance on Holy Writ and the writings of the Ancients (which took place in many cultures), when scholars committed texts to memory, and based what they wrote on elaborate citations, preferably in the original tongue. This tradition continues in some scholarly writing. The most extravagant example of it in English is Robert Burton's *The Anatomy of Melancholy* of the mid-seventeenth century, half of which was written in untranslated Latin citations. During that century, it was assumed that whatever was published was written for the ages, and for the elite who could read.

That tradition lingers in the schools to this day. A school textbook carries with it the assumption that it contains the uncontroverted truth. Even the name, *text*book, implies this assumption. The *New England Primer*, Webster's Speller, Ray's Arithmetic, and McGuffey's

Readers (first published in 1837) and the various histories of the United States published after the Revolution and during the nineteenth century, all were offered to students as official texts, containing the truth. A textbook, accordingly, should never contain anything subject to question or controversy. Teachers should never, never offer anything controversial to their students, because they, like the texts, were supposed to be perfectly virtuous, and, like the Prophets, to deal with unalterable, permanent truth. The textbook controversies of the present, of course, stem from this tradition.

This history explains in part why the Progressive movement disappeared. It attempted to carry into the lower schools the questioning tradition of the nineteenth-century university, which to this day worries our cultural, political, and intellectual conservatives.

Building America, a liberally oriented social studies journal, appeared in 1935 as a publication of the Society for Curriculum Study. In 1947, when it was published through the Association for Supervision and Curriculum Development, it was demolished by conservative attacks.

The Impact of Committee and Commission Reports

So far, we have dealt here with the ideas and influences of the Progressive movement. These were given expression in textbooks, as we have indicated, but the rhetoric that they grew out of was offered in a number of reports by national committees and commissions, often composed of or led by individuals of very high national status. The story of these groups has been told in several well-known historical accounts. It will suffice here to indicate their influence on educational materials and practice.

The most influential of these reports have been the most prescriptive. The reports of the Committee of Ten and the Committee of Fifteen of the 1890s, before the Progressives, had a direct effect on the offerings in the elementary and secondary schools of the United States, which continue to reflect them. There were others. The report of the Commission on Economy of Time in Education (headed by Abraham Flexner, who previously had led the reform of medical education), led to the elimination of astronomy from the secondary schools, and contributed to the great decline of enrollments in Latin and Greek (the latter now having disappeared almost entirely). The report of the Commission on the Reorganization of Secondary Education, *Cardinal Principles of Secondary Education*, functioned as a kind of manifesto (or perhaps an agenda), was widely discussed, and was influential on the writing of textbooks such as those described earlier here.[17] In the early 1940s, two reports by the Educational Policies Commission, *Education for ALL American Youth* and *Education for ALL American Children*, sought to sum up what had by then become the conventional Progressive wisdom.[18] The reports were widely discussed on college campuses and in the central offices of some school districts. Earlier, the Twenty-sixth Yearbook of the National Society for the Study of Education, *Curriculum Making: Past and Present*," had set in motion what became the curriculum field.[19]

The more prescriptive of the various reports by the national committees and commissions had the greatest effect on school practice, and hence on the demand for textbooks and other materials. The reports that had such an impact may now be listed. They include the reports of the Committee of Ten on secondary education and of the Committee of Fifteen on elementary education, the Commission on the Reorganization of Secondary Education (which issued the *Cardinal Principles of Secondary Education*), and James B. Conant's *The American High School Today* (although this volume was published in 1959, after the period discussed here). Other reports have been forgotten, or have dissolved into little more than rhetoric. Of the reports issued since 1980, if this generalization holds, only the *Paedeia Proposal* of Mortimer Adler is likely to have a detectable effect on school practice, including the materials of instruction.

The list of forgotten reports is long, though many of them were widely read and discussed in their own time. The list includes the publications of the Progressive Education Association, the publications of the Commission on Life Adjustment Education, and the various polemics of the 1950s. The lesson seems evident: to have an effect, be specific and prescriptive.

The reports of several of the committees and commissions were echoed in several of the large city and state school systems in the work of large, expensive curriculum committees, which consisted of teachers released from the classroom for the purpose, aided by university consultants. These committees published courses of study, sometimes voluminous. George Reavis, then Curriculum Director for Cincinnati, once described in a lecture the process that was widely used. The committee worked for a year, for example, on the Language Arts offering, issuing a mimeographed preliminary report. This report was distributed for trial and criticism to the teachers of the school district. Following revision, it was issued in final, printed form, and became the official course of study for the district, and was, in Reavis's term, "installed."

These voluminous courses of study were circulated throughout the nation. Some of them, notably the State of Pennsylvania "telephone book" (so nicknamed because of its size and appearance), became source material for courses of study in other school systems.

By 1945, it had become evident that this approach to changing the actual classroom offering had a very limited effect, and in many cases no effect at all. The large, expensive courses of study gathered dust on the classroom shelves. My personal experience as a junior high school teacher late in the 1930s is illustrative. I read most of the course of study before offering a course in science for the first time. I glanced at it once or twice during the next semester, and forgot about it. By then, I had developed a course of my own, which included the general topics contained in the course of study, but which differed from it in approach and much substance. Why? Because I had found what "worked" for me and the students I faced. Many teachers must have made the same decision. The difficulty was that these courses of study did not fit any classroom in particular.

Neither did the textbooks. While some teachers, no doubt, simply followed the book, I and the teachers I knew at that time used them as reference books. Used that way, the more books the better. In my science classes, I had access to five different science series. They formed the nucleus of a classroom library, but they were far from being the main resource, since the offering was intended to be a "hands-on" experience.

The Impact of Developments in Testing

However, another approach had a very substantial effect on classroom practice: the development of mental testing and the development of achievement testing. Both had begun early in the century, and began to have widespread effects on school practice during the 1920s. Tests of mental ability, or "intelligence," were (and are) used widely to estimate the students' potential for academic achievement. By 1920, in Detroit, they were used to form ability groups, usually three in number for a given grade. The Detroit "X", "Y", and "Z" groups were used widely by the end of the 1920s, and they continued to be used in the schools despite growing criticism. They had their effect on textbooks. Arthur Gates, for example, strongly recommended the use of ability groups for instruction in reading:

1. Forming Ability Classes.
Determining Reading Ability. In a school in which the number of fourth-grade pupils is large enough to form several grade classes, it is usually advantageous to divide the pupils into classes as homogeneous as possible in capacity and ability. For this purpose, the following tests are recommended:
    1. An individual or group intelligence test.
    2. Two or more of the *Gates Silent Reading Tests for Grades 3 to 8* . . .
    3. *The Modern School Achievement Test in Level of Reading Comprehension.*[20]

The practice of ability grouping was attacked by the Progressives, but it is still widely practiced. The opponents of this practice cite research in support of their position, but a great many teachers prefer to continue it. Accordingly, some elementary school texts have been especially written for children of low reading ability—a fifth-grade social studies text, for example, written at a third-grade reading level.

The texts, too, were based on research. As Gates said (in the First Grade *Manual* of the *Work-Play Books*):

The Work-Play Books are designed to put into effect the principles of a modern philosophy of education and the laws of the psychology of learning. They are the outcome of more than ten years of research.[21]

In 1958, Gates continued to base his judgments on such research. He told me in conversation, for example, that the average reading scores for elementary school children on his tests had increased a full school grade between the 1937 and 1957 renorming and revision of the Gates Reading Tests. The norming population of 1957 was huge— 100,000 children. During the period after 1930, of course, the techniques of testing and of statistical analysis were very considerably refined, and the scope of achievement testing was greatly broadened.

What many hoped would be the definitive research on the nature and results of the Progressive movement was published in 1942 as the five-volume report of the Eight Year Study, but the effect of this publication was almost entirely obliterated by the events of World War II. The Eight Year Study has left very little residue, although the report by Eugene R. Smith and Ralph W. Tyler, *Appraising and Reporting Student Progress*, had a substantial effect on the development of the techniques of evaluation.[22] This pivotal book illustrated how such a quality as critical thinking could be measured, and in doing this, gave the first behaviorally oriented description of this process. This, and the other approaches developed by the Evaluation section of the Eight Year Study at The Ohio State University (under Tyler's direction) had the effect of transforming the field of achievement testing. It may well be the most enduring contribution of the Eight Year Study.

The Legacy of the Progressive Era

What, then, is the legacy? Some of the residue of the Progressive era continues to appear in classroom practice and in the materials of instruction. Here are some examples:

1. Testing and evaluation are here to stay, though the modes of estimating actual and potential accomplishment continue to evolve.

2. The materials of instruction are much broader than they were a half century ago, though they continue to be mainly print-driven and verbal.

3. Many teachers believe that a supportive (but not overly permissive) classroom climate is not only more pleasant for teachers and students, but is more productive of classroom learning.

4. The public continues to believe that some form of educational material is basic to school learning, and seems willing to pay a much higher cost than was earlier the case. The public has supported the acquisition of instructional hardware ever since the invention of the telephone, the phonograph, and the motion picture. They live in hope that some concrete device will solve the difficult problems of education.

What has disappeared, or become less common?

1. The Activity Movement and the Project Method. Despite a brief reencounter with these practices during the Open School fad of the early 1970s, few teachers make use of them at present. An occasional teacher makes use of the Dalton Contract (not mentioned here, but descriptions are easily available in the literature).

2. Democracy in the classroom. Under the pressure brought by the press, politicians, and therefore the public, teachers have felt constrained to reassert their authority in the classroom. This has led to a virtual disappearance of cooperative planning and other practices requiring that the student take part in deciding what to learn in school. Achievement test scores, not teachers and students, dictate the nature and content of the student's school experience.

3. Respect for children. The rhetoric of school reform, as this is written, deals not with children as human beings, but with the structure and organization of schools and the incentives to be offered to teachers. The factory model of education has become the dominant metaphor: input, process, output. The Progressive ideal of respect for the child as a growing human being has largely disappeared from public discourse.

Given the nature of school reform movements, it seems likely that many of those currently being undertaken will come to seem atavistic, and that a later wave of school reform will affirm much of what the Progressives held dear. It is to be hoped that what is fruitful about the reforms of the 1980s will not be lost, as was the rigor of the 1890s during the Progressive era, and that the more imaginative and effective aspects of the Progressives will be reaffirmed and extended. There is reason to hope that the developers of the materials of instruction, including textbooks, may be among the leaders of the next wave of educational reform. The textbooks have always been specific and prescriptive; as they illustrate how authentic instruction can be accomplished, they can help to make it happen.

The question that emerges from this review is this: Do textbooks determine the curriculum, or do they reflect it? Before 1900, it appears that textbooks *were* the academic curriculum, especially in the elementary schools. Since then, as teachers became better educated and the schools broadened their purposes and took in more of the population, textbooks have come more and more to reflect the curriculum, not to lead it. While remaining major sources of information and ideas, by 1950 textbooks had found their place in a greatly broadened array of resources.

Of course, schools vary enormously in the breadth of resources they use. It is not possible to determine the actual school practice in detail; Bagley's attempt in 1930, and several equally small studies since then, are all that are available, and they are not adequate to the scope of the question. It is important, as Fraley points out,[23] not to confuse the rhetoric with the reality. It is likely, however, that by 1950 most schools offered much more than the textbook as the source of academic learning in the curriculum.

In any case, textbook publishers must follow the market; they do not make it. As the Progressive era ended, it seems clear that the textbooks did not make the curriculum; they reflected it. Experience shows that textbooks can influence practice in fairly minor ways, but they are still chosen by schools and school systems, and they must compete for the attention of potential purchasers.

40   TEXTBOOKS AND CURRICULUM: 1930-1950

FOOTNOTES

1. John Dewey, *The Child and the Curriculum* (Chicago: University of Chicago Press, 1902).

2. Ralph W. Tyler, "The Place of the Textbook in Modern Education," *Harvard Educational Review* 11 (May 1941): 329-34.

3. Ibid., pp. 335-37.

4. Jeanne Chall, *Learning to Read: The Great Debate* (New York: McGraw-Hill, 1967).

5. William Bagley, "The Textbook and Methods of Teaching," in *The Textbook in Modern Education*, ed. Guy M. Whipple, Thirtieth Yearbook of the National Society for the Study of Education, Part 2 (Bloomington, IL: Public School Publishing Co., 1931), pp. 7-26.

6. Jeanne Chall, Sue Conard, and Susan Harris-Sharples, *An Analysis of Textbooks in Relation to Declining SAT Scores* (Princeton, NJ: College Entrance Examination Board, 1877).

7. *The New England Primer*, Twentieth Century Reprint, facsimile (New York: Ginn & Co., n.d.).

8. *McGuffey's Eclectic Primer*, rev. ed. (New York: American Book Co., 1909).

9. William H. Elson and Lura E. Runkel, *The Elson Readers Primer* (Chicago: Scott Foresman, 1927).

10. George S. Counts, *Dare the School Build a New Social Order?* Pamphlet 11 (New York: John Day, 1932).

11. Harold Rugg, *A History of American Government and Culture* (Boston: Ginn & Co., 1931). See also, idem, *An Introduction to American Civilization* (Boston: Ginn & Co., 1929).

12. Frank Abbott Magruder, *American Government: A Consideration of the Problems of Democracy* (Boston: Allyn and Bacon, 1930).

13. John R. Clark, Arthur S. Otis, Caroline Hatton, and Raleigh Schorling, *Modern School Arithmetic, Eighth Grade* (Yonkers-on-Hudson, NY: World Book Co., 1938).

14. Commission on Secondary Education of the Progressive Education Association, *Science in General Education: Suggestions for Science Teachers in Secondary Schools and in the Lower Division of Colleges*, Report of the Committee on Science in General Education (New York: Appleton-Century-Crofts, 1938).

15. Ronald Lippitt, "An Experimental Study of the Effect of Democratic and Authoritarian Group Atmospheres," in *Studies of Topological and Vector Psychology 1*, University of Iowa Studies, Studies in Child Welfare, vol. 16, no. 3 (Iowa City, IA, 1940), pp. 45-195.

16. Angela E. Fraley, "Core Curriculum: An Epic in the History of Educational Reform" (Doct. diss., Teachers College, Columbia University, 1977).

17. Commission on the Reorganization of Secondary Education, *Cardinal Principles of Secondary Education*, U.S. Office of Education Bulletin 35 (Washington, DC: Government Printing Office, 1918).

18. Educational Policies Commission, *Education for ALL American Youth* (Washington, DC: National Education Association/American Association of School Administrators, 1944); idem, *Education for ALL American Children* (Washington, DC: National Education Association/American Association of School Administrators, 1948).

19. National Society for the Study of Education, *Curriculum-Making: Past and Present*, ed. Guy M. Whipple, Twenty-sixth Yearbook of the National Society for the Study of Education, Part 1 (Bloomington, IL: Public School Publishing Co., 1926).

20. Arthur I. Gates and Jean Y. Ayer, *The Work-Play Books, Fourth Grade Manual* (New York: Macmillan, 1932), p. 23.

21. Arthur I. Gates and Jean Y. Ayer, *The Work-Play Books, First Grade Manual* (New York: Macmillan, 1931), p. 1.

22. Eugene R. Smith, Ralph W. Tyler, and the Evaluation Staff, *Appraising and Recording Student Progress* (New York: Harper, 1942).

23. Angela E. Fraley, *Schooling and Innovation* (Boston: Tyler Gibson, 1981).

CHAPTER III

Textbooks and the Curriculum in the Postwar Era: 1950-1980

DAVID L. ELLIOTT

The Challenge

During this postwar period (1950-1980), the standard American public school curriculum met its greatest challenge in the federally funded, subject-oriented curriculum projects of the late 1960s and early 1970s. While textbooks reflected but had not yet come to exemplify that curriculum, they too were greatly influenced by these projects. This chapter describes how the challenge to curriculum and textbooks was met by the emergence of nationally marketed, multigrade textbook programs that became the dominant shapers of the curriculum.

The Legacy from the Previous Era

Following World War II, the Progressive era came to a close and further development of education for problem solving never appeared.[1] Instead, early progressivism came to be replaced by an increasing concern for course content, a concern clearly represented in two popular contemporary doctrines, "life adjustment" education and "social reconstructionism." The curriculum based on these doctrines emphasized preselected units of study constructed around either personal or social problems known to be recurrent in our society. A decade or so later, a lingering uneasiness about the Progressive movement found expression in a concern about children's learning of basic skills and led to enriched classrooms and materials, especially textbook programs supplemented with audiovisual materials and equipment.[2]

Nonetheless, elements of the progressive heritage were revived, at least in a small number of classrooms, and survived into at least the

42

early 1970s. Examples of this torch-bearing were found in the correlated and fused curricula of the 1950s, in which subjects such as English and social studies or mathematics and science were presented together in order to take advantage of their interrelationships, and in the later interest in "open education" late in the 1960s.[3]

A SOCIETY IN FLUX

The aftermath of World War II brought Cold War competition with the Russians and fear of communist expansion at home and abroad. It also brought an expanding industrial economy and the need for trained and intelligent manpower. Both of these developments had a profound effect on the schools of this country. Cremin wrote that "any one of these in and of itself would have loosed fantastic pressures on the schools. Taken together, however, and compounded by a growing dissatisfaction among the intelligentsia, they held the makings of the deepest educational crisis in the nation's history."[4]

Postwar America was very different from the one that had given rise to progressive education. There was rampant individualism, which was often called nonconformity. The economy was harnessing vast new energy sources and extending the uses of automation that made earlier notions of vocational education obsolete. New information was being generated at a phenomenal pace, thus "thrusting to the fore the school's traditional responsibility for organizing and transmitting knowledge of every sort and variety."[5] And as if all this ferment were not enough, the next decade brought the Civil Rights movement and related desegregation and antipoverty efforts that were to put even more demands on the schools.

The explosion of knowledge was to give rise to interest in the structure and strategies of the subject fields, to new studies in children's learning and development, and as we shall see, unprecedented nationwide efforts in school curriculum reform. In the meantime, critical appraisal of the schools and their roles in educating young people coming from many quarters—much of it from critics outside the ranks of professional educators such as Rudolph Flesch (*Why Johnny Can't Read*), Arthur Bestor (*Educational Wastelands*) and Hyman Rickover (*Education and Freedom*)—focused public attention on the schools and the education of the nation's children and youth.[6]

THE ROLE OF TEXTBOOKS

In their chapter on "The Controversial Past and Present of the Text," McMurray and Cronbach reminded us that textbooks have played a major part in Western education for 500 years, years that have "brought fundamental changes in educational outlook."[7] Referring to the reformers of earlier decades, they held that "present-day criticism of the text arises largely because many writers contend that in its present form or perhaps in its essential nature, the printed text is unsuited to the new aims of education." Nevertheless, they found schools were purchasing and using more texts than ever before and so inferred that the textbooks of the time must have been compatible with the approaches of most educators. Throughout the 1940s and 1950s, however, most critics of the schools were not factoring textbooks into the equation of criticism and calls for reform. The brunt of critics' attacks was brought to bear on teachers, teaching approaches, and subject-matter content. For example, in the first edition of *Why Johnny Can't Read*, Rudolph Flesch took issue with the "look-say" method for teaching reading, and it was not until his second volume, *Why Johnny Still Can't Read* that he mounted a direct attack on textbooks by denouncing the "dismal dozen" reading series.[8]

Nevertheless, there were some critics who were taking textbooks to task for containing preselected subject matter that was oversimplified and organized in ways that made it difficult to tailor instruction to individual learners. In the 1960s, Dale found textbooks still being criticized for being inflexible, for promoting uncritical memorization, and for stressing training rather than education, with lessons of limited relevance to learners' needs.[9] It was not until later in that decade, however, that a major round of challenges to the dominance of the textbook took place in the form of federally sponsored subject-matter projects. In the instructional approaches of these projects and the writings of their staff members, the answer to the question raised by McMurray and Cronbach was that the textbook, at least in its present form, was indeed unsuited to the new aims of education.[10]

The Response

The curriculum projects of the 1950s and 1960s that were mounted in response to general dissatisfaction with school programs certainly had the potential to make a successful challenge to the type of day-to-day classroom instruction represented by the textbook. Before these projects came along, many and varied strategies and tactics were employed as the schools responded to the criticisms. Administrative measures such as nongraded classrooms and team teaching were tried, along with technological innovations such as educational television and programmed instruction, and with other approaches such as the use of behavioral objectives and accountability schemes based on achievement tests, to name just a few. In addition, there were the projects supported under the provisions of the 1957 National Defense Education Act that emphasized science, mathematics, and foreign languages and were later expanded to include history, geography, reading, civics, and English.

Unprecedented levels of financial support from both the federal government and private foundations were given to curriculum improvement efforts in elementary and secondary schools. The Elementary and Secondary Education Act gave rise to hundreds of local and regional efforts to improve programs. An emerging concern over the effects of poverty on the development of preschool and school-age children gave rise to a wide range of early childhood and "compensatory" education programs, the most notable of which were Head Start and Follow Through. The National Science Foundation sponsored projects in mathematics, science, and social studies.

SUBJECT AREA CURRICULUM PROJECTS

It was these subject-matter projects that collectively became one of the most concerted and comprehensive educational reform efforts in our nation's history. Starting in the late 1950s with the Physical Science Study Committee, a number of curriculum projects were initiated. Most of the projects were influenced by the Woods Hole Conference in 1959. The publication of a report of that conference, *The Process of Education*, in which Jerome Bruner appeared to reaffirm the importance of "learning by doing" of the earlier Progressive era, but with the added dimension of having the "doing" (discovering) guided early on by inquiry approaches and by the "structures" of the knowledge disciplines.[11]

By 1964, there were seven elementary/junior high and five high school projects, and by 1966 there were twenty-six projects. In the typical format of these projects, university scholars, in some cases teamed with professional educators, mounted elaborate and ambitious efforts to produce new curricula in a wide range of separate subject areas. Writing sessions were followed by trial testing of materials in schools. Dissemination was accomplished through the production of teacher's manuals and student materials and equipment and through in-service institutes and workshops for teachers. In some cases, the materials were later published and marketed by commercial publishers, usually without a teacher training component.

In these projects, participating scholars initially intended to update content of elementary and secondary science, but soon found that "explicit ways of controlling and manipulating information had to be taught if any integrity of content was to be achieved."[12] That is, in order for children to understand the knowledge in any subject area, it was found that they had also to be introduced to what Bruner called the "structure" of that subject area, or the ways in which things are related within it. The science curriculum products had modernized content, up-dated and selected to permit in-depth study; a rich variety of multimedia materials; and emphasis on science process—on "doing" science through "hands-on" learning activities—and on the use of unifying themes.[13]

One result of all these efforts was a proliferation of separate subjects, including new ones not previously taught (e.g., astronomy, anthropology).[14] This situation was undoubtedly due to the fact that most of the new curriculum projects were initiated or strongly influenced by scholars from individual disciplines rather than by elementary and secondary educators, in marked contrast to the situation in the 1950s when correlated and fused subjects had brought the content of closely related disciplines together so that similarities and interrelationships could be more readily understood.

Thus it was that most projects rejected the traditional fact-oriented ways of teaching mathematics, science, and social studies in favor of an emphasis on hands-on discovery and inquiry. Other projects applied modern principles of linguistics to the teaching of reading, English language arts, and the teaching of foreign languages.

Many projects found the textbook format too confining for their purposes and the products of most elementary science projects (e.g., Elementary Science Study [ESS], Science Curriculum Improvement Study [SCIS], and Science—A Process Approach [S—APA] and some in elementary social studies (e.g. "Man: A Course of Study" [MACOS] and "Our Working World") were published as multimedia materials packages. However, the adoption of new textbooks was the central method of spreading the new curricula at the secondary level (e.g., the physics text of the Physical Science Study Committee [PSSC] and the biology texts of the Biological Science Curriculum Study [BSCS]). A good many of the projects also realized the importance of teacher's guides and preservice and in-service training for teachers, although when the materials kits and textbooks were picked up by commercial publishers this latter component was not emphasized either by the publishers or the users. This neglect of teacher training was probably the weakest link in this whole curriculum reform movement and a key cause of its demise. Longstreet saw in the process emphases of the new curriculum products "a profound restructuring of what was educationally valuable," a substantial shift from conventional instructional methods, and thus a significant alteration of teacher-student relationships.[15] Teachers and textbooks were no longer to be "unquestioned distributors of truth; they were, instead, to be questioned, tested, and doubted." The role of the student was to shift from passive consumer to active producer of concepts and generalizations, so that teacher-pupil relationships and the ways the teacher imparted knowledge would have to be changed. Unfortunately, this perspective reached relatively few classrooms. In practice, public school teachers tended to adopt the new materials and perspectives without essentially modifying their traditional ways of teaching. "The new processes and perspectives dropped by the wayside."[16]

The Result

Following a brief flurry of enthusiasm, the new curricula and their related materials failed to take root in the schools. Materials from federally funded projects of the 1960s and 1970s were not selected for classroom use (only 25 percent of teachers used a minimum of one program). The dominant instructional material continued to be the conventional textbook, the social studies curriculum was mostly history and government, with geography at K-8. The dominant modes of instruction continued to be large-group, teacher-controlled recitation and lecture based primarily on the textbook, and the "knowing" expected of students was largely information-oriented. To be successful, students had to reproduce not only the content but the language of the textbook.[17]

Thus it was that most of the products of the subject-matter projects were neither widely adopted nor did they stand the test of time. Any number of explanations have been offered for this failure. As indicated above, Longstreet noted that the process emphasis and alteration in teacher and pupil roles advocated by most projects did not take root and teachers tended to adopt the new materials without essentially modifying their traditional ways of teaching. Marker held that the programs were too difficult to implement, had unrealistic user expectations, lost their on-site advocate, and/or faced problems from misapplication.[18] Engle argued that the main reason the "new social studies" programs were not being used was that teachers "are poorly prepared by their own education to confront the controversy and uncertainty that is the real bone and sinew of scholarship" and that democratic ideology "is not as universally accepted by our people as our language would lead us to believe."[19] Welch reviewed studies of science curriculum development, including the characteristics of the curriculum products and the development strategy that went into producing them, factors influencing their adoption and use, and evidence of their impact on schools and students, and concluded that the science classroom of 1979 was little different from that of twenty years earlier.[20]

Textbooks in the 1980s

Walker saw the "commercially packaged kits designed to accompany individualized programs [as] the greatest challenge to the conventional textbook" during the 1960s and 1970s.[21] For the most part, this challenge was unsuccessful, although, as indicated earlier, textbooks based on the work of many of the curriculum projects (e.g., BSCS and PSSC) were published and the subject-matter content and learning exercises of many of the science and social studies textbooks were noticeably influenced, at least for a few years, by the research and development work of those two decades.[22]

Most changes in textbooks that occurred during the 1970s and 1980s were more evolutionary than revolutionary, and took place in response to a wide range of influences. Generally speaking, there was a slow, steady movement toward individualization of instruction, especially in reading (stapled sheets, cards, booklets, and other aids that could be used separately). In addition, supplements to textbooks in the form of audiovisual materials and equipment, programmed instruction, computer-assisted instruction, films, and video recordings blossomed. Textbooks grew in size and became more colorful and more highly illustrated. Basic skills programs, especially competency-based approaches, were mounted across all of the basic subjects. Concern over misrepresentation and underrepresentation of minorities (and later of women, the handicapped, and the aged) led to significant revisions in the pictorial (and some of the narrative) content of textbooks starting in the 1960s. Interest in career education resulted mainly in inclusion of information relevant to careers in mathematics, science, and social studies textbooks.

In 1979, a conference on "The Textbook in American Education" was held at the Library of Congress "to review the state of knowledge regarding the textbook in American education and society, and through this review to stimulate future inquiries."[23] In her conference paper, Chall concluded that middle and secondary school textbooks might have been too easy, a condition she saw as a commentary on the use of readability formulas in writing and editing textbooks.[24] She did, however, see changes in textbooks in response to concern for tightening of requirements and stressing of essentials in reading in the late 1960s, in writing in the mid-1970s, and in mathematics in the mid-1970s (when dissatisfaction with the "new math" led to a demand for greater emphasis on skill in computing than on concepts and understandings). Similar "back to basics" concerns were expressed about social studies and science texts, which had moved away from an emphasis on facts and dates to an emphasis on concepts and generalizations.

In another conference paper, Porter reported that content analyses of elementary mathematics textbooks showed (a) that a "core curriculum in fourth grade mathematics does exist," especially with respect to computational skills associated with "back to basics"; (b) that variation in content covered in different textbooks, especially in "optional curriculum" topics, "could result in variation in content taught in the classroom"; and (c) that, in general, "content decisions that are left to the teacher require a comparatively high level of expertise in mathematics." The content decisions left to the teacher "may be those that teachers are least prepared to make."[25]

As a result of a study of cognitive levels in the "complex numbers" sections of secondary textbooks printed between 1961 and 1984 and the "decimals" sections of textbooks printed in the mid-1980s for grades three through six, Nicely concluded that widely used textbooks "rarely pose real problems."[26] Two studies of secondary mathematics textbooks published between 1961 and 1980 concluded that, if problem solving is to be a major focus of school mathematics during the 1980s, the textbook will be inadequate as (the sole) instructional resource to help students acquire these higher-level cognitive processes.[27]

Aukerman described and illustrated the origins and methods and materials of some 101 approaches, most of which were available in commercially published textbooks or similar materials.[28] Beck found "much evidence that basal reading programs represent the state of the art of reading instruction" (both content and methods).[29] Chall reported that two widely used traditional basal reading series contain lessons built around stories, word method, an emphasis on comprehension, little phonics or writing, and heavy dependence on the teacher. One newer series that began with phonics contained lessons built around phonic elements, greater variety in teaching new words, and similar emphasis on comprehension.[30] Bond and Dykstra summarized and discussed the findings of twenty-seven studies of the relationships between various approaches to beginning reading instruction and student achievement in reading.[31] Finding no statistically significant differences across approaches, they concluded that to improve reading instruction "it is necessary to train better teachers rather than to expect a panacea in the form of materials."

Patrick and Hawke compared social studies textbooks from 1980 and 1960 and found that the most widely used textbooks were alike in format and style, and contained similar information and interpretations.[32] The most striking changes were in the slick use of graphics and general attractiveness. Skill development lessons were more frequent in elementary texts; content coverage was stressed in secondary texts. Generally, there was more diversity in pedagogy—ranging from "read-recite"/narrative chapters and end-of-chapter questions to more use of primary source materials, of tabular and graphic data, and of more varied end-of-chapter activities. On the other hand, Agostino and Barone compared social studies textbook programs published in the late 1970s and early 1980s with those published a decade earlier and found that few of the "new social studies" innovations of the earlier programs found their way into those published later.[33] A group from People for the American Way examined thirteen commonly used textbooks and found them encyclopedic and comprehensive in scope, with too much stress on facts and too little on concepts, methods, or critical thinking about American public values, the conflicts among them, and the necessity for continually making choices.[34]

Schneider and Van Sickle surveyed thirty-six major publishers of social studies instructional materials to determine the degree of change and diversity in content or instructional methodology and found a retreat from the dramatic changes of the 1960s and early 1970s due in large part to a general concern for basic education, but also a concern for the "humanizing" of social studies.[35] Ravitch compared the "expanding environments" content of most current K-3 social studies programs with the study of mythology, legends, biographies, hero tales, and great events of Western literature and history that made up the curriculum before the 1930s, and suggested that the earlier content be restored in the interest of promoting "cultural literacy."[36]

Fitzgerald carried out a comprehensive study of junior and senior high school U.S. history textbooks published since 1900 and found that pedagogical fads, influences of political interest groups, and other prejudices of the time have led to revising history texts to reflect current values, thus losing continuity and precluding generations of students from sharing any common reading of the past.[37] Today's textbooks are written by committees and designed to be simplistic and to offend no one, making them incredibly dull. True scholars have little or no role (or interest) in the writing of textbooks any longer. This latter judgment was upheld by Downey, who suggested that one reason for the poor quality of secondary U.S. history textbooks is that the scholarly community has not taken an active interest in them. He asserted that U.S. history textbooks ought to be reviewed more regularly and suggested minimal criteria to apply in such reviews.[38]

Jackson examined forty-four secondary-level geography texts published from 1900 to 1970 to determine how long ideas persisted even though they had been abandoned at the university level.[39] Environmental determinism, as the basic explanation of man's activities on earth, was used as an index of change and not until the 1960s did determinism begin to be widely questioned in secondary level texts—at least twenty years after it was abandoned as a central theme at the university level.

Graves analyzed eight language arts textbooks and teacher's editions at both the second- and fifth-grade levels to determine how much and in what way writing was taught.[40] He found that, although writing opportunities were introduced and mechanics emphasized, "the entire (writing) process area was left untouched by the texts." Neither prewriting, composing, nor postcomposing activities were "suggested with strength or substance," nor was the learner's capacity for voice development or self-critical capability developed. Donsky studied the learning activities in three representative English language arts textbooks from each of three periods between 1900 and 1969 and found declining trends in the written word and increase in oral language exercises, with grammar and sentence construction remaining essentially unchanged.[41]

Elliott and Nagel found that nine elementary science series published between 1984 and 1986 emphasized the *products* of science through topic coverage, memorization of content, and cookbook-style hands-on activities with predetermined results, rather than science *process*.[42] Pauling discussed and illustrated problems he found with high school chemistry textbooks: too much information presented at too advanced a level, too many errors, and the inclusion of complex and confusing topics (e.g., molecular orbitals).[43] Rigden criticized textbooks as a major source of a common view that advances in science do not depend on inspiration and imagination but come (only) from straightforward logical thinking that is not only "smooth and unerring [but] routine and inevitable. . . . Scientific knowledge is the overriding concern of textbook writers; the *quest* for that knowledge is ignored."[44]

Conclusion

The challenge to the textbook as the main source of instruction that was mounted in the 1960s and 1970s largely failed. True, the contributions of university scholars in the curriculum projects trickled down and resulted in some expansion and updating of subject-matter content. General science, for example, has been replaced by large infusions of life, earth, and physical science; and some social studies programs have certainly shown the influence of input from the social science disciplines. In addition, a rich collection of supplementary materials has been built up, including print material, films, videorecordings, maps and charts, and three-dimensional models. Many of these materials are offered by the same publishers that produce the textbook programs and are intended for use with those programs.

What has not carried over from the curriculum projects of the 1960s and 1970s is the stress on inquiry and discovery, the promotion of student initiative in asking questions and seeking answers using the conceptual tools and "ways of knowing" of the knowledge disciplines. Problem solving is missing from mathematics, writing from language arts, "hands-on" laboratory inquiry from science, the study and discussion of social and political problems from social studies, and a range of varied evaluation approaches that tap more than factual recall from programs in all subject areas.

Also missing from the preceding era are activities and projects, the use of community resources, the interrelating of knowledge across subject fields, democracy in the classroom, and a respect for children (and teachers) as individuals capable of acting both independently and in cooperation with others to manage their own learning (and teaching) and solve problems.

So it is that, despite the mustering of an unprecedented array of resources from the federal government, private foundations, universities, professional organizations, the textbook prevailed. Textbooks not only grew in size and improved in aesthetic appeal, but came to be packaged with a set of ancillary components such as teacher's editions, workbooks, quizzes and tests, and (in some cases) supplementary books and audiovisual and manipulable materials. Moreover, textbook programs appear increasingly to have taken over the role of multigrade level curriculums in the various subject areas, replacing local courses of study and becoming substitutes for teacher initiative and creativity in program planning, particularly at the elementary level where one teacher is responsible for at least five or six subject areas.

These developments are consistent with Eisner's characterization of the textbook and its ancillary materials as serving multiple functions that reinforce its central role in determining curriculum content largely because textbooks provide expertise, are "time savers," and provide security for both teachers and students in outlining content scope and sequence.[45]

Footnotes

1. Foster McMurray and Lee J. Cronbach, "The Controversial Past and Present of the Text," ed. Lee J. Cronbach, *Text Materials in Modern Education* (Urbana: University of Illinois Press, 1955).

2. Roma Gans, "The Progressive Era: Its Relationship to the Contemporary Scene," in Bernard Spodek and others, *Open Education: The Legacy of the Progressive Movement* (Washington, DC: National Association for the Education of Young Children, 1970), pp. 39-50.

3. See Vincent R. Rogers and Bud Church, *Open Education: Critique and Assessment* (Washington, DC: Association for Supervision and Curriculum Development, 1975), pp. 7-16, and Spodek and others, *Open Education.*

4. Lawrence Cremin, *The Transformation of the School: Progressivism in American Education, 1876-1957* (New York: Alfred A. Knopf, 1961), pp. 338-39.

5. Ibid., p. 356.

6. Rudolph Flesch, *Why Johnny Can't Read and What You Can Do About It* (New York: Harper & Row, 1955); Arthur Bestor, *Educational Wastelands* (Urbana: University of Illinois Press, 1953); and Hyman G. Rickover, *Education and Freedom* (New York: E.P. Dutton, 1959).

7. McMurray and Cronbach, "The Controversial Past and Present of the Text."

8. Rudolph Flesch, *Why Johnny Still Can't Read* (New York: Harper & Row, 1981).

9. Edgar Dale, "Instructional Resources," in *The Changing American School*, ed. John I. Goodlad, Sixty-fifth Yearbook of the National Society for the Study of Education, Part 2 (Chicago: University of Chicago Press, 1966), pp. 84-109.

10. For example, see Robert Karplus, *One Physicist Looks at Science Education* (Berkeley, CA: Science Curriculum Improvement Study, 1983).

11. Jerome S. Bruner, *The Process of Education* (New York: Alfred A. Knopf, 1960).

12. Wilma S. Longstreet, "The School's Curriculum," in *The Elementary School in the United States*, ed. John I. Goodlad and Harold G. Shane, Seventy-second Yearbook of the National Society for the Study of Education, Part 2 (Chicago: University of Chicago Press, 1973), p. 252.

13. Wayne W. Welch, "Twenty Years of Science Curriculum Development: A Look Back," in *Review of Educational Research*, 7, ed. David C. Berliner (Washington, DC: American Educational Research Association, 1979), pp. 282-306.

14. John I. Goodlad, *The Changing School Curriculum* (New York: Fund for the Advancement of Education, 1966).

15. Longstreet, "The School's Curriculum," p. 252.

16. Ibid., p. 253.

17. James P. Shaver, O. L. Davis, Jr., and Suzanne W. Helburn, "The Status of Social Studies Education: Impressions from Three NSF Studies," *Social Education* 43 (1979): 150-53.

18. Gerald W. Marker, "Why Schools Abandon 'New Social Studies' Materials," *Theory and Research in Social Education* 7 (1980): 35-56.

19. Shirley H. Engle, "Late Night Thoughts about the New Social Studies." *Social Education* 50 (January 1986): 20-22.

20. Wayne W. Welch, "Twenty Years of Science Curriculum Development."

21. Decker F. Walker, "Textbooks and the Curriculum," in *The Textbook in American Society*, ed. John Y. Cole and Thomas G. Sticht (Washington, DC: Library of Congress, 1981), pp. 2-3.

22. See EPIE Institute, *Product Reports* (New York: Educational Products Information Exchange Institute, 1975-1980).

23. John Y. Cole and Thomas G. Sticht, eds., *The Textbook in American Society: A Volume Based on a Conference at the Library of Congress on May 2-3, 1979* (Washington, DC: Library of Congress, 1981).

24. Jeanne S. Chall, "Middle and Secondary School Textbooks," in *The Textbook in American Society*, ed. Cole and Sticht, pp. 24-27.

25. Andrew C. Porter, "Elementary Mathematics Textbooks," in *The Textbook in American Society*, ed. Cole and Sticht, pp. 19-20.

26. Robert F. Nicely, Jr., "Higher Order Thinking in Mathematics Textbooks," *Educational Leadership* 42 (1985): 26-30.

27. Robert F. Nicely, Jr., "Mathematics Instruction: A Decade of Change." *International Journal of Instructional Media* 12 (1985): 127-36; Marilyn N. Suydam and Alan Osborne, *The Status of Pre-college Science, Mathematics, and Social Science, 1955-1975*, Vol. II: *Mathematics Education* (Columbus: Center for Science and Mathematics Education, Ohio State University, 1977), pp. 98-101.

28. Robert C. Aukerman, *Approaches to Beginning Reading* (New York: John Wiley & Sons, 1971).

29. Isabel L. Beck, "The Basal Readers," in *The Textbook in American Society*, ed. Cole and Sticht, pp. 14-16.

30. Jeanne S. Chall, *Learning to Read: The Great Debate* (New York: McGraw-Hill, 1967).

31. Guy L. Bond and Robert Dykstra, "The Cooperative Research Program in First-Grade Reading Instruction," *Reading Research Quarterly* 2 (1967): 5-142.

32. John J. Patrick and Sharryl D. Hawke, "Curriculum Materials," in *Social Studies in the 1980s*, ed. Irving Morrisett (Washington, DC: Association for Supervision and Curriculum Development, 1982), pp. 39-50.

33. V. R. Agostino and W. P. Barone, "A Decade of Change: Elementary Social Studies Texts," *Social Studies Journal* 14 (1985): 20-29.

34. J. D. Carroll, W. D. Brodnax, G. Contreras, T. E. Mann, N. J. Ornstein, and J. Stiehm, *We, The People: A Review of U.S. Government and Civics Textbooks* (Washington, DC: People for the American Way, 1987).

35. Donald O. Schneider and Ronald L. Van Sickle, "The Status of the Social Studies: the Publisher's Perspective," *Social Education* 43 (1979): 461-65.

36. Diane Ravitch, "Tot Sociology: or What Happened to History in the Grade Schools," *American Scholar* 56 (1987): 343-54.

37. Frances Fitzgerald, *America Revised: History Schoolbooks in the Twentieth Century* (Boston: Little, Brown, 1979).

38. Matthew T. Downey, "Speaking of Textbooks: Putting Pressure on the Publishers," *History Teacher* 14 (1980): 61-72.

39. R. H. Jackson, "The Persistence of Outmoded Ideas in High School Geography Texts," *Journal of Geography* 75 (1976): 399-408.

40. Donald H. Graves, "Language Arts Textbooks: A Writing Process Evaluation," *Language Arts* 54 (1977): 817-23.

41. Barbara von D. Donsky, "Trends in Elementary Writing Instruction, 1900-1959," *Language Arts* 61 (1984): 795-803.

42. David L. Elliott and Kathleen C. Nagel, "School Science and the Pursuit of Knowledge—Deadends and All," *Science and Children* 24, No. 8 (1987): 9-12.

43. Linus Pauling, "Throwing the Book at Elementary Chemistry," *Science Teacher* 50 (1983): 25-29.

44. John S. Rigden, "The Art of Great Science," *Phi Delta Kappan* 64 (1983): 613-17.

45. Elliot W. Eisner, "Why the Textbook Influences Curriculum," *Curriculum Review* 26, No. 3 (1987): 11-13.

CHAPTER IV

Textbooks and Challenge:
The Influence of Educational Research

JEANNE S. CHALL AND SUE S. CONARD

We will be concerned in this chapter with ways in which educational research has influenced the development of textbooks, how educational research findings have affected what authors and publishers of textbooks have produced, and also how research findings have affected the preferences of those who select and use textbooks.

Our position, that research has contributed significantly to policy and practice regarding textbooks, is consistent with Richard Shavelson's more general perspective of the research-practice relationship expressed in his presidential address to the American Educational Research Association in 1988.[1] As he describes, in some instances the connection may neither be clear nor the applications immediate and direct. But in the case of textbooks, evidence of a clear link and an almost instant responsiveness abounds.

We present here three case studies concerning issues in the development and use of textbooks. The first concerns the question of whether to stress oral or silent reading; the second, whether easier or harder textbooks are better; and the third, whether or not to teach phonics. The issues relating to oral versus silent reading and to the teaching of phonics are concerned mainly with reading textbooks for the elementary school. The third issue, optimal difficulty, includes content textbooks at all levels of education—elementary through college. All three issues touch on basic processes of learning and teaching, and all have been debated and studied for as long as we have had educational research.

We selected only three issues to make possible historical overviews of the effects of research on practice and, conversely, the effects of practice on research. For two of the cases, the teaching of phonics and the difficulty of textbooks, one can find considerable empirical evidence. The oral/silent reading issue has not been studied as extensively. But it contains many of the research-practice tensions that seem to characterize those educational practices that are influenced by educational research.

Overall, the three cases are presented not as definitive, tested historical realities, but as exemplars and as cautionary tales from which we may learn to do better today than in the past.

Silent or Oral Reading? The Application of Thorndike's Research on Comprehension

THE RESEARCH

Our first example comes from the classic research by Edward L. Thorndike entitled "Reading as Reasoning"—one of the most far-reaching studies on reading.[2] The study, essentially clear and simple, asked middle-grade students to read silently several expository selections and to answer questions on them—questions of general import, facts, word meanings, and inference. An analysis of their responses, and particularly their errors, revealed that many of the children failed to comprehend the passages. They had difficulty with the meanings of many of the words and with reasoning through the meaning of the passages. The major implication drawn from the study was that the instruction provided in schools for these children was not sufficient for the task they were given in the research—reading silently for understanding. The predominant mode of reading practice in schools at the time, oral reading, was not sufficient for developing the ability to read with comprehension. It was recommended that students, particularly those in the middle and upper elementary grades, should have more silent reading for comprehension practice. Since no one really knew what the best way to teach comprehension was, Thorndike suggested it might help to have the students practice reading silently selections such as those used in his study and answer similar kinds of questions.

APPLICATION OF THE RESEARCH

Thorndike's recommendation to emphasize silent reading practice in the intermediate and upper elementary grades received early acceptance by authors and publishers of textbooks and other curriculum materials. They accepted, also, his suggestion to use short selections followed by comprehension questions. In time, the questions evolved into a multiple-choice format, instead of the open-ended form originally used.

Indeed, Thorndike's suggested procedure for practice in reading comprehension helped create a whole new industry in educational publishing—the self-teaching, consumable workbook; the dittoed, then xeroxed, worksheet; the self-administering reading kits with their short selections and questions; and, more recently, computerized exercises in reading comprehension.

Why was there so quick, so pervasive, and so enduring an application of Thorndike's research? Why is his article, "Reading as Reasoning," still being read? Probably because of the "truth" it contains. It was not hard for teachers to realize that silent reading practice was needed to balance the then heavy emphasis on oral reading. And his suggested methods provided a useful way to assess students' "understanding" of what they read by noting whether they answered the questions correctly. Also, when most reading instruction began to be done in three within-class groups, the silent reading of short selections and the answering of questions about those selections seemed a constructive use of time by the groups that were working independently of the teacher. Multiple-choice format, answer keys, and, beginning with the late 1950s, color coding of the reading difficulty (readability) of the selections were useful aids for the teacher.

OVERGENERALIZATION OF THE RESEARCH

Questionable applications of Thorndike's research can be found almost from the time of its publication and continue to the present. Although Thorndike's research was conducted on intermediate grade pupils, it was also applied to the primary grades. Silent reading was soon considered the ideal reading mode, even for first grades, although no hard evidence supported it.[3] Silent reading was recommended in the teacher's manuals of most basal reading textbooks for the primary grades, no doubt on the assumption that what is good for the middle grades should be good for the primary grades. Thus, beginning in the 1920s and continuing until today, most basal reader manuals emphasize silent reading right from the start in grade one, although theoretical, intuitive, and practical knowledge indicates the greater value of oral reading in the early grades. When oral reading is suggested in the teacher's manuals, its purpose is quite vague.

Authors and publishers of reading textbooks not only overgeneralized the grades for which Thorndike's research was valid, but they also overgeneralized the type of content for which it was appropriate. Thorndike's test passages were from nonfiction, expository writing. The reading textbooks and other curriculum materials asked the same kinds of questions on narrative fiction and even poetry, neither of which had been tested in the original research and both of which require a different kind of comprehension.[4]

By the early 1980s, the use of silent reading exercises was so prevalent that Durkin found from systematic observations of middle-grade classrooms, as well as from analyses of basal reader manuals, that teachers' time was devoted mainly to assigning and correcting questions or testing comprehension rather than to discussing and teaching it.[5]

SUMMARY

Thus, Thorndike's ingenious research has had profound effects on reading instruction through the reading textbooks and other instructional materials. Some of the effects have been productive. Others have been less than productive.

It is important to note, however, particularly in a time of much questioning of the value of educational research for educational practice, that Thorndike's research has had a broad and enduring effect—some of it good, some not so good. The negative effects, as we see them, come not from any flaws in the research, but from the tendency of users of the research to overgeneralize its findings without additional research evidence.

How Difficult Should Textbooks Be? The Application of Vocabulary and Readability Research

Research on text difficulty and students' learning has also had considerable effect on textbooks. This area of research began early in the present century, about the same time as the studies of silent reading, and developed along two parallel lines of inquiry: research on vocabulary difficulty and research on comprehension difficulty or readability. Both areas investigated objective measures of evaluating difficulty and the use of these measures to predict the approximate ability individuals would need for reading and understanding what was read. Vocabulary researchers concentrated mainly on reading textbooks for the primary grades while readability studies were more often concerned with written and spoken text for all levels.

The earliest vocabulary studies were undertaken just shortly after the publication of Edward Thorndike's word-frequency lists for the English language in 1921.[6] To establish difficulty, the number of new words and the rate and extent of introduction were counted. Generally, these counts were then used to compare the difficulty of two or more series of basal readers or various editions of one series. As criteria for their conclusions and recommendations, vocabulary studies relied heavily on word lists developed by Thorndike and other researchers.[7]

Readability research was also interested in vocabulary as an indicator of difficulty, but examined the contributions of many other factors as well. One early study by Gray and Leary identified eighty-two variables associated with difficulty.[8] In addition to defining and measuring factors related to difficulty, many readability researchers also developed formulas, statistical devices for predicting the difficulty of text for readers of known reading ability. Chall and Klare describe over fifty such formulas developed by these studies, together with their applications and evidence of their validity and reliability.[9]

Several descriptive and comprehensive reviews document the large body of research in both vocabulary and readability, including those by Clifford, by Klare, and by Chall.[10] Recent updates of the latter two reviews are also available.[11]

What were the findings of these many studies conducted during the 1920s and 1930s? Essentially, both vocabulary and readability studies found that certain characteristics of both reading and content textbooks at all levels influenced students' comprehension. They also found that most textbooks published during these years were too difficult for the majority of both elementary and secondary students. They were, therefore, quite consistent in their recommendation that books used in every grade be made easier.

APPLICATIONS OF FINDINGS

Historical accounts show an almost immediate reaction by textbook publishers to these recommendations. Beginning in the late 1920s, the vocabulary load of reading textbooks decreased with each subsequent edition. Comparative studies document the introduction of fewer and fewer new words and more and more repetitions of them.[12] Within a period of ten years, the average number of different words in second-grade readers decreased from 1,147 to 913.[13] During this same period new words introduced in first-grade readers decreased from 644 to 462 and within the following ten years, to 338.[14] This simplification of vocabulary in reading textbooks continued through the 1950s and into the first half of the decade of the 1960s, during which new words in first-grade readers were repeated on an average of six to ten times immediately following their introduction.[15] Reading textbooks for the upper elementary grades also became easier. The vocabulary in sixth-grade basals decreased consistently from 1947 to 1967, and Gates described the vocabularies of fourth-grade basals published during the early 1960s as so limited as to be most appropriate for average third-grade students.[16]

Changes in the difficulty of content textbooks beginning in the late 1920s paralleled those found in reading books. Horn identified this downward trend in difficulty in social studies textbooks as early as 1937, and Chall, Conard, and Harris documented a continuation of the movement toward ease in this content area some thirty years later and in literature and grammar and composition books as well.[17]

IMMEDIATE AND ENDURING CONSENSUS

The mounting of evidence on the simplification of textbooks leads to the questions of why authors and publishers moved so quickly and so in concert to produce easier and easier books and why this trend continued for fifty years. One explanation for the unusually strong influence of these studies is their cumulative property.[18] That is, the potential of vocabulary and readability studies to affect practice was enhanced by their continuity from the earliest, least-mechanical word counts to complex and linguistically aware formulas. As Clifford describes, subsequent studies built upon, modified, or extended findings from their predecessors so as to constitute a "family-tree" of research rather than a pile of studies.[19]

A second hypothesis is related to the applied nature of vocabulary and readability research and its close association with problems defined by teachers. One of the earliest readability studies was, in fact, in response to concerns about difficulty expressed by junior high school science teachers.[20] Since these studies were conducted upon textbooks, it was relatively easy to apply their findings to other textbooks. This supposition is further supported by the prompt adoption by publishers of the methods and tools used and developed in these studies. Historically, reviews of the applications of vocabulary and readability research as well as publishers' own accounts demonstrate extensive use of vocabulary lists and readability formulas to determine and often alter the difficulty of their products.[21]

A third hypothesis is that this research was a necessary, although not a sufficient, condition for the changes in textbooks. That is, one must look also to the educational climate and demands of the times that gave rise to the research. The 1920s and 1930s were a time of the expanding high school, and teachers found existing textbooks too difficult for many of their "new" students, those who were staying on in school longer than had their parents. It was also a time of more immigration into the United States and thus of more students in elementary grades who had limited proficiency in the English language. The mismatch between the reading abilities of such students and the difficulty of their books was, therefore, a very real and pressing concern.

It is possible, then, that the democratization of education in general and the impetus to make instruction available and suitable for all students set the stage for the research on vocabulary and readability measurement as well as for its wide acceptance and application in schools and publishing houses. And with the existing social and educational environment, easier textbooks as outcomes of the use of this research were virtually assured.

OVERAPPLICATION OF THE RESEARCH

While the recommendations of vocabulary and readability research and the prevailing views of the 1920s and 1930s interacted to encourage publishers and authors to produce easier textbooks, did they also provide the support for the proliferation of this trend?

In the case of research, the answer to this question is "no." It should be remembered that almost all of the vocabulary studies were comparative; that is, they were able to tell which books were more or less difficult in a relative sense. Only a few vocabulary researchers actually tested the books they studied with students, and only a single study provided criteria for optimal difficulty in terms of the rates of vocabulary introduction and repetition from such testing.[22]

Similarly, readability formulas were quite reliable tools for telling how difficult books were for a given group of readers, but not for prescribing how difficult they should be. Thus, while information on relative difficulty was provided for schools and publishers by this research, only one study was designed to provide criteria for judging when limits had been reached. And yet, the specifications for primary readers from Gates's study were met quite early (in the 1940s) and were quickly exceeded in spite of cautions and warnings about overapplication from many well-respected vocabulary and readability researchers.[23]

Without available evidence from research, it is possible that schools turned to publishers for such information since publishers were considered more knowledgeable than schools in areas concerning books and difficulty. In turn, publishers seem to have perceived the consensus of their customers to be "easier is better," for easier books were selling, and they competed among themselves for larger market shares by publishing easier books. Thus, producer and consumer may have interacted to reinforce mutually the downward spiral of difficulty.

CHANGES IN THE TREND

It was not until the early 1960s that educational views on difficulty seemed to change. Ideas from changing psychological perspectives began to emphasize the importance of the very early years to learning and the need to teach more and teach it earlier.[24] National concern that the American educational system might be lagging behind that of the Soviet Union also gained momentum. At about the same time, research findings on beginning reading instruction began to suggest the need for more difficult books at the earliest levels.[25] As they had in the earlier years, publishers reacted to these influences, and by the middle of the 1960s, evidence of a reversal of the trend toward ease began to appear. Willows, Borwick, and Hayvren noted a fivefold increase in the rate of vocabulary introduction in first-grade readers from 1962 to 1972, and increasing difficulty in sixth-grade readers from 1967 through 1975 was reported by Chall, Conard, and Harris.[26]

By the late 1970s, concern for the overall quality of education had reached national proportions and continued to accelerate.[27] The "dumbing" of textbooks became the watchword for reform, just as "easier is better" had been the clarion call many years before.

SUMMARY

This account offers another example of the relationship between educational research and practice and, particularly, of the interdependence and mutual reinforcement that exists among the research on text difficulty, the educational publishers, and the views of the educational community. Evidence in this case is especially strong, for it spans over half a century of documentation. From the 1920s until the 1960s or 1970s, depending on subject and grade, publishers used research findings and the tools of research to develop easier books, as requested by the schools. Beginning in the 1940s, further simplification was not supported by research, but was continued, perhaps because of the momentum of the trend toward ease, the preferences of teachers and administrators, and/or the competitiveness among various publishing houses.

Publishers' "overuse" of readability and vocabulary research went even further. Because ease was preferred by schools and the requirement of some selection committees for a particular level of difficulty, they edited or wrote "to" a formula or word list by replacing hard words and shortening sentences, although the researchers warned against such practices.

At the present time, both research and the educational climate support more difficult and challenging textbooks.[28] Our prediction is that within only a few years comparative studies of the difficulty of textbooks will show movement in this direction. And yet, this trend may again go beyond an optimal level if new research is not undertaken to define standards and establish limits.

How Should We Teach Beginning Reading?
The Application of Research on Phonics Instruction

Another example of the influence of research on textbooks is that of the place of phonics, or decoding, in the teaching of beginning reading. Although the phonics issue has been studied from the beginnings of educational research, we will be concerned mainly with the 1960s and 1970s, when influences of the research on practice were evident.

During the late 1960s, after a decade of controversy set off by Rudolf Flesch's *Why Johnny Can't Read*,[29] a series of research studies was undertaken to determine whether a stronger or weaker emphasis on phonics or decoding was warranted. These studies included syntheses of the past research and classroom comparisons of beginning reading methods with a greater or lesser emphasis on phonics.

THE RESEARCH

During the 1960s, the two research studies that had the strongest impact on practice were Chall's *Learning to Read: The Great Debate* and the twenty-seven U.S. Office of Education first-grade studies.[30] The first was a synthesis of past research from the classroom, laboratory, and clinic, and included also analyses of basal readers and other reading programs and visits to classrooms. The second was based on twenty-seven individual comparisons of different beginning reading methods with greater or lesser amounts of phonics. Both these large-scale studies concluded, as did others at the time, that a greater emphasis on decoding in the early grades produces better results.

APPLICATION OF THE RESEARCH

Ten years later, the amount of phonics included in the majority of commercially published reading programs increased considerably, and most basal reading programs introduced the teaching of phonics earlier than they had in the 1960s.

Evidence for these changes comes from Popp's analysis of beginning reading programs published after 1967 as compared to those published in the 1960s.[31] In general, Popp found a stronger code-emphasis (phonics) in the post-1967 programs than in the earlier ones. For example, the first-grade basal readers published in the late 1950s and early 1960s taught consonant sounds and blends and, perhaps, consonant digraphs. In comparison, the first-grade reading programs published in the late 1960s and early 1970s taught all these plus short and long vowels, vowel digraphs, diphthongs, vowels controlled by r, l, and s, and high-frequency compound words. Even programs still favoring an emphasis on meaning taught greater amounts of phonics in their 1970 edition than in those published during the 1950s and 1960s. If one adds the publication of many separate phonics workbooks, games, and kits, one must conclude that a considerable change had taken place in the publishing of early reading programs following the research on beginning reading of the late 1960s.

In a series of analyses of the rise and fall of reading scores on the National Assessment of Educational Progress, Chall hypothesized that the increase in scores of the nine-year-old cohort from 1971 to 1980 could be attributed to stronger beginning reading programs that included reading in kindergarten, more systematic phonics, more challenging basal readers, and more remedial assistance.[32] The tapering and decline from 1980 to 1986 seemed to be associated with an increased emphasis in the primary grades on word meanings, comprehension, and "higher cognitive processes," and less emphasis on phonics and the reading of connected text. These changes in emphasis are evident in the basal readers of the 1980s and their manuals.[33]

The Uses and Misuses of Educational Research

The previous discussions demonstrate that educational publishers, at least the larger ones who publish basal readers and content area textbooks, are users of educational research.

If a publisher invests about $25 million to develop a reading series, one can assume that some attention will be paid to research evidence. But the authors and publishers of textbooks are also very much aware of the demands and preferences of schools and textbook adoption committees. Both research and "the market" intensify the stresses and strains of developing quality textbooks. In their desire to be responsive to the recommendations from research and to the criteria from selection committees, they tend further to be reactive rather than inventive.

The large proportion of publishers' financial resources invested in developing reading series seems to create an atmosphere of "hard sells" and appeals that are reminiscent of religious conversions. Both publishers and schools often speak in terms of "believing" or "not believing" in literature, in skills, in phonics, or in whole language. One seldom hears questions raised regarding the evidence to support these preferences.

This strong zeal comes also from the nature of reading instruction itself. Reading is essentially the bread and butter of education and of educational publishing, and it becomes the focus of criticism when educational outcomes are below what is desired. Hence, few teachers can afford to place themselves in the position of being the judge of what is best in reading instruction for the children they teach. Most teachers rely on what the scholars and experts say is best, and on what the authors of the reading programs, who are usually reading experts, bring out.

In the matter of state textbook adoptions, the rhetoric is anything but scholarly and objective. During adoption hearings, publishers' representatives often make inflated claims about their programs and derogatory statements about competing programs based on selected research evidence, interchanges more likely to be associated with political campaigns.

The use of educational research by educational publishers is far from simple or clear-cut. It tends to go through rhetoric and argumentation, not only among publishers, adoption committees, and teachers, but among researchers who subscribe to different viewpoints. It is common to hear reading researchers say that textbooks are wanting because publishers do not apply the available research fast enough. Indeed, about three years is usually the minimum time needed to develop a textbook from inception to marketing. Would we be better off if the research could be applied faster? Maybe. But we believe the problem may be more associated with the varied findings of educational research. Much of the research contradicts other research on the same issue. The problem in using educational research for educational publishing seems to us to be knowing what research to use, and when and how to use it. Publishers must also know what research findings to leave alone. What authors and publishers of textbooks need is a synthesis and interpretation of the research relevant to their work. Otherwise publishers may be worse off than they were before they knew the research.

Still another characteristic of educational research makes continued practical uses of it by publishers difficult. Research is usually not replicated over time, in different situations, with different kinds of children and teachers. Thus, as our examples show, it is easy for findings to be overgeneralized—to ages and grades not tested.

Special Interest and Ideologies

Perhaps one of the strongest factors in both the uses and misuses of research for the development of textbooks lies in values, preferences, and ideologies. Such preferences are found particularly in the area of reading, which has been subjected to conflicting views for hundreds of years. One view popular today and from the 1920s to the 1960s holds to a conception of reading as a natural process, similar to spoken language, that is learned best by "just being read to and by just reading," with little or no direct teaching.

The other major view is that reading develops and changes, that it needs to be learned, and that direct teaching of a different kind at different stages of development is needed.

No amount of research in linguistics or in neurology, no amount of developmental and experimental research, or no amount of data from national reading scores seems to convince proponents of the "natural" view that beginners do better with programs that follow the second view, i.e. when they are taught more directly rather than discovering reading on their own.[34]

Although each view encompasses some aspects of the other, there is a tendency for the rhetoric to spread to accusations or accounts of dire consequences that may be expected from following the other.

And textbooks get caught up in these debates, claiming to hold one or the other view.

To conclude, educational research has had a considerable influence on the development of textbooks. It has contributed to the way children are taught, to the way their textbooks are organized and written, to how much they learn, and to what and how much they read. Most of these influences have been beneficial, but there have also been negative effects, overuses, and misuses of research findings among researchers and publishers. These, we believe, can be reduced by a greater spirit of cooperation, a more open exchange and sharing of knowledge, and by joint efforts to monitor the application of research findings to textbooks and the effects of these applications.

FOOTNOTES

1. Richard J. Shavelson, "Contributions of Educational Research to Policy and Practice: Constructing, Challenging, Changing Cognition," *Educational Researcher* 17 (October 1988): 4-11, 22.

2. Edward L. Thorndike, "Reading as Reasoning: A Study of Mistakes in Paragraph Reading," *Journal of Educational Psychology* 8 (June 1917): 323-32.

3. For example, see Guy T. Buswell, *Non-oral Reading: A Study of Its Use in the Chicago Public Schools*. Supplementary Educational Monographs 6 (Chicago: University of Chicago Press, 1945).

4. Jeanne S. Chall, *Learning to Read: The Great Debate. An Update* (New York: McGraw-Hill, 1983).

5. Delores Durkin, "What Classroom Observations Reveal about Comprehension Instruction," *Reading Research Quarterly* 14 (1978-79): 481-533.

6. Edward L. Thorndike, *The Teacher's Word Book of 10,000 Words* (New York: Teachers College Press, 1921).

7. Ibid.; Edward L. Thorndike, *A Teacher's Word Book of 20,000 Words* (New York: Teachers College Press, 1931). See also, Arthur I. Gates, *A Reading Vocabulary for the Primary Grades* (New York: Teachers College, Bureau of Publications, 1926) and Edward W. Dolch, "The Combined Word Study List," *Journal of Educational Research* 17 (January 1927): 11-19.

8. William S. Gray and Bernice E. Leary, *What Makes a Book Readable?* (Chicago: University of Chicago Press, 1935).

9. Jeanne S. Chall, *Readability: An Appraisal of Research and Application* (Columbus: Ohio State University Press, 1958); George R. Klare, *The Measurement of Readability* (Ames: Iowa State University Press, 1963); idem, "Assessing Readability," *Reading Research Quarterly* 10 (1974-75): 62-102.

10. Geraldine J. Clifford, "Words for Schools: The Applications in Education of the Vocabulary Researches of Edward L. Thorndike," in *Impact of Research on Education: Some Case Studies*, ed. Patrick Suppes (Washington, DC: National Academy of Education, 1978); Klare, *The Measurement of Readability*; Chall, *Readability: An Appraisal of Research and Application*.

11. Klare, "Assessing Readability"; George R. Klare, "The Formative Years," in *Readability: Its Past, Present, and Future*, ed. Beverley L. Zakaluk and S. Jay Samuels (Newark, DE: International Reading Association, 1988), pp. 14-34; Jeanne S. Chall,

Sue S. Conard, and Susan H. Harris, *An Analysis of Textbooks in Relation to Declining S.A.T. Scores* (New York: College Entrance Examination Board, 1977) ERIC ED 148 865; Edgar Dale and Jeanne S. Chall, *Readability Revisited and the New Dale-Chall Readability Formula* (in press); Jeanne S. Chall and Sue S. Conard, *Textbooks and Challenge: An Inquiry into the Educational Effects of Easier and Harder Textbooks* (in press).

12. Chall, *Readability: An Appraisal of Research and Application*; idem, *Learning to Read: The Great Debate*; (New York: McGraw-Hill, 1967); idem. *Learning to Read: The Great Debate. An Update*.

13. John A. Hockett, "The Vocabularies of Recent Primers and First Readers," *Elementary School Journal* 39 (October 1938): 112-15.

14. Hockett, "The Vocabularies of Recent Primers and First Readers"; Chall, *Readability: An Appraisal of Research and Application*.

15. Dale M. Willows, Diane Borwick, and Maureen Hayvren, "The Content of School Readers," in *Reading Research: Advances in Theory and Practice* 2, ed. G. E. MacKinnon and T. Gary Waller (New York: Academic Press, 1981), pp. 100-175.

16. See Chall, Conard, and Harris, *An Analysis of Textbooks in Relation to Declining S.A.T. Scores*, for a comparison of vocabularies in readers published from 1946 to 1967. See also, Arthur I. Gates, "Vocabulary Control in Basal Reading Material," *Reading Teacher* 15 (November 1961): 81-85.

17. Ernest Horn, *Methods of Instruction in the Social Studies* (New York: Charles Scribner's Sons, 1937); Chall, Conard, and Harris, *An Analysis of Textbooks in Relation to Declining S.A.T. Scores*.

18. Clifford, "Words for Schools: The Applications in Education of the Vocabulary Researches of Edward L. Thorndike."

19. Ibid., pp. 26-27.

20. Bertha A. Lively and S. L. Pressey, "A Method of Measuring the Vocabulary Burden of Textbooks," *Educational Administration and Supervision* 9 (October 1923): 389-98.

21. Jeanne S. Chall, "The Beginning Years," in *Readability: Its Past, Present, and Future*, ed. Beverley L. Zakaluk and S. Jay Samuels (Newark, DE: International Reading Association, 1988), pp. 2-13; Dale and Chall, *Readability Revisited and the New Dale-Chall Readability Formula*; Chall and Conard, *Textbooks and Challenge: An Inquiry into the Effects of Easier and Harder Textbooks*.

22. Testing of vocabularies was reported in Luella Cole, *Teaching in the Elementary School* (New York: Farrar and Rinehart, 1939), and Edward L. Thorndike, "Improving the Ability to Read," *Teachers College Record* 36 (October, November, December 1934): 1-19, 123-44, 229-41; Arthur I. Gates, *Interest and Ability in Reading* (New York: Macmillan, 1930).

23. Gerald A. Yoakam, "The Reading Difficulty of School Textbooks," *Elementary English Review* 22 (December 1945): 307, Horn, *Methods of Instruction in the Social Studies*, p. 162; Gates, "Vocabulary Control in Basal Reading Material," p. 81.

24. Benjamin S. Bloom, *Human Characteristics and School Learning* (New York: McGraw-Hill, 1976).

25. Chall, *Readability: An Appraisal of Research and Application*.

26. Willows, Borwick, and Hayvren, "The Content of School Readers"; Chall, Conard, and Harris, *An Analysis of Textbooks in Relation to Declining S.A.T. Scores*.

27. *On Further Examination: Report of the Advisory Panel on the Scholastic Aptitude Test Score Decline* (New York: College Entrance Examination Board, 1977). For example, see reports such as National Commission on Excellence in Education, *A*

70 THE INFLUENCE OF EDUCATIONAL RESEARCH

Nation at Risk: The Imperative for Educational Reform (Washington, DC: U.S. Department of Education, 1983). See also, John I. Goodlad, *A Place Called School* (New York: McGraw-Hill, 1984).

28. Chall and Conard, *Textbooks and Challenge: An Inquiry into the Educational Effects of Easier and Harder Textbooks.*

29. Rudolf Flesch, *Why Johnny Can't Read* (New York: Harper and Row, 1955).

30. Chall, *Learning to Read: The Great Debate*; idem, *Learning to Read: The Great Debate. An Update*; Guy L. Bond and Robert Dykstra, "The Cooperative Research Program in First Grade Reading," *Reading Research Quarterly* 2 (Summer 1967): 5-142.

31. Helen M. Popp, "Current Practices in the Teaching of Beginning Reading," in *Toward a Literate Society: A Report from the National Academy of Education*, ed. John B. Carroll and Jeanne S. Chall (New York: McGraw-Hill, 1975), pp. 101-146.

32. Jeanne S. Chall, "Literacy: Trends and Explanations," *Educational Researcher* 12 (November 1983): 3-8; idem, "New Reading Trends: The NAEP Report Card," *Curriculum Review* 25 (March/April, 1986): 42-44; idem, "Could the Decline Be Real? Recent Trends in Reading Instruction and Support in the United States" (Paper prepared for the NAEP Technical Review Panel, Center for Education Statistics, U.S. Department of Education, August, 1988).

33. Nancy Neill, "Analysis of Basal Readers for District Textbook Adoptions," (Unpublished paper, Graduate School of Education, Harvard University, Cambridge, MA, 1987); Linda A. Meyer, C. N. Hastings, and R. L. Linn, *Assessing Early Reading with New Decoding and Comprehension Measures* (Champaign, IL: Center for the Study of Reading, University of Illinois, 1988).

34. Jeanne S. Chall, "Reading and Early Childhood Education: The Critical Issues," *Principal* 66 (May 1987): 6-9.

Section Two
THE TEXTBOOK INDUSTRY

CHAPTER V

Writing and Editing Textbooks

M. JEAN YOUNG

In 1890, the state of California decided to produce its own text-books. But once they produced a textbook for each subject, they concluded that publishing textbooks cost the state more than it would cost private publishing houses and that, in general, teachers found the state-produced textbooks unsatisfactory.[1] Thus it was clear that because of cost and quality considerations, the state would leave publishing up to private industry. Over the years this has created a unique and sometimes uneasy alliance between the state, charged with providing public education, and private industry whose existence depends on profit. The main question is, how can you trust a profit-making industry to do what is best to create textbooks to help educate our children?

Some of the answers to this question lie in the way textbooks are authored and edited and in the ideals and philosophies of the authors and editors who decide what gets into textbooks. I came to understand these issues over the course of nine years from 1978 through 1986 while I was a science textbook editor and later a developer of instructional materials on a freelance basis.

This chapter is to a large degree the story of the making of *Modern Biology*, the 1981 edition. I was the editor of this textbook and the nine ancillaries that accompanied that edition. At the time it was being considered for another edition in 1978, *Modern Biology* sold 60 percent of the market and set the standard for general high school biology texts. It got a lot of attention from Holt, Rinehart and Winston, the publishers, and educators, parents, communities, and the media. In spite of this attention it was not produced differently than any textbook that came out of Holt, Rinehart and Winston in the years when I was there. The story of *Modern Biology* therefore represents the writing and editing of any major textbook at that time.

Publishing has changed a lot in some ways since I left Holt. I was involved in the development and production of other textbooks and their ancillaries after I left Holt. I have weaved this information into the story in order to give an updated version of writing and editing that is as complete as possible.

The "uneasy alliance" between the state and the publishers of textbooks created tension in the predominantly idealistic educators who were the authors and editors of *Modern Biology*. While both authors and editors had a primary concern to make the textbook profitable, they were also concerned about creating a textbook that would help teachers teach and students learn.

Authors are chosen by publishing companies for two reasons. The author is often well-known in his or her field, is affiliated with a prestigious organization (e.g., a biology teacher who is a member of the National Association of Biology Teachers), and/or has a well-known pedagogy. The other reason is that they are associated in some way with education. Textbook authors are always members of an author team that usually includes at least one teacher and may include one teacher educator.

An often overlooked group of people who have a direct and important impact on what goes into the textbook are the consultants. These influential people check the textbook's content and pedagogy. They are either experts in their field or teachers in the field that the textbook covers. Often the teachers are chosen by geographic area. For example, since the influence of such states as Texas and California on what goes into textbooks is well-known, the list of textbook teacher consultants, located in the front of every school textbook, will always include one or two consultants from these states.

Developmental or content editors at Holt were usually former teachers. Every editor I worked with at Holt, with only one exception, was a former teacher. Even some of the copy editors and production and art staff were former teachers. All of us, authors and consultants included, wanted to produce good textbooks—textbooks students could learn from and that gave them up-to-date and pertinent information.

Textbook Development

In this chapter I emphasize the various influences that come into play when a textbook is produced. These influences make textbooks different, and all too often make them more similar than different. Slightly different factors influence each of the several stages of textbook development.

The first step, before any production phase, is to determine whether or not to publish a book at all. In the case of *Modern Biology* (MB), the question was not whether to produce another edition. Instead, the question concerned the extent to which the new edition would have new material. Because information on most biology subjects tends to be obsolete even before another edition can be produced, MB was reviewed for another edition after the previous edition had been out only two years.

During the time I was at Holt, we would sometimes only revise a portion of a science textbook to make it current. I was told recently that this practice is no longer used for science books, because publishers found it no longer practical in the competitive sense. The main concern here is that the information base for some books has a higher turnover than for others. When updating a science book, a publisher is faced with so much new information that even a three-year update cycle may not be sufficient. Many publishers of science textbooks now send customers update sheets or newsletters free of cost.

As with any publication, before deciding when and to what extent to revise MB, we made a cost-effective analysis. Information was gathered about former and current sales figures, and what states and districts were going to be adopting textbooks in this subject area by the time the book reached the marketplace. Special attention would then be paid to those markets in terms of covering the state syllabus or local curriculum guides.

A significant part of the preproduction phase, and one that has greatly expanded since I was an editor, is marketing. One of my last tasks at Holt was to be involved in videotaping focus group sessions behind a one-way mirror. Teachers in a given subject area were asked to attend a meeting where they would comment on textbooks. In this case we were finding out about one of our science textbooks by asking teachers what they thought of the textbook in general, its features, and so on. Along with our textbook were several textbooks on the same subject from other publishers. Participating teachers were not told what publisher we represented. We taped two groups of ten teachers each. This information was then going to be used in subsequent revisions.

Whenever I went out to give talks to teachers as part of my job at Holt, I told them that, contrary to what many people thought, what was in textbooks was a result of what teachers made known they wanted in textbooks. If what they wanted was not in textbooks, it was either because not enough teachers wanted it or because not enough teachers made their wants known. Focus groups, surveys, feedback from sales representatives, are all now used to find out what teachers want. I am sure that if enough teachers said they wanted pictures of dogs on page 14, publishers would have at least one picture of a dog on page 14 of every school textbook produced.

Along with these marketing activities, editors at Holt also did intensive studies of the competition. Before initial discussions of how the 1981 edition of *Modern Biology* (MB '81) would be revised, I analyzed every aspect of other best-selling biology textbooks. I made lists and charts of every conceivable feature and kind of content that we could use to improve our revised edition. We wanted to use whatever seemed to be working well for other publishers in our revised edition. We also wanted to find out what they did that was not working well to ensure our competitive edge and to do something new that would make our textbook better.

In the preproduction phase we also gave consideration to what illustrations we could include in the textbook within the confines of our budget. Decisions we made were based on pedagogy, aesthetics, and, of course, cost. For example, we felt a photograph made with an electron microscope or conventional microscope should be accompanied by a drawing so that students could understand better what was being depicted. We also went "all out" cost-wise in choosing unit openers. The publishing executives had the final say on these unit openers as well as on what would go on the cover because of the belief in the importance of pictures to attract the customer. As I recall, we paid about $500 (a lot at the time) for a wonderful unit opener which later appeared in three other biology textbooks.

The last part of the preproduction phase was to have an authors' meeting. The marketing phase and textbook analyses provided information about how to revise a textbook, or what to include in a new textbook. Then it was the task of authors and editors to produce the manuscript. For the MB '81 authors' meeting we had established parameters ahead of time such as keeping the general phylogenetic format (zoology and botany content covered phylum-by-phylum). The actual authors' meeting on MB '81 entailed deciding upon schedules for when chapters would be due and who would be writing which chapters.

The amount of influence authors have on textbook content and pedagogy varies widely among subject matter areas and grade level. In general, the more specialized the field and the higher the grade level, the more influence an author is likely to have. Except for the original author of MB, no other author has had a greater influence on that book than James Otto. MB was first published as *Biology for Beginners* in 1921 and was written by Truman Moon. Otto became a third author for the first time in 1947 along with Moon and another author, Paul Mann. Otto's influence was so great that even though he died in 1972, after having done work on the 1973 edition, his name also appeared on the 1977 and 1981 editions. It was Otto's editions that set the standard for biology textbooks for four decades. Few authors enjoy this kind of influence today. But those chosen for a specific pedagogical slant largely determine what is in textbooks.

Multiple-member teams are also important considering the time constraints they are under to produce the manuscript. While work on MB '81 began in 1978, the development phase occurred in only eight short months. Another consideration may be the age of the author. Publishers do not want to have to break in a whole new team with every edition, so they try to have an overlap for consistency over the years. Who produces what part of the manuscript and how much of the manuscript varies, depends on such things as expertise, amount of revision needed, and time constraints.

The time constraint is of paramount importance, not only because of time needed to revise the text based on input from consultants and authors but also because of the "bound book date." After a decision has been made to produce a textbook a bound book date is set. A lot can go awry in the production schedule but the bound book date is written in stone. This means that a date has been set and the final stages have to be completed or the giant web presses, used in printing the book, will be at a standstill at the rate of thousands of dollars a day for the publisher. It is the senior editor's job to make sure the book is ready. In order to do so, the content editor must direct the activity of the authors.

I remember well the influence of time constraints in producing

MB. One example comes particularly to mind. The eighth and last unit arrived from the author but the editors (content and senior editor) had decided to restructure the unit. I stayed at home one day from the office and cut and pasted manuscript to fit the revised structure. It took me fourteen hours, but the next day we had our first draft which was then whisked off to consultants for review.

At Holt, the science textbook authors were given ample opportunity to provide feedback on galleys sent to them for approval. However, editors have the last word because they are updated on feedback from customers, are aware of how much and what can go into the book, get feedback from consultants, and are responsible to meet the bound book date. One author complained bitterly about "the short, choppy" sentences of the 1978 edition of MB. But, the editor had purposely rewritten the sentences to comply with demands from customers for a lower reading level.

Some authors decide not to continue writing a textbook from edition to edition for various reasons. For one thing, again, it is a tremendous time commitment. One author for MB '81, a family man and a high school teacher, decided one edition was enough for him. Furthermore, he was unhappy with the amount of royalties he was getting. Unlike other publishing situations, a team produces school textbooks. More time, effort, and money is put into marketing and production by school publishers; therefore, they get a greater share of the profit and authors a lesser share. But, elementary/secondary textbook publishers also sell more books than most trade or college publishers.

The larger publishing team includes all those engaged in marketing activities, a small research staff, executives, and the production team. The production team at Holt consisted of a content editor who interacted directly with the authors, a copy editor who had the responsibility of making sure the manuscript was grammatically correct and clear, a photo researcher, an art director, a production manager, and a senior editor who was in charge of making sure we all met the bound book date while also producing good textbooks. As content editor, I appreciated the cooperation and collegiality of the group with whom I worked. During the two years of our association, I cannot remember even one altercation among us. This was important because the orchestration of producing a textbook is a complex combination of working on a time schedule to put together a manuscript, pictures, art, glossary, index, commentary for the teacher's edition, special features, and ancillary materials such as laboratory manuals and workbooks.

The influence of editors on textbooks varies widely depending on factors too numerous to delineate in this chapter. As the content editor, I enjoyed quite a bit of influence for MB '81. Knowing what worked and did not work in the classroom made me and other former teachers effective content editors. While working on MB, I also visited classrooms and talked with biology teachers. Lest it be thought that editors remain school educators, I want to point out that even the contact I had with classroom teaching during the production of MB '81 was ·not enough. Therefore, I relied heavily on our teacher consultants who made recommendations on how to change the manuscript to better meet the needs of students. I still had the mentality and the idealism of the school educator, but had been greatly influenced by the profit motive. It was not that I became callous, but rather that I perceived textbooks more on a nationwide level and considered the vastly different kinds of teachers, students, and contexts for whom we were developing textbooks.

A case in point of this national outlook is that we understood the mistake made in promoting "teacher-proof" materials, but at the same time understood that some teachers were better prepared to teach biology than others. This has not changed over the years. One science editor told me recently that there were some science teachers who are grateful for so-called "dumbed down" textbooks, knowing they could not handle much else. Publishers now try to provide so much of a variety that every teacher, however prepared, can use the textbooks. Lincoln said "You can't please all the people all the time," but publishers try to.

THE DEVELOPMENT PROCESS

To say that the development team now goes on to produce the textbook is to grossly simplify what actually happens. While the team does have an influence, feedback from consultants and from the "field" (those factors outside the publishing house such as customers and pressure groups) all have input into the final form of the textbook.

The teacher consultants of MB reviewed the manuscript for pedagogy; the university professors reviewed the subject matter content. In all cases, they had the final word, and the manuscript was changed according to their suggestions. The variance here was in the amount and number of comments given by individual consultants. That is not to say that the reviewers saw the final manuscript. They made suggestions for first drafts which may have or may not have resembled the final manuscript. Much was left up to the discretion of the editor who often depended on other textbooks as resources and other kinds of feedback.

Editors often get direct feedback in letters from customers. More often than not, the letters I got at Holt related to what the customers perceive to be errors in the textbooks. Nonetheless, these letters were always appreciated. (Any feedback from the field was appreciated.) Some letters, however, were silly. One irate biologist sent us a long list of what he perceived to be errors. Unfortunately, he had gotten a first printing of MB which still had some typographic errors as most first printings then did. Such errors constituted most items on his list. There were a couple of genuine minor errors, but the rest were matters of opinion. For example, we had many letters about the number of ATPs (adenosine triphosphates) released as a result of cellular respiration. College biology texts, which were often used as a last word in such controversies since they were written by recognized experts in the field, showed either 36 or 38 ATPs being released. We went along with college textbooks produced by Holt to be consistent. So, we continued to get letters asking us how we could possibly be so ignorant as to say that 38 ATPs were produced.

That is not to say there are no real errors in textbooks. *Education Index*, which provides an index by subject matter and author, has a section under textbooks called "errors." These errors can also stem from policies of the publishing company. One might call not mentioning that the Pilgrims came to North America as a result of religious persecution an error, but it was the policy of one publishing company, however ill advised, not to discuss religion in history textbooks for schools.

Holt came to know a lot about including controversial topics during the time MB '81 was being produced. At that time the controversy over whether or not to include creationism in textbooks was at its peak. We even had a news team from ABC's "Nightline" come in to interview the science executive editor. I watched the interview being taped then stayed up late to see what appeared on the show. The executive editor had, in my opinion, done a good job answering some difficult questions. On the show his answers were edited to the point where he appeared ridiculous. The editing made it seem that he was not taking a stand regarding evolution, although he had actually said that evolution is a theory and that Holt textbooks presented it in that way. The show was clearly designed to make publishers the "bad guy" no matter what was said.

That same year NSTA (National Science Teachers Association)

79

and NABT (National Association of Biology Teachers) both came out with policy statements about creationism. It is a religious belief, they stated, and evolution is a scientific theory. This, to many publishers, including Holt, closed the controversy. Our responses to complaints from creationists simply called their attention to these policy statements.

The only other controversial topic we dealt with was the topic of human reproduction. We had a simple formula. We named the parts of reproductive systems and described meiosis (cell division that gives rise to sperm and eggs), without referring to the relationship between the two.

In addition to getting more than enough feedback from certain parts of the field, Holt textbook sales representatives from all parts of the country were sending us reports on what they found out through interacting with teachers. They told us, in writing, what teachers thought was good, what was bad, what they wanted more or less of. They told us about illustrations, subject matter content, and pedagogy. One group of sales representatives was designated as the advisory panel and spent time with us in the preproduction phase, giving us extensive information and making recommendations. Typical of such comments was the statement that our laboratory manual was considered to be too "cookbook." Most teachers said they wanted manuals that involved more of an inquiry approach. However, some teachers did not have access to laboratory equipment they would need in order to do some of our experiments. So, for each chapter we gave them an experiment and a paper-and-pencil activity.

Several writers on the topic of textbook selection have put the onus of improving textbooks on people who select textbooks.[2] Knowing the extent to which the field has influence it is easy to see why.

Not all the influence on MB '81 came from the field. Publishing staff members who worked on textbooks—the artists, photo researchers, copy editors, and production staff—used information from the field coupled with their own artistry and greatly influenced MB. For each, the influence was a result of about half information from the field and half artistry. Artists, however, probably had the most aesthetic influence. They contributed the general look of the textbook, specifically color and style. All the editors and staff had input into final choices but the artists provided the options.

Photo researchers worked from author and editor specifications. They tried to find the best photos possible while keeping to the predetermined budget. Through studies of competing textbooks, the editor determined what kind of photos, how large, and so on, must be included in order to be competitive. (Currently, color photos are a must.) Again, the content editor made the final choice but the photo researcher provided the options.

Photos also accounted for racial and minority balance in the textbook. Long before MB '81 was being produced, influence from the field resulted in greater representation of women and blacks in textbooks. Especially in our careers sections we made sure we had a balance, but sometimes this got a little unrealistic. As one Holt author pointed out, we had a female airplane pilot in a career page photograph, even though at the time there was only one female commercial airline pilot.

Copy editors contributed to the general readability of the manuscript. They rewrote and recommended changes in the manuscript that made it have a better reading flow. They also kept track of vocabulary words and word usage. The final word for readability came from applying readability formulas to the manuscript so that we could know whether or not it was on an appropriate grade level. The results of the readability tests were the most requested information from potential customers. Because of the potential volatility of the readability question, we had to hire an independent consultant to apply the readability formulas to the manuscript.

The production staff, as the liaison between the printer and the publisher, selected typefaces and made sure the textbook met specifications developed by the National Association of State Textbook Administrators. The Advisory Commission on Textbook Specifications regularly publishes a manual with detailed specifications for publishers to follow in producing a textbook. Such specifications include paper, cover, and binding requirements. The typefaces, space between letters (leading), and number of words per line must also meet specifications for readability.

TEXTBOOK PROGRAM AND ANCILLARIES

For an editor, producing a textbook is a little like giving birth. The proud mothers and fathers have undergone a gestation period of about two years of production and have spent many nights and weekends before seeing their final creation. But there is little time to enjoy the results of the creative process because shortly after giving birth to the textbook the "ancillaries" (as publications other than the textbook are called) must be produced. Because the ancillaries must be ready to accompany the textbook, they are developed and produced in a matter of months. A cadre of freelance writers and editors, and now development houses, are employed to have these ancillaries ready in time.

For MB '81 we had as many as seven freelance writers and editors working on the ancillaries. All of them had a background in teaching and all of them had a good idea of what "works" and what does not work in the classroom. The problem was, that because of the time constraint, most of the test items and some of the laboratory activities did not get field-tested. Since most of the laboratory activities were classics that had been included in biology laboratory books since their advent, this was not a major problem. In addition, some of the potentially difficult laboratory investigations were properly developed. For example, one of the authors of the laboratory manual spent considerable time developing a cloning laboratory in conjunction with an expert. Some new laboratory activities, however, were never seen by any student until they were published.

The textbook and the various ancillaries have come to be known as the "textbook package." A textbook program may include several publications for the pupil: pupils' edition of the textbook, workbook, laboratory manual. There are also several publications for the teacher: teacher's edition of the textbook, workbook, laboratory manual with teaching guidelines and answers to questions; test booklets; a teacher's resource book; overhead transparencies; posters; a computer program accompanied by a user's manual. Many of the separate ancillaries are given away as incentives to buy a class set of the pupils' edition. The practice of producing so many ancillaries started when I was at Holt. The increasing demand for more and more "giveaways" has now increased the price of the textbook, and has resulted in an increased reliance on development houses to produce ancillaries.

Postproduction

After the ancillaries were produced, it was time to watch sales figures to see how well the textbook was selling and to get feedback on what new features had been accepted and which had not. It was also a time to go to professional gatherings such as the National Science Teachers Association (NSTA) convention to give talks and to provide in-service training on how to use the new book. When textbooks are sold, the sales representative agrees to provide training on how to use the textbook. Sometimes the editor was sent to provide the training.

With MB '81 we found ourselves somewhat scooped by a new biology textbook put out by Scott Foresman. They used a phylogenetic approach as did MB, but had remarkably beautiful photos and art, and they tried a new format. They concluded discussion of a topic at the bottom of the page; there was no need to turn the page to conclude the reading and no beginning of topics, or ending, in the middle of a page. Teachers loved it. There were also teachers who had been teaching from MB so long that they decided to buy the new Scott Foresman book just for a change. (I was told recently that their success with this book was short-lived, however.)

Another way we came up short on MB '81 was in producing regional field guides to accompany the textbook. Numerous teachers told us that they used local flora and fauna to teach biology and that they would like to have a field guide that was directly coordinated with the textbook. We developed five field guides that ended up not being sold but were used solely as giveaways—incentives to buy the textbook. Some teachers said they liked them and used them; others seemed to have just stored them away on a shelf.

When I traveled to various places giving talks and providing training on how to use MB '81 and its ancillaries, the most frequent question I was asked was about the reading level. Beyond that I was asked about the placement of human body and frog inserts (several page inserts in the text showing the various organ systems—a Holt trademark). A textbook is made in pieces called "signatures." To place an insert anywhere except between signatures is extremely expensive. Unfortunately, the signature breaks were not convenient and the frog insert ended up among the fishes.

A View from Academe

I have tried to relate the perceptions I had while an editor at Holt and later as a freelancer. Looking back on my career in publishing, I now have a very different perspective. I recognize that we did much that I would never do now, but I am still proud of MB '81. We did not succumb to irrational requests from pressure groups and customers but sought and followed experts' suggestions. We were especially careful to include correct and up-to-date information. Within the confines of a readability formula, it is at least clearly written and coherent. (This is not to say that it could not be better.) There are, however, many instructional design features I would change, many of which are described and listed in a booklet Charles M. Reigeluth and I wrote for the Phi Delta Kappa "Fastback" series.[3]

My general impression of MB '81 now is that it is a great encyclopedic version of general biology for high school students. In fact, many teachers have told me that they have a class set of MB in their rooms for students to look up information even though they do not use it as a primary textbook for the course. Mainly because of state requirements, it was important to "cover" everything. This made subject-matter content king. For example, we did not include a chapter on behavior, but included that topic in separate sections. The reason was that not many places included behavior in their syllabus, but for those who did, it was "covered." These decisions were made because a general biology textbook that included everything would be infinitely large.

My experience with the publishing industry has helped me with my research on selection and use of textbooks in that I can understand the constraints under which publishers operate. Particularly, it seems that publishers have to sit on a fence between being too innovative and not being innovative enough. To the extent they are convinced that an innovation will be accepted by teachers, they will be purveyors of educational innovations. Take behavioral objectives as an example. Although their importance had already been emphasized by Tyler and others, behavioral objectives gained more general notice with the publication of Bloom's *Taxonomy of Educational Objectives* in 1956. About the time that objectives were first being discussed in the *Journal of Teacher Education*, they were beginning to be included in teacher's editions of textbooks. As the number of journal articles peaked (in 1974), objectives were being used on a regular basis in pupils' editions along with the introduction to each chapter. By the time MB '81 was produced, we were coding test items in the text manual to match the objectives at the beginning of the chapters.

For MB '81 we also tried out an innovation in the teacher's edition first, a fairly common practice. For each chapter we designed a structural overview of the information in the chapter. These overviews later became known as "concept maps." In MB '81 it was largely ignored by teachers and not carried through in subsequent editions. This is a case where a good idea was incorporated into the textbook on a trial basis. I wonder how long it will take concept maps to get into textbooks again now that they are better accepted. The point is that publishers cannot be innovators on a large scale because of cost considerations even though they are willing to try innovations that will improve textbooks.

Some problems with textbooks seem to be real and others are problems only for some people. What is "bad" is not the same to all people. So what are some of the *real* problems?

1. Research can tell us how students can learn better from textbooks, but publishers do not look to this kind of research for criteria for producing textbooks. They listen to teachers. Research has shown that teachers do not always know what they need, so publishers try to fulfill the perceived needs of the marketplace, not necessarily the actual needs.

2. There are myriad problems with state requirements for content coverage, specifically in the way results are reported. Often there is a set of questions regarding what topics are covered in the textbook or what aspects of pedagogy are included in the textbook by page number. If the textbook mentions that topic, it is reported. For example, a state or district might ask if American Indians are discussed. The text might say "American Indians are the indigenous population of North America." The report would show the page number where this statement is made, indicating that the topic of American Indians was covered. A Washington Post reporter, quoting results of a report done by Tyson-Bernstein, states: "To make sure the books 'mention' this material, textbook selection committees, faced with large stacks of competing series, often just look through the index to see if a topic appears."[4]

3. Research on textbook selection has revealed that the most widely used criteria for selecting textbooks are copyright date and authors' credentials. Suffice it to say here that this is probably the worst way to select textbooks in that these criteria are, for the most part, meaningless.

When I recently asked several publishers what they wanted most from academe they all said, without hesitation, they wanted teachers to be trained to use and select textbooks. They said they put into textbooks the kinds of methods and materials that attempt to compensate for lack of good teacher education, which is what "easy to manage" textbook packages are all about. Much has already been learned about how students learn from text. We in academe need to inform teachers how to use textbooks to enhance student learning and to research further how different students learn best from textbooks and under what circumstances. Then, we must train teachers what to look for when selecting textbooks for their students.

Finally, I would like to see the use of nonfiction books, newspapers, magazines, videos, computer programs, as well as more than one textbook for any given subject in classrooms. To not use a textbook at all would deprive students of learning how to use books as information sources, but to rely so much on one textbook is equally onerous. Learning is a project for a lifetime. Beyond the classroom, we never use a textbook again. So, why do we train our children to rely on one textbook as the main source of written information on a given subject?

Footnotes

1. E. J. Townsend, "The Textbook Question," *Education* 11 (1891): 556-65.

2. See, for example, Roger Farr and Michael A. Tulley, "Do Adoption Committees Perpetuate Mediocre Textbooks?" *Phi Delta Kappan* 66, no. 7 (1985): 467-71; Jean H. Osborn, Beau Fly Jones, and Marcy Stein, "The Case for Improving Textbooks," *Educational Leadership* 42, no. 7 (1985): 9-16; Caroline B. Cody, *A Policymaker's Guide to Textbook Selection* (Alexandria, VA: National Association of State Boards of Education, 1986); Harriet Tyson-Bernstein, "Textbook Adoption: The Enemy Is Us," *Curriculum Review* 26, no. 4 (1987): 9-11.

3. M. Jean Young and Charles M. Reigeluth, *Improving the Textbook Selection Process*, Fastback #275 (Bloomington, IN: Phi Delta Kappa Educational Foundation, 1988). A good source of information for text design is David H. Jonassen's two-volume series, *The Technology of Text* (Englewood Cliffs, NJ: Educational Technology Publications, 1982).

4. From Lawrence Feinberg, "Textbooks, 'Themeless, Dull'," *Washington Post*, 23 April 1988, p. A10.

CHAPTER VI

The Small Publisher in a National Market

M. BLOUKE CARUS

This chapter deals primarily with elementary basal textbook publishing, namely publishing in the basic subjects of reading, language arts, mathematics, science, and social studies for kindergarten through the eighth grade.

I will be discussing how small publishers try to cope and to survive in an increasingly complex field of textbook publishing, a field littered with acquisitions and withdrawals rather than new entries and success stories.[1] Indeed, the past few years have shown that the small basal publisher cannot exist for long without some kind of external support from a parent or outside source. Our purposes here will be (a) to explain why the smaller basal publishers have such difficulty surviving, despite the urgent need for innovation, alternatives, and improved quality, and (b) to describe conditions under which small textbook publishers can enter the basal market.

For purposes of discussion, small publishers will be considered anything less than $30 million in annual sales; medium sized publishers, $30 million to $100 million; and the giants, anything over $100 million.

The field is complex because many of the educational problems that have surfaced in the past few decades have some kind of instructional and textbook dimensions. Each one of these educational problems is knotty and complex in itself and cannot be solved by any simplistic procedures or by layering new elements of reform on existing textbooks, as has been done so often in the past.

The problems are so profound and pervasive that they are not only troublesome to small publishers. They are also causing major difficulties for all publishers. As a result, the entire industry is in turmoil, and this is especially telling for small publishers who have very limited capital and cannot afford any serious market misalignments.

For example, the selection of content in any of these basic subjects is problematical. There is a new and encouraging demand for cultural literacy as educators are taking E. D. Hirsch more seriously these days.[2] However, cultural literacy is very difficult to fulfill in the basal areas because of our pluralistic society and because most of the classic literature, folk tales, fairy tales, and anecdotes about famous people were written by and about white males. At the present time there is an equally strong and appropriate demand for ethnic, racial, and sexual balance in all elementary textbooks. To meet this demand the amount of classical literature and stories about white males used in the past would have to be significantly reduced. The net result is that important compromises must be made between these two opposing constraints.

The Need for Consensus

The United States is one of the few countries without a ministry of education that ordinarily dictates curriculum content. For a variety of reasons, we have not yet developed methods to arrive at consensus for resolving controversies about what should be taught.[3] There is an urgent need for such consensus, and this is one of the most perplexing of all the problems in the basal textbook industry. In a period of rapid change, publishers can no longer simply update existing textbooks, or survey the wants and needs of adoption committee members in the larger states, or put in different names, faces, and problems, and expect to get away with it as they have done too often in the past.

There are a variety of means to achieve consensus, subject by subject, and I think the current scene is quite illustrative of two reasonably successful attempts to reach consensus. In the field of mathematics, the National Council of Teachers of Mathematics (NCTM) has shown leadership in developing a solid set of recommendations on what should be taught from kindergarten to the twelfth grade. For example, in the elementary grades, instead of the main emphasis on the basic operations of arithmetic, the NCTM recommends a broad based introduction to functions (algebra), geometry, probability and statistics, graphing, and estimating. NCTM also offers guidelines for using this knowledge to solve problems and to develop higher-order thinking skills.[4]

In the field of reading, a national commission report (*Becoming a Nation of Readers*), sponsored by the National Institute of Education, is finally bringing order out of chaos.[5] Until the publication and wide dissemination of this booklet, the research and effective practices had not been summarized and put into a form that provided an intelligible guide to help teachers and school districts distinguish good textbooks from bad ones. Although there are a few countertrends, such as the whole language movement,[6] because of *Becoming a Nation of Readers* many districts throughout the United States are using these new criteria to evaluate reading textbooks, to the great benefit of all concerned.

At the heart of the controversies about content is also the increasingly expanding information explosion. The problem of developing a common language, commonly held concepts and historical images, and commonly held background knowledge is not trivial, as Hirsch has so well articulated.[7] There is, therefore, an urgent need for scholars, organizations, and the wisest people in America to deal with this issue so that we can soon develop a means of arriving at what all students should know when they graduate from secondary education.

The lack of consensus also applies to pedagogy and classroom organization. During a period when educational research is coming into its own and there is an urgent need to translate effective teaching principles and the results of the important educational research into instruction that can be used widely as a part of textbook programs, the small publisher is taxed to the limit to know what to include and how to structure lessons. Because of the increasing demands for improved test results by the informed lay public, publishers can no longer get away with simplifying the lesson plans and making things easier for teachers (better known as "dumbing down"). Now, for the first time in many decades, all publishers must really think things through in making the thousands of decisions regarding content and pedagogy. Making such decisions requires many resources that small publishers of textbooks usually do not have.

The lack of consensus about what should be taught and how it should be taught has bizarre consequences, as the recent California adoption in mathematics illustrates.[8] In general, publishers have great difficulty interpreting textbook adoption criteria of the large states or districts, as well as those of the adoption committees themselves. Also, the adoption committee members are usually volunteers who are not familiar with the research, or are not subject matter specialists with a broad liberal education, and most difficult of all, they are not given the time to wade through the enormous amount of materials in order to make intelligent selections. The usefulness of state adoption committees seems to be a thing of the past, and it seems much wiser to allow local districts the power to select materials with which they can live.

Educators and, in turn, publishers, are caught in the dilemma of producing significantly improved results under social conditions that are more difficult than ever before. Even more perplexing is the fact that parents, the taxpayers, and the public have witnessed declining test scores and significantly increased costs over the past two decades, and are therefore skeptical about increasing taxes further without some kind of assurance that there will be a pay-off in better results and in students who will be employable upon graduation from high school or college. This means that the textbook business will no longer be business as usual, but rather that the companies, large and small, that expect to survive and grow in the future must contribute toward improved results or they should not be in the business. To achieve these results requires a real understanding of effective instruction, a wide knowledge of educational research, an awareness of the current classroom environments, and what is needed to improve them, and manageability of instruction. In addition, there are frequent complaints about the need to improve instruction and to provide strategies for learning problem-solving and higher-order skills. All in all, during the next decade it will take a brave publisher to enter the elementary basal textbook business, unless some of these major issues are resolved and stability returns to education and to the education market.

The root cause of the instability is the current educational reform movement, one of the largest, longest, and most fundamental reform movements of this century, and perhaps since the beginning of public education in America. It blossomed with the 1983 report of the National Commission on Excellence in Education (*A Nation at Risk*) and a dozen other major commission reports. Instead of withering away as have other reform movements in past decades, the current movement has reached the business community and many powerful leaders in the private sector who recognize that our country will not be competitive unless basic changes are made in education.[9] With the crescendo of calls from foundations, media, academics, and business, the movement for restructuring education seems to be widely felt. As David Kearns of Xerox has written:

Public education in this country is in crisis. America's public schools graduate 700,000 functionally illiterate students every year, and 700,000 more drop out. Four out of five young adults in a recent survey couldn't summarize the main point of a newspaper article, or read a bus schedule, or figure their change from a restaurant bill.

At a time when our preeminent role in the world economy is in jeopardy, there are few social problems more telling in their urgency. Public education has put this country at a terrible competitive disadvantage.

The task before us is the restructuring of our entire public education system. I don't mean tinkering. I don't mean piecemeal changes or even well-intentioned reforms. I mean the total restructuring of our schools.

Why do I, a businessman, the head of one of the world's great corporations, care about education? I care about education for the same reason that every parent in America does—education is the future. It's the future of our way of life. Thomas Jefferson believed that education was the *sine qua non* of democracy. Without education, democracy would falter and eventually fail. He was right.[10]

The international comparisons in reading, writing, science, and mathematics[11] will continue to provide incentives to improve instruction until American education is educationally competitive with the other industrialized nations. I believe a strong case can be made that textbooks must play an important if not crucial and essential role in this reform movement for a variety of reasons.

Textbooks, no matter how complete and effective, cannot substitute for good teaching. However, superior textbooks can provide a lot of assistance to elementary teachers of all abilities who are trying to accomplish a Herculean task. In order for elementary teachers to provide for their students, they ideally should have a solid liberal education with wide reading and some real-world experiences to support their instruction in *all* of the basic subjects. The current reform movements in teacher education are a bright spot on the horizon of educational reform,[12] but they will take many years to implement fully, and it will take decades before the new and much better educated teachers become a significant percentage of our teaching force. In the next few decades, therefore, we will have to cope with teachers who are predominantly neither the best and brightest of the academic student population, nor familiar with educational research, nor well prepared for teaching under current conditions.

For all these reasons, there is an urgent need to develop the best textbooks ever, because of so many forces coming to bear on educational change. Textbooks could provide not only the support, but could become a catalyst for improved instruction if given the opportunity. If reform continues on an upward path, textbooks could serve as the vehicle to provide the conclusions of educational research, proven classroom practices, the most effective classroom management, and a better and more judicious choice of content; and they could provide for more and better homework, ways to work with parents, reference ideas, and supplementary materials. In this publisher's view, textbooks *do* have an important and an essential role to play, especially in these times of extremely rapid educational changes.

Entry of Small Publishers into
Basal Publishing

Even though a strong case can be made that small publishers encounter great obstacles in entering the basal textbook publishing field, a number of small nonbasal publishers publish supplementary materials. As any casual observer can see at the national conventions of the major educational associations, hundreds of small publishers and suppliers have found markets for their products and sell in some way to teachers and to schools. These small publishers have found a market niche in the school business and are profitable in doing so. If they develop enough confidence in their products and their knowledge of the market, if they have access to marketing experience in the basal textbook business, and if they have sufficient capital, they could very well enter the basal publishing business.

There are a number of advantages of starting small and avoiding the constraints of the basal textbook business. One of the advantages is that a publisher can stake out a territory or establish its reputation and stick with it over long periods of time, as Open Court has done, starting in the early 1960s. With luck and good timing, one can survive as a niche publisher at the beginning, and therefore not have to pay the price of the enormously expensive constraints of the major basal publishers. If the niche truly fulfills a basic educational need, and the publisher has developed a strong following and a reputation, then the publisher can change to full line basal publisher and be much more secure in the firm's investments than a new entry could ever possibly be.

In order to survive in a very competitive market of medium-sized and large publishers, small publishers cannot and probably should not imitate the large publishers, because they can never match the resources, especially representation and sales power at the local levels. Rather, a small publisher should look toward current and future unmet needs that the larger publishers have difficulty providing.

During the current upheaval in educational reform,[13] the many unmet needs create opportunities for the smaller publishers who eventually may choose to become basal publishers. There are needs for supplementary materials for classroom libraries, for materials to help parents become more effective in educating their own children, for materials to help teachers teach thinking skills and higher-order skills, for more effective materials in the sciences and social studies, for useful software based on sound educational research, for research-based textbooks for training the new generation of teachers, and for improved materials for testing and assessment.[14]

Big publishers tend to build up a medium-sized infrastructure to support all of their marketing and other activities. They therefore tend to become somewhat bureaucratic and lethargic, and have difficulty in adapting readily to rapid changes needed to accommodate the educational reform movement. In addition, the basal textbook giants are, for the most part, fairly large publicly held companies that suffer from the often destabilizing effects of frequent management changes and takeover possibilities.

Smaller publishers, on the other hand, can provide strengths to buttress the weaknesses of the large publishers. If properly conceived and organized, small publishers can provide better adaptability and decision-making ability; they can become risk takers and innovators because everything is on a smaller scale; they can provide for more unity, consistency, and for longer-term commitments; and they can become very aggressive in pursuing market niches. Therefore, we see the proliferation of small publishers as a healthy phenomenon, and we hope that from time to time they will enter the basal markets as they become strong enough and have the opportunities to do so.

Implications of Lack of Resources for Small Publishers

Basal textbook publishing has a variety of dimensions that make it difficult for any publishing firm to sustain itself with less than $30 million in sales per year, without large infusions of capital or cash from external sources to bring sales up to that sustainable minimum. For example, to develop and publish a basal reading program for kindergarten to eighth grade, the estimated costs are anywhere from $15 to $45 million, which includes student books, teacher's guides, workbooks, tests, management systems, teacher's resource guides, supplementary workbooks and other materials, etc., now usually over

200 separate items. With the current market demands for revisions every two to three years, which also cost from $1 to $10 million, the stakes become very high indeed. For all the other basal subjects, the costs are estimated to be somewhat lower, in the neighborhood of $10 to $20 million each. Thus a small publisher should have access to capital to develop each one of the basal programs before even thinking of entering this field.

Another major investment needed for entry into the market, and to be considered seriously in that market, is for a national field force with a strong infrastructure to call on school staff and adoption committees and to train teachers. A sales representative will cost up to $100,000 per person to support and will be expected to have annual textbook sales between $500,000 and $1,000,000. However, small publishers cannot possibly afford a field force to cover most of the schools in the country as the large publishers do, so that the smaller publishers cannot personally call on all potential customers but rather must be extremely selective.

It is also essential to provide strong sales support or marketing activities, which include such things as sampling of complete sets of materials, the normal promotional activities (such as advertisements, catalogues, and publicity), market research, etc. The sampling expense has become essential and is one of the largest marketing costs; however, teachers and adoption committees have become addicted to receiving samples, and there is little that can be done to alleviate that practice under present circumstances.

For all of these reasons, marketing costs for small publishers usually exceed 30 percent of gross sales, whereas the large publishers are able to maintain marketing costs of below 20 percent of gross sales. This is a heavy burden for the smaller publisher.

Publishers almost have to become omniscient so as to gather the knowledge and insights to be able to meet the real and perceived needs of teachers who are at the receiving end of the information explosion and the educational reform movement. The costs to gather this information in a timely manner are high. For example, the condition of teaching is such that teachers are busier than ever and are pressed to the limit of their time and energy, and they need all the help that can be provided, such as textbooks. They do not have time to study the materials in class, they do not take teacher's guides home as a rule, so they need guides that are truly useful when they pick them up for each daily lesson. This puts an added burden on the publisher to provide a lot of know-how about current best practices and educational research, about how teachers really operate and should operate, rather than copying old models and old methods that are now discredited or wasteful of classroom time.

Textbook publishers have the burden of meeting many constraints all at the same time, which means high risks and especially high costs for the small publishers. For example, there is a real need for better materials based on changing needs, which have been and will continue to be hard to implement, such as the demand for cultural literacy; the demand for ethnic and sexual balance; the demand for improved test results; the need for more individual attention with the realization that smaller class sizes are prohibitively expensive; the demand for teaching strategies; and demands in all the other categories of educational reform.

Although we are not hearing much about it, the new technology in computers and software will ultimately be part of basal publishing and will create a whole new revolution in instructional practices and textbook publishing. This may take a few years, but investments in electronic publishing will be significant. They will raise the ante once more and destabilize the industry again for at least the next decade. These costs of entry and updating will increase the break-even point of basal publishers.

Another continuing cost for publishers is the result of the ongoing social revolutions. The last two decades or more have been especially difficult for all textbook publishers because all the large political groups have "discovered" that textbooks are a major contributing factor for creating stereotypes of social behavior that are passed on from one generation to the next. As the blacks raised their social consciousness during the early 1960s—followed by other racial and ethnic groups such as Orientals, native Americans, and Hispanics, and then by the feminists, the elderly, and the handicapped—each group claimed that it was not adequately represented in elementary textbooks, which was of course true. Finally, in the past few years, many Americans are realizing that stories about the religious aspects of American life have been all but eliminated in American textbooks for fear that the publishers might antagonize one religious group or another, or the antireligious groups. There is now a general recognition that almost all textbooks should put stories and information about the religious elements back into textbooks, so currently there is a new demand that needs to be satisfied all over again.[15] This confusion and lack of means to arrive at consensus in the selection of content seems never to end and cries for some kind of resolution. Because of the current social turmoil, I expect this dilemma for publishers, which causes almost insuperable difficulties for the smaller publishers, to continue during the foreseeable future.

As school districts demand better results, higher test scores, and better student motivation, publishers will have to spend more on training teachers to use their materials more effectively. In addition to the need for large investments in the programs themselves and the need for frequent revisions, small publishers do not have the resources to keep track of the changing world of education, to translate educational research and the best practices into teachable and manageable programs, to provide a strong field organization to deliver the programs and provide customer feedback and satisfaction, and to keep track of the ongoing politicization of the textbook field. We do not see any of these problems suddenly disappearing in the near future, and therefore the costs will continue to escalate. Small publishers will find it difficult to enter the basal markets except under extremely favorable conditions.

FOOTNOTES

1. The past few decades have seen numerous changes in the field of textbook publishing with the acquisition of many of the smaller companies by the giants. Open Court and McDougall-Littell are surviving, growing, and becoming mid-sized text publishers, whereas many of the other prominent publishers have been acquired by the larger firms. These include Allyn & Bacon, Follett, Harper & Row, Lippincott, Economy, SRA (Distar Program), Cambridge, Laidlaw, American Book Company, Ginn & Company, D. C. Heath, Holt, Rinehart & Winston, Rand McNally, Charles E. Merrill, Prentice-Hall, Silver Burdett, and Addison-Wesley. The giants that remain are Gulf & Western, a combination of Simon & Schuster, Ginn, Allyn & Bacon, Prentice-Hall, Silver Burdett, and the former Esquire companies (Globe Book Company, Cambridge, Modern Curriculum Press); Harcourt Brace Jovanovich, which acquired Holt, Rinehart & Winston; Longman, which acquired Addison-Wesley; Raytheon (D. C. Heath); Houghton Mifflin, which acquired Rand McNally; and Scott, Foresman and Co., which acquired Silver Burdett and Southwestern in the 1970s. Scott, Foresman and Co. has now been acquired by Time, Inc. One of the other giants, Macmillan, which had previously acquired Harper & Row and Laidlaw but closed them in 1988, is now in the process of acquisition by the Maxwell Communication Corporation, the London publisher.

2. E. D. Hirsch, *Cultural Literacy* (Boston: Houghton Mifflin, 1987).

3. Harriet Tyson-Bernstein, *A Conspiracy of Good Intentions* (Washington, DC: Council for Basic Education, 1988).

4. National Council of Teachers of Mathematics (NCTM), *Curriculum and Evaluation Standards for School Mathematics* (Reston, VA: National Council of Teachers of Mathematics, 1989). What is "best" is obviously subjective, but the NCTM Commission on Standards for School Mathematics has come to grips with what can and should be taught for the needs of tomorrow's citizens. Although California and Texas have made admirable progress in raising the sights for textbooks and instruction, I believe the NCTM model is the best one to achieve national consensus on what should

96   THE SMALL PUBLISHER

be taught and how. Genuine scholarship and wisdom is urgently needed to achieve consensus in all basal areas.

5. Richard Anderson, Elfrieda Hiebert, Judith A. Scott, and Ian A. G. Wilkinson, *Becoming a Nation of Readers: The Report of the Commission on Reading* (Champaign, IL: Center for the Study of Reading, University of Illinois, 1985).

6. Jeanne S. Chall, "Learning to Read: The Great Debate 20 years Later—A Response to 'Debunking the Great Phonics Myth'," *Phi Delta Kappan* 70 (March 1989): 521-38.

7. Hirsch, *Cultural Literacy.*

8. M. Blouke Carus, "California and Textbook Reform: Too Little Too Late, Too Much Too Soon" (Paper presented at the Annual Meeting of the American Educational Research Association, Washington, DC, 1987). ERIC ED 276 128.

9. "The Decline of America's Work Force," *Business Week*, 19 September 1988, pp. 100-101.

10. David T. Kearns and Denis P. Doyle, *Winning the Brain Race: A Bold Plan to Make Our Schools Competitive* (San Francisco: ICS Press, 1988).

11. Curtis C. McKnight, F. Joe Crosswhite, et al., *The Underachieving Curriculum: Assessing U. S. School Mathematics from an International Perspective* (Champaign, IL: Stipes Publishing Co., 1987).

12. The Holmes Group, *Tomorrow's Teachers: A Report of the Holmes Group* (East Lansing, MI: Holmes Group, 1986); Carnegie Forum on Education and the Economy, *A Nation Prepared: Teachers for the 21st Century* (Hyattsville, MD: Carnegie Forum, 1986); National Commission for Excellence in Teacher Education, *A Call for Change in Teacher Education* (Washington, DC: American Association of Colleges of Teacher Education, 1985); Marc Tucker, "Peter Drucker, Knowledge Work, and the Structure of Schools," *Educational Leadership* 45 (February 1988): 44-46; idem, "Better Teachers: The Arts and Sciences Connection," *Change* 18 (September/October, 1986): 12-17; Lee Shulman, "Assessment for Teaching: An Initiative for the Profession," *Phi Delta Kappan* 69 (September 1987): 38-44; Mary Liepold, "A Nation Prepared? The Carnegie Forum and NSTA Have Some Suggestions," *Science and Children* 24 (October 1986): 13-14.

13. Reform movements are underway especially in Arkansas, California, Florida (Miami), Illinois, Indiana, Massachusetts, Michigan, Minnesota, Missouri, New Jersey, New York (Rochester), North Carolina, South Carolina, Texas, and Wisconsin (Milwaukee). As Chairman of the Education Committee for the Illinois Manufacturers Association, I have been involved with education reform efforts in Illinois in general and in the Chicago Public Schools in particular. We have been working with leaders in business and industry, city officials, school board members, teachers and school administrators, and the state legislature in an effort to bring about reforms that will be beneficial to all Illinois students, and which will in turn benefit Illinois business and industry.

14. See, for example, Robert Rothman, "Schools Urged to Develop Wider Set of Assessments," *Education Week*, 14 September 1988; idem, "Bennett Is Urged to Probe 'Dumbing Down' of Tests," *Education Week*, 20 April 1988; Linda Lenz, "New Reading Test Set for Schools," *Chicago Sun-Times*, 13 March 1988; Ed Roeber and Peggy Dutcher, "Michigan's Innovative Assessment of Reading," *Educational Leadership* 46 (April 1989): 64-69.

15. Paul Vitz, *Censorship: Evidence of Bias in Our Children's Textbooks* (Ann Arbor, MI: Servant Books, 1986). Vitz is basically sympathetic to all of these needs, but there are no individuals who can speak for each of the groups. Therefore, there are hundreds, if not thousands, of judgment calls—any one of which can be a cause for rejection of the entire series.

CHAPTER VII

Small Publishers: Filling Market Niches

SHARRYL DAVIS HAWKE AND JAMES E. DAVIS

"My students could learn better if someone would write a . . ."
"Why doesn't anyone publish a . . .?" "A company could make a
fortune if it would just polish up these materials I've developed and
sell them."

These statements are the stuff of which niche publishing is made.
Unmet needs, publishing gaps, and creative ideas are a niche
publisher's motivation and raison d'etre. While a large or mid-size
publisher aspires to generate sales of $10 to $100 million plus, a niche
publisher may aspire (at least initially) to generate sales of $1 to $5 or
$6 million. While a basal publisher thinks in terms of print runs of
50,000 to 150,000 volumes, a niche publisher thinks in terms of 3,000
to 10,000 volumes. While a larger publisher dreams of sweeping 40
percent of a major state basal series adoption, which might total as
much as $10 million, a niche publisher dreams of a single school
adoption of $5,000 or $6,000.

Although the goals and expectations of niche and mid-size or giant
publishers are vastly different, they play in the same ball park. Sharing
the arena with the "big guys" is both a blessing and a curse for niche
publishers: the unfilled voids left by larger publishers provide
opportunities for them, yet the customer's expectation for the
"freebies" and discounts offered by big publishers is their albatross.
Nevertheless, the educational publishing industry has always had
niche publishers, and they seem likely to continue to be part of the
industry picture. In this chapter we will examine the role, nature, and
likely future of this part of the publishing industry. Because literature
on the topic is virtually nonexistent, our writing draws primarily on
our own recent experiences as niche publishers and now curriculum
developers, as well as our earlier experiences as teachers and
researchers. Although many of our examples come from the field of
social studies—our content area—we believe the examples are
applicable in other subject fields.

97

What Is Niche Publishing?

In our minds, niche publishers are distinguished both by their size and their goals. We define their size (in dollars) as under $10 million in yearly sales. In reality, many stay around $3 to $7 million in yearly sales. Although they share profit goals similar to their larger colleagues, many do not aspire to grow into large companies. Instead, their goal is often to be innovative and flexible and to avoid being bogged down by large staffs and high percentage overhead costs.

Niche publishers are specialists, not full-line publishers. Their offerings tend to fall into the following categories:

* materials focused on current "hot" topics or new content,
* materials based on innovative pedagogy,
* materials aimed at specific populations,
* materials with innovative formats, and
* materials aimed at local or regional markets.

It is impossible to count accurately the number of publishers in the niche category. Many of them do not belong or report their financial statistics to the American Association of Publishers. They also come and go rather quickly in the industry. However, our educated guess is that there are several hundred niche publishers producing precollege materials in all subject areas as we enter the last decade of this century.

While each niche publisher's story is different, there are important similarities in many of the stories, most of which are laced with a certain Horatio Alger flavor. We present here a hypothetical history of a niche publisher—a history that is a composite of several actual stories.

History Alive! *The Story of a Niche Publisher*

Jane Williams was one of those teachers principals dream about— creative, energetic, knowledgeable. During the five years she taught third grade at Central Elementary School, she did more to enrich the teaching of history than all the other teachers combined. For example, she frequently involved students in historical art projects, creating models for them to make large cutout images of important historical people or of ordinary people in other time periods. Jane also constructed several simple dioramas of historical scenes in which students displayed their cutout characters. Students often used their creations in classroom dramas about events and eras. Jane's students regularly reported history studies to be their favorite subject; their social studies test scores went off the scale; and other teachers admired her ability to capture the students' imaginations. From time to time, Jane would make hands-on materials for other teachers to use in their history lessons.

While serving on a social studies textbook selection committee, Jane talked with several sales representatives from the textbook companies about her materials and asked them why their companies did not provide hands-on materials. Discouraged by their lack of interest in such materials, Jane decided to devote one summer to producing a limited quantity of some of her historical figures and dioramas. With a student helper, she created and hand painted twenty-five figures of ten different historical characters and made thirty dioramas. Jane named her products *History Alive!* With permission from the school district, she set up an exhibit table at the countywide teacher in-service meeting in August. Within four hours all Jane's *History Alive!* inventory had been purchased, and she had $4500 in her pocket.

Buoyed by this success, Jane spent the next school year trying out new ideas for her figures and dioramas in her classroom and exploring ways to turn her ideas into a business. After much searching, she found a printer who would print her oversized cutouts. The unit cost was high, but Jane realized she could not make all her products by hand. The teachers who bought her hand-made products were so pleased with them that Jane was sure she could charge more for commercially printed versions.

By the following summer Jane was ready to turn entrepreneur. With confidence she quit her teaching job, spent the summer creating more products, had them printed, and developed some brochures describing her *History Alive!* products. When the school year started, Jane was ready. She loaded her products into her car and set out to go school to school, district office to district office, to sell her products. When possible, she took orders on the spot and filled those orders on the weekend from the inventory in her garage. When customers were reluctant, she volunteered to come back and demonstrate the product with students. This sales technique nearly always resulted in an order. By the end of the year, Jane's telephone message recorder was filled every Friday evening with orders or inquiries resulting from word-of-mouth publicity.

Jane's year-end financial statement was impressive. She had made a 30 percent profit. By reinvesting most of her profit and getting additional financial backing from the bank, Jane was able to manufacture a greater volume of her original products and add a few new ones to her inventory for the next school year. Realizing the limitations of school-to-school selling, Jane also prepared a brochure mailing to schools in surrounding states to test the mail order potential for her *History Alive!* products.

Assessing the results of her second year, Jane determined that in the new schools she called on during the year, her sales were as strong as in her first year. However, in schools she called on for the second time, she had few sales, seemingly because she had few new products to offer and because teachers were sharing with their colleagues the materials they had purchased the first year. The mail order experiment had barely paid for itself, indicating that *History Alive!* products needed a "personal sell."

Although still retaining profits of almost 25 percent, Jane knew she was at a crossroads. She could continue her present operation—be her own sales force, take her current products into new territories, and expect to retain good profits. However, this choice lacked challenge, and Jane was convinced that there were ways to reach more customers. After much thought, Jane decided to take two steps. One was to hire a writer/editor who could produce new products while she was selling or creating new markets. The second step was to get other people to sell her product line for her. By the end of the summer she had her first employee, a product developer, and she had contracted with five independent sales representatives to carry the *History Alive!* product line.

Jane's third-year financial statement showed a two-fold increase in sales but a sharp decline in profits—down to about 8 percent. Overhead costs and sales commissions were cutting into profits. Jane was not discouraged because she recognized she had taken two major steps in adding a developer and starting a sales force. She believed the payoff for both these steps would come in the following year. Having been freed from the daily routine of sales calls, Jane also had time during the year to talk to customers and to create new product ideas. She believed the time had come to expand her inventory beyond cutouts and dioramas into books—historical storybooks that would enrich the dull historical narrative in social studies textbooks. Jane was sure her idea would work but discovered that books are not cheap to develop. Both sales representatives and teachers told her that to be competitive the books had to be full-color and hardbound. Jane took their advice.

By offering her home as collateral, Jane was able to get financing to create seven of these books. When school started, Jane's sales force, now expanded to ten representatives, had four of the books to show people and three more on the way. The initial response seemed positive, but as the year progressed, Jane got more and more phone calls from the sales representatives saying that customers were expecting free samples of the books and discounts on multiple orders. The sales representatives also clamored for a flashy catalog to mail and to leave with customers. The year-end financials showed the company's sales slightly increased but profits only at about 5 percent. "Next year," said Jane, "we will reap the rewards of the new products."

In the fourth year, revenues from the line of history storybooks did indeed increase, three-fold. But sales from the historical cutouts and dioramas fell off significantly. Sales representatives complained that these products were now old hat, and other companies were starting to produce them. In fact, one of the large textbook companies had begun to make similar looking figures and were giving them away with adoptions of their textbook series. The bottom line was that *History Alive!* was still respectably profitable, but Jane again had some tough decisions to make. Her choices were many. She could enter new regions of the country through the expansion of sales force. She could develop more products along the same lines of the hands-on materials and storybooks. Or, she could apply the same format ideas of hands-on materials and storybooks to new subject areas such as science or reading. Any of the new endeavors would require more capital. Would the expansion pay off in increased profits?

To confound Jane's dilemma, she got a phone call one day from a mid-size publisher who was interested in acquiring her company. The offering price was attractive and included employment for Jane for one year, if she would move across the country to the company's headquarters. While the money was attractive, Jane had not started *History Alive!* just to make money. She had started it because she had an idea that would improve education. At the same time, the realities of the business world were not lost on Jane. Keeping *History Alive!* profitable was going to be an uphill climb. With other companies now "cashing in" on her idea, was she losing her niche?

Jane Williams sold *History Alive!* She plans to use the profits from the sale to start another niche company. Wiser now, Jane knows that the realities she will face with her new company will not be vastly different from those she faced with *History Alive!*

Realities of Niche Publishing

Although the story of *History Alive!* is hypothetical, some of its elements seem to occur in every niche publisher's story. Niche publishing companies are generally started by entrepreneurs, often people who have been involved with education as teachers, federally funded developers, or sales representatives for other publishers. Most niche entrepreneurs are motivated by a combination of commitment to better education and a belief that their ideas can be made profitable. Rarely does the entrepreneur have experience in all aspects of the publishing business—development, manufacturing, sales, marketing, financial management, people management—and yet the entrepreneur is called upon to do or manage all those functions, at least initially.

Very often the niche company produces a tidy profit in the first year or two. With the entrepreneur doing most of the work, expenses are low. If a product has merit, there are always educators—early adopters—who are eager to buy and try new teaching materials. Unfortunately, this phase is usually short-lived, maybe a year or two. Then the realities of the marketplace start to come into play—sales penetration has to be broadened, new products have to be produced to build inventory, cheaper and often better quality manufacturing processes are necessary, flashier marketing materials are required. Customers begin to demand all the incentives provided by large publishers—free samples, discounts, no-cost in-service programs. No longer is the entrepreneur able to work out of a garage as a one-person show. Having realized the goal of getting a company started, now the entrepreneur has to face decisions about growth, decisions that often involve more personal financial risk. Rarely is the niche publishers' problem a lack of ideas. Instead, the problems are those of finances, management, and ways to broaden sales.

Perhaps the most bitter-sweet situation faced by a niche publisher is realizing that his or her idea has been usurped by a mid-size or large publisher. The idea brought to life, nurtured, and made profitable by the niche publisher is "adapted" by a large publisher and sold, often for a lower price, or given away as an incentive for buying the company's more expensive basal products. Suddenly, the niche is gone! While a niche publisher may be flattered to have his or her product instincts affirmed by the large company, this kind of flattery can be financially disastrous.

A specific case in point is the area of state studies in elementary and middle-school social studies. Although for more than sixty years the curricula of school districts across the country have called for the study of the student's own state at fourth grade, major publishers produced only generic, regional geography textbooks for this grade level. Publishers contended that the limited market for a single state study precluded profitability. In the past ten years, several niche publishers developed and profitably sold state studies programs in several formats. The availability of these programs created a demand from customers for these products, a demand which had not previously been voiced because customers did not believe it feasible to expect to buy state materials from commercial publishers. In addition to an increased demand, the larger publishers recognized that niche publishers were making profits from state studies products. They began to acknowledge that such products could be profitable. They further reasoned that even if the products were not profitable, they could serve as an effective incentive to attract customers to the rest of the company's social studies textbook series from which profits were assured. Thus, a niche that was opened and nurtured by niche companies is being closed at this time by competition from larger companies.

What happens to a niche publisher when the niche begins to disappear? Some publishers, like the hypothetical Jane Williams, are acquired by larger companies. However, acquisition is not the end of other niche publishers' stories. For some, buying offers are never made. These companies must either close up shop or move on to create or nurture other niches.

The Future of Niche Publishing

Niche publishers have been a source of innovation in education publishing since its beginning. Some companies that started out as niche publishers have become major forces in the industry. While increased size does not preclude innovation, experimental ideas become more problematic in large companies whose bread and butter are basal textbooks. Do the recent mergers and acquisitions of large publishers bode well or ill for niche publishing?

Some observers believe the increased size of merged companies will make these companies even less willing to experiment with untested content, pedagogy, or materials for special populations. This rigidity should open the door for niche publishers to develop products to meet needs or create markets unaddressed by the large publishers. The question for the niche publisher is not whether opportunities will exist but whether the opportunities will last long enough for him or her to make a profit and move on to another niche. The fierce competitiveness among the larger publishers will make them more observant of the success of niche publishers and entice them to incorporate more quickly the innovations of these companies.

Does this mean that niche companies will become the unacknowledged research and development branches of large companies? To some degree this seems to us a likely possibility, at least for many niche publishers. In addition, niche publishers cannot escape the pressures of the marketplace. As Jane Williams discovered, at some point in every niche company's growth, the entrepreneur encounters the same demands as the larger companies for inventory growth, sales support, marketing expansion, manufacturing cost control. The niche company generally lacks the deep pockets of the larger, merged companies or even mid-size companies with parent company backing. If niche companies do not prosper in the era of the mergers, it will not be because they lack ideas. It will be because they lack the financial resources to compete. They will face either being bought by the larger companies, or worse yet, simply have their ideas usurped.

This scenario would seem to paint a rather bleak picture for niche publishers. However, we do not believe the picture is entirely bleak. We think it only suggests some realities that niche publishers need to acknowledge.

Niche publishers only have about a three- to five-year opportunity to publish and make a profit from a new product innovation. By the end of about five years, the financially successful innovation will be either acquired or usurped by other companies. This reality need not be negative for the niche publisher if he or she understands from the beginning that no niche product will carry him or her to retirement. A niche publisher must constantly be developing new products and opening new markets.

Costs in a niche company demand rigorous control. Short print runs and low sales volume give the niche publisher no economies of scale; manufacturing costs of both products and marketing materials can quickly run up the unit cost of products. While customers may be willing to pay somewhat more for an innovative or specialized product, even niche products must be within the expectations of school budgets. The entrepreneurial urge to take a manufacturing or marketing risk must be held in check when it comes to cost decisions.

Niche publishers must avoid the temptation to match the "bells and whistles" of the large publishers' products. The attraction of niche products is uniqueness—products the customer cannot buy elsewhere. Niche publishers often seem most successful in their first revision of a product—the edition in which mistakes or glitches of the first printing are worked out and the product's attractiveness is improved. Very often after the second edition, they try to add the slickness, packaging, and gimmicks used so effectively by the large publishers. This attempt can lead to trouble for the niche publisher who does not have the resources (or often the expertise) to make these additions. Costs rise, but sales do not rise proportionately.

Niche publishers must avoid, in general, the costly demand to provide schools and teachers with free samples, classroom pilot-test materials, and discounts. Distributing these kinds of marketing costs across a small inventory of products can easily put the cost of a product out of the competitive range. Although some sales will be lost through a firm policy that precludes "freebies" and discounting, niche publishers (unless they have deep pockets) must simply avoid competing with the large publishers in these sales games.

The successful addressing of the four realities above can, in our view, help assure a healthy number of niche publishers serving the vital function of bringing innovation to education in years to come. However, we do not feel the burden of fostering this innovation should fall entirely on niche publishers. Although niche publishers compete in a capitalistic marketplace, educators need to be cognizant of the high risk taken by this segment of the industry. Educators should always demand from niche publishers an accurate, high-quality product, but they can help foster innovative or special market publishing by not demanding free samples, discounting, and extras, such as in-service programs. School decision makers should encourage niche companies to put their resources into high quality products that meet needs unaddressed by other companies, be willing to pay for extras such as samples and in-service training, and buy the product for the need it meets rather than for the "deal" the niche publisher agrees to cut.

The need for innovative, special market products has never been greater than it is in today's schools that deal with highly varied populations, citizen expectations for attention to specific issues, and pressures to raise achievement levels. The niche publisher can help schools meet these demands by being responsive to limited markets— markets not initially of interest to larger publishers. However, to make this possibility work, the niche publisher and school personnel need to understand each other. Schools need to be willing to spend time describing their needs to the publisher, and the publisher, in turn, must be willing to publish materials that do not have a ready-made, national market. Schools need to adopt a different way of thinking about niche publishers—thinking that focuses on quality and the meeting of student needs rather than discounts, in-service activities, and entertainment. The forging of this new kind of public/private partnership can benefit both niche-filling publishers and school-based educators. Together they can more effectively meet the ultimate goal of providing the most effective learning resources possible for American students.

CHAPTER VIII

The Elementary and High School
Textbook Market Today

JAMES R. SQUIRE AND RICHARD T. MORGAN

Current Characteristics of Educational Publishing

Close to forty educational publishers generated sales of instructional materials of around $1.7 billion to American public and private schools in 1987. In addition, many smaller publishers offered supplementary items, so total education sales were close to $2 billion.[1] Today's schools presently expend around $34.17 per pupil for textbooks and related materials (less than 1 percent of school budgets). In 1986, such expenditures ranged from a high of $68 per pupil in Washington, D.C. to a low of $19 per pupil in Utah.[2]

Eleven percent of all textbook expenditures occurred in California and 7.3 percent in Texas, the two states often alleged to dominate textbook decisions because of the size of their markets. However, sales are spread throughout the country, with the ten largest states accounting for only half of the industry revenues.[3] Approximately half the revenues are achieved in "open territory" where local schools and teachers select instructional materials directly. The other half are achieved primarily in the South and West where statewide committees prescreen textbooks and determine a limited number (usually from five to ten) which can then be purchased. Although the number of states engaged in statewide adoptions (twenty-two) has not changed for fifteen years, the importance of these states to the industry has grown as the American population has moved south and west and the total textbook market in these regions has climbed from 40 to about 50 percent of the national market.

RANGE OF MATERIALS

Of the more than $1 billion expended by elementary schools on textbooks and related materials in 1986, some 40.4 percent was spent

107

on instructional materials in reading, more than twice the total dollars expended in elementary school mathematics (15.5 percent). Much less was expended on elementary social studies (6.4 percent), elementary science and health (8.4 percent), elementary language arts (8.3 percent), spelling (6.4 percent), handwriting (0.5 percent) and literature (0.7 percent). Indeed, reading and language arts, when combined with spelling and literature, account for about 60 percent of elementary school instructional dollars, just as language arts teaching dominates instructional time throughout the first six years of schooling.[4] And these totals *do not* include expenditures for library books, newspapers, and other materials not directly associated with reading instruction. Expenditures for other kinds of elementary school teaching are limited: music, 1.8 percent; dictionaries, 1.2 percent; and miscellaneous purchases, 10.3 percent.

The $700 million market for high school subjects is even more diversified. Vocational titles (business, industrial arts, home economics) comprise the largest segment of the market.[5] The nation's schools offer hundreds of different courses in the vocational areas, but, except for introductory courses in business education, enrollments in any single subject are limited. Sales in each of the central academic high school subjects regularly secure between 10 to 15 percent of industry revenue in the secondary school market: social studies, 13.9 percent; mathematics, 13.7 percent; literature, 12.5 percent; foreign languages, 10.3 percent (5.9 percent in Spanish, 3.4 percent in French); and English composition and grammar, 8.0 percent. But, again, except for multiple-year programs in composition or literature, the secondary school market is fragmented into a large variety of courses so that the potential market for any single textbook is far smaller than a textbook intended for an elementary school grade. This is one reason why, historically, author royalties for high school textbooks are substantially higher than for elementary school books, ranging from a 4 percent royalty at the primary level (where the potential return is vast) to 6 to 8 percent for junior high school titles, and 8 to 10 percent for high school. (Royalties on college textbooks, written for even smaller potential markets, exceed substantially those paid on high school books).

COSTS OF PUBLISHING

Although the total revenue expended by schools may seem large, the percentage of dollars committed to instructional materials has not exceeded 1 percent of total school expenditures for the past two decades.[6] Historical data suggest that schools once committed three times the present percentage for textbooks, but this level of expenditure declined during the 1960s. The average expenditure of $34.17 per pupil per year for all textbooks seems sharply limited if one realizes that today's costs to install, say, a basal reading program are likely to exceed the total amount. Indeed, the cost of an average college textbook title is about $30. With the cost of purchasing a single secondary school textbook about $20, the total funds available limit the frequency with which schools can purchase new textbooks and the prices that publishers can charge. Still, the acceleration in the cost of textbooks has been far less than in other aspects of our culture. In the days when a Broadway theater ticket seldom exceeded $4.40 or $5.50, one truism widely held among publishers was that the cost of a book should not exceed the cost of a theater ticket. With a new ticket high of $55 announced for Broadway in 1989, one looks in vain for a related parallel to the costs of educational books.

Financial data on the current operations of educational publishers help to explain the restrictions under which today's publishers operate. Table 1 presents operating data for 1986 as reported by the Association of American Publishers.

TABLE 1

OPERATING COSTS OF EDUCATIONAL PUBLISHERS
(15 REPORTING)

Cost of Sales (in percent)		Publishing Expense (in percent)	
Printing, paper	22.1	Editorial[b]	6.5
Plant cost (plate investment)[a]	7.5	Production	1.9
Royalties	4.5	Marketing[c]	26.2
		Fulfillment[d]	7.0
		Administration	9.3
Total	34.1	Total	50.9

[a] Investment in type, illustration, graphic design, film used in printing, and maintenance for duration of edition, often as long as fifteen years with successful texts

[b] Editorial personnel in-house and outside; conferences, travel, consultant fees associated with product development, research, field tryouts

[c] Personnel and consultant staff to sell programs; offering of in-service programs; program support items and promotional material; field conferences for customers, complimentary teacher editions and related items

[d] Order entry, customer service, inventory control, and distribution

Source: Association of American Publishers, *Annual Industry Statistics* (Washington, DC: Association of American Publishers, 1988.)

Industry statistics, then, reveal that the average school publisher in 1988 obtained around 15 percent pretax profit (or less than 9 percent return after taxes) on an investment in relatively high-risk textbooks, only slightly more than is possible with low-risk municipal bonds. Small publishers (sales below $30 million), essentially uneconomical in today's high-cost markets because of the expense of marketing and fulfillment, reported no profits in 1987 and suffered major economic problems in production and distribution. The largest publishers achieved 19.5 percent pretax profits—a reasonable return, but hardly a windfall. And these bottom line figures have been falling in recent years. They clearly explain why so many small and medium-size publishers are unable to operate profitably under today's conditions. And those unfamiliar with business need to remember that margins after taxes tend to be only around half of the pretax profit.

Of the total sales dollars, 22.1 percent goes for printing and paper, 7.5 percent for plant cost (investment in plates), 26.2 percent goes for marketing cost (including the free teacher manuals and inspection copies, the staff development services, as well as other "freebies" that many schools expect); 7 percent goes to fulfillment; and 9.3 percent pays for administration. These percentages have not changed substantially over the years.

Editorial costs of 6.5 percent include allocation for field testing and research, hardly a large amount, and author royalties of 4.5 percent. If sales of textbooks currently total around $2 billion per year, as this report suggests, educational publishers currently are paying close to $100 million annually in royalties, and 80 percent of this total normally goes to the authors involved in the more widely used programs.

Cost restrictions hamper publishers as much as they do schools, and offer one reason for the widespread lack of innovative products. During the early years of the Right to Read Program in Washington, a much touted exemplary reading program cost $180 per pupil to install. Schools that were then budgeting an average of $12 per pupil for all instructional materials could not even consider such an alternative. Similarly, much of the early promise of audio-visual or computerized products has been lost because schools simply can not afford the alternative without major outside assistance.

Given the high total investment and relatively low overall return on educational publishing, the data explain not only the increasingly limited number of publishers, but why publishing is increasingly dominated by large companies. Smaller publishers seldom can expend

40 percent of their funds in marketing and distribution of textbooks. The data also point to the basic conservatism of the industry. Few publishing executives will gamble recklessly with their investors' money. Thirty or forty years ago it may have been economically feasible to publish textbooks adapted for use in local or regional schools, say the Southwest or the Southeast, or in religious schools. Nonintegrated "southern" texts were quite common until the mid-1960s, and Catholic programs in basic academic subjects disappeared about the same time. Today's publisher, however, finds it essential to market substantially the same books in California or Texas as in Michigan or Florida. This is why it seems that the adoptions in Texas may be dictating the content or methods used in Connecticut or Idaho. However, publishers repeatedly report market research indicating that the teachers in adoption states tend to seek the same characteristics in textbooks as those in "open territory," and that except for occasional regionalisms (southwestern or New England culture, for example), demands are relatively uniform throughout the United States.[7] Market research, often involving direct interaction with teacher customers, will tell a publisher whether a requirement in California or Florida is likely to be acceptable in Michigan or Massachusetts, or whether changes recommended by a R&D laboratory or a professional subject-matter association will be accepted by classroom teachers. Economics alone prevents publishing textbooks for a single market segment. To do so today would almost certainly require an anticipated market share in excess of 50 percent of all sales, and no responsible publisher would gamble on such overwhelming success, even though, on occasion, a few textbooks are this successful.

Similarly, small specialized markets—"thin" markets in the vernacular of publishing—are unlikely to attract substantial investment unless subsidized (as were many of the curriculum projects of the U.S. Office of Education and the National Science Foundation in the 1970s.) For example, Hispanic enrollments in our schools are clearly sufficiently large to support publication of several Spanish-English instructional programs; not so, however, for separate programs for speakers of Finnish or of various Asian languages.

Even the basic curricular areas have seen a decline in available textbook programs. In the 1960s, for example, nine different programs in elementary school music were offered to American schools; today's rising costs and limited expenditures in this low priority curricular area sustain only three major commercial programs. Similarly, the number of basal reading programs has declined from sixteen to eighteen a decade ago to only eight or nine submitted in recent adoptions. This decline in the number of programs is directly related to the consolidation in educational publishing.

The Development of Educational Publishing

How did the educational industry develop to its present state? The origins date back to colonial America. Venezky, Woodward, and Graham, among others, have studied the history of publishing with respect to basal readers.[8] But more revealing, perhaps, are comments in histories of reading instruction published by Gray, by Smith, and by Venezky,[9] and the analysis by Elson[10] in her review of nineteenth-century textbooks as "guardians of tradition." Readers have been especially important in the history of educational publishing as they have been in education. It is no surprise, then, that the first books were ABC's for children, the Psalter, and the Primer, first published in England during the sixteenth and seventeenth centuries, and heavily saturated with religious content. These were the forerunners of the Hornbook, the first piece of instructional material mentioned in American records in 1678.[11] Shortly thereafter, most primers began to be published in America, although the *New England Primer*, the first title designed specifically for use in the colonies, was published in London. Emphasizing alphabetic rhymes and pictures, the *New England Primer* achieved widespread popularity that continued well into the next century when reading materials took on a moralistic and nationalistic emphasis. Noah Webster's *American Spelling Book* became the most popular reader through the first quarter of the nineteenth century. Providing lessons in moral instruction, it reached a total distribution of more than 24,000,000. As late as 1866, it was reported selling 1,596,000 copies annually.[12]

But other readers followed Noah Webster's, such as Caleb Bingham's readers beginning in 1796 and Lyman Cobb's readers around 1835. At the lowest levels they focused on one or two syllable words and by the third book on selections from the speeches and writings of major American and British authors. And almost every reader was accompanied by a related speller.[13] Sets of readers and spellers then followed—George Hilliard's, Lindley Murray's, John Russell Webb's readers, and, most influentially, the Quaker readers of Samuel Wood.[14] By the time of the first appearance of the famous McGuffey readers between 1836 and 1844, an emphasis on moralistic lessons and alphabetic and phonetic methods had been well established.[15]

Textbooks for other academic classes followed—rhetorics, foreign languages (the first Latin book appeared in 1726), arithmetics, geographies, histories. Literature textbooks were the last to arrive largely because the subject became an acceptable course for study only in the late nineteenth century. Science textbooks were used, but a vast expansion of offerings did not emerge until the twentieth century.[16] Most of the early texts for secondary schools were written by European authors and imported. American authorship, primarily university professors for high school subjects, did not become commonplace until the nineteenth century.

Most textbooks during the nineteenth century were issued by separate publishers and on occasion the publishers and authors were the same. Throughout the last century, the McGuffey eclectic readers—graded in difficulty, providing controlled introduction of vocabulary, sentence length, and word repetition—became the most widely used textbooks in the history of America, "the schoolbooks for millions."[17] Over 122 million copies were sold, and, from 1836 to 1920, more than half the school children of America learned to read from these books. From the McGuffey tradition, the concept of the graded reader, and, ultimately, the concept of grading in all subjects, was established.

The basal reading programs also subsequently introduced aids for teachers, questions for students, and "notes" for teachers on how to teach the beginnings of an instructional program.[18]

During the long dominance of the McGuffey readers, few competitive programs were successfully introduced, but by the early decades of this century the Ward readers (1894), the Beacon readers (1912-1913), and the Elson readers (1909-1914), among others, were tailored to new tastes. At the same time, a wide range of textbooks for elementary school mathematics and for most academic high school subjects appeared, and an increasing number of educational publishers offered complete lists of textbooks for all subjects and grades. Conditions stimulated reasonable diversity and numerous small family-owned publishers emerged. Each would have its own reading, spelling, and arithmetic programs, and often titles for every high school course. Many of these publishers emerged around the great university centers—Boston and Cambridge, Philadelphia, New York City, and Chicago. The publishing of textbooks was influenced by academia well into the twentieth century. Today's publishers are far more diversified and are as likely to be located in California, Texas, or Florida as anywhere. And teachers today inevitably expect one or two authors on any textbook to be associated with schools. Indeed, all teacher authorship is sometimes seen as a virtue. The days of university domination have long since ended.

Although consolidation, merger, and acquisition have long been characteristic of the publishing industry, and one of the ways in which smaller publishers become larger, not until the 1960s were many educational publishers acquired by multinational corporations as an analysis of the operating data will indicate. Substantial economies in scale, particularly in distribution and sales, occur as companies grow larger. Middle-sized publishers (with revenues of $10 to $45 million) are particularly pressed to maintain needed inventory and provide field representatives to call on customers throughout the nation. Thus, publishers have grown large and fewer in number. Further, the prospective revenues to be secured in electronic publishing (yet to be realized) and the obvious community of interests between those in publishing and those in other areas of communication have promoted consolidation of firms in "the knowledge industry," just as growing internationalization of commerce has led to multinational companies entering the fray.

The promise of widespread international sales of textbooks has seldom been realized except by certain college fields. School textbooks are too laden with national cultural values to "transport" easily. Still, achieving access to the large North American textbook market continues to attract foreign investors, particularly those in other English-speaking countries. With only a few exceptions (most notably Addison-Wesley in mathematics and Ginn and Company in reading), American textbooks are used primarily in American schools in this country and in American schools abroad.

Today, educational publishers tend to be fewer in number and, more frequently, a part of large corporations. Only an occasional family owned publisher, like Open Court, remains. Indeed, the company devoted exclusively to book publishing is now an exception. Still, publishers insist that editorial decisions remain within the province of those who have educational expertise.[19]

That there is also room for new companies that begin with limited products and focused marketing goals is indicated by the rise during the past two decades of firms like the McDougal-Littell Company. Thus, the evolution of educational publishing continues.

Characteristic also of the current scene is the rise of scores of independent contractors who develop, edit, and/or design textbooks to the specifications of publishers. Normally staffed by experienced editors, writers, graphics and design personnel, such developers provide publishers with ways of securing needed expertise on programs without maintaining extensive and expensive internal staffs.

Influences on Content, Design, and Scope of Textbooks

Schooling in America is largely a domain for local and state decision making. Yet, development and publication of textbooks involves national considerations. Publishers thus must develop textbooks that are usable throughout America, not just in one or two states. How publishers attempt to seek a national consensus on the content, scope, and sequence of instructional programs involves analysis of state and district requirements, study of standardized and specialized assessment tests used to evaluate learning, interaction with teachers (it is estimated that 80 percent of programs today are selected by teachers),[20] assessment of readability (sometimes involving children), interpretation of current research and development, and consultation with experienced authors and curriculum leaders in the field.

PREPUBLICATION

The development of a major instructional program requires a basic rationale prepared in advance, a detailed specification of the philosophy of the instructional design, and an indication of key instructional features. Usually the prospective authors and key editorial personnel, all subject specialists, are responsible for such a prospectus. These guidelines normally precede market studies that are often designed to check them. In many companies, senior authors as well as senior editors participate jointly in such advanced specifications and in developing a rationale to indicate why the proposed new program will be superior in some ways to programs currently available. Publishers regularly engage professional and scholarly leaders on projects of this kind and just as regularly listen to their advice. But always the successful publisher checks the advice secured from academicians against the attitudes of school practitioners.

Surveys of market needs are inevitably part of the development process, as are analyses of existing competitive products. But the needs must be clearly interpreted. No experienced publisher would base decisions only on what a survey of customers or salesmen say they want (most of which reflect only what they have already seen). It is not what teachers say that is important but what they mean. Interpretation is everything.

Reviews of recent research are inevitably part of the process, at least for more responsible publishers. So are interpretations of what has been learned from publisher representatives and consultants who work daily with teachers and administrators in classrooms in every city and town. Indeed, one of the unrecognized strengths of the large publisher is his awareness of the teaching needs facing customers throughout the nation, even in small schools and remote areas. This accumulated knowledge is perhaps more responsible than any other factor for the continuing strength of many of the large publishing companies in certain subject areas, and for the fact that those responsible for publishing the most widely used programs twenty-five years ago are often publishers of the more widely used programs today (e.g., Scott Foresman or Harcourt Brace Jovanovich in literature; Houghton Mifflin in high school mathematics; Holt in high school science).

Creation of a rationale, then, is mandatory if a program is to proceed, and key authors participate extensively in its development. Some of the ideas for a program advanced at these early stages may seem at times "pie in the sky," but experienced publishers learn not to winnow ideas too quickly. Not all the ideas that authors present are likely to prove feasible, but all should be considered.

Market studies, then, can be undertaken with a particular kind of instructional program in mind, or even of particular market segments. On occasion, model lesson plans, units, or samples of instructional features, are developed to test customer reaction. Sometimes they are tested with children in a classroom.

Generally, content specifications are part of the overall plan: the percent and kind of literature desired, the need for nonnarrative informational pieces, the importance of belles lettres or of literature from the Hispanic or black tradition, the ways selections may be organized, the percent of a lesson to be devoted to problem solving, and so forth.

These are not idle considerations that can be left to the end of the process. Most experienced publishers know that the classroom teacher's judgments on the quality of a textbook and on how well children will respond to it are critical in program selection. It often is the first aspect of programs considered and is one reason, after the early primary grades, why the quality of illustration and the topics are priority considerations. It also explains why current trends (even fads) in education receive such attention. Publishers have learned that teacher committees examining textbooks will often assume adequacy if not excellence in basal content and approach, but will look to see how such much-discussed topics as acid rain, cultural literacy, thinking process, or collaborative learning are embedded within a program.

The program rationale also specifies the desired instructional outcomes such as knowledge to be acquired and the skills and processes to be taught, tested, and reviewed. Will the thinking process be handled as a separate strand or will it be embraced within writing and oral language activity? Most textbook programs are designed to stimulate learning that is as predictable as possible in a variety of classroom settings and are built around lessons and units written to achieve desired, prespecified learning outcomes. Writers and developers must have a clear sense of purpose before they initiate their work. Providing this sense of direction is clearly the responsibility of overall program editors and authors.

Without such a basic rationale, it is not possible to estimate pages, percentages of art, typographic layout, and the like, and to provide the tentative cost estimates that can be weighed against estimated return. In a very real sense, the visual design of a textbook program follows, not precedes, the content and instructional design; yet type face, page design, art and layout, heading, and so forth, can do much to enhance both the appeal and the "learnability" of programs, as recent studies by Thomas Anderson and Bonnie Armbruster in the social studies have made clear. Finally, given the size of the financial investment in textbooks, publishers frequently find it desirable to "field-test" or "try out" certain aspects of the program—a new decoding strand in a reading program, for instance, or the reaction of children and/or teachers to some new science lessons for a particular grade. Sometimes prototype units are developed and tested following development procedures pioneered by the federally sponsored R&D laboratories of the 1960s and 1970s,[21] or extensive data are collected on what works and what does not work in existing programs. Recently, for example, one publisher was so concerned at Durkin's report that teachers seldom used the carefully prepared prereading portions of lesson plans (devoted largely to the significant tasks of activating prior knowledge, establishing a set for reading, and predicting what may follow), that he organized an extensive ten-week study of grade 1 and grade 4 teachers in four sites throughout the country and provided for classroom observation, teacher interviews, as well as other kinds of data collection.[22] Because most studies of this kind are proprietary and related to competitive product development, they are seldom published. But this does not mean they are unimportant.

The authors of textbook programs, almost always competent in the subject and the teaching of the subject, work with experienced editors in evaluating reactions and reports and in revising manuscript. Experienced marketing and sales personnel are normally asked to study the programs as they develop and to interpret probable teacher acceptance. Because large programs, such as those in elementary reading or elementary mathematics, can involve more than 100 or 150 separate item titles, all of which must be published simultaneously, a single author or two cannot be responsible for writing all manuscript. Still, they can help in specifying what is needed for every title, can write model lessons, and can review all manuscript. (Thirty years ago publishers often could issue multiple-year programs serially and schools would install them year by year. Then authorship by a small team was feasible and frequent. Now schools want to see all components of a program before adopting.)

When authorship teams do not contain all of the expertise required for program development, publishers will engage consultants to advise on special dimensions of a program—on the Holocaust or Jewish history, for example, or on the treatment of evolution. Employment of multicultural teams to advise on treatment of minorities in content and illustration has been a common practice, as has been the practice of securing regional reactions from educators to assure widespread acceptance.

One problem, of course, is that textbook authors are seldom held as accountable for the quality of textbooks which bear their names as they are, say, for scholarly studies or research reports. Publishers, thus, bear the responsibility. Indeed, seldom is the authoring of a distinguished textbook considered as support for candidates who are being considered for university promotion, even though some have improved the learning of a generation of students. Dora V. Smith once observed that not until the literature written for children was seriously reviewed and the authors held accountable for the quality of their writing did literature for children begin to improve. Much the same is true of textbooks today. Not until authors find their professional reputation affected by the textbooks that bear their names will many of them attend sufficiently to quality concerns.

POSTPUBLICATION

The publisher's responsibility does not end with publication of the instructional program. Training of sales and consultant personnel is needed if communication with customers is to be clear and persuasive. Promotional materials must be designed, advertising planned. Especially important for large instructional programs are the installation services—the staff development for administrators, supervisors, and teachers that will support successful initial use. Where programs are innovative to any degree, such consultant services can extend throughout the entire first year of use. Even four or five years later, school districts that encounter difficulties (lower test scores, parent criticism) will frequently call on the publisher for support.

Then, new editions must be planned. Many school boards in this country have regulations prohibiting the adoption of textbooks with copyrights older than three years. Thus change is mandated by the customer even when not required for instructional purposes.

The postpublication investment in textbooks, therefore, is considerable, particularly for the large multiyear programs, and the return on investment is slow. Not only is three to four years required to produce many textbook programs in advance of publication, but a minimum of six years must pass before most school districts have an opportunity to select the program, since the adoption cycle throughout the nation extends over such a period.[23] Small wonder then that publishers try to time the date of textbook introductions of programs to coincide with the dates of major state adoptions, as in California and Texas. They thus hope to ensure an earlier return on their investment. In this way such large states influence the timing of program introductions much more than they influence content.

THE SELECTION OF TEXTBOOKS

The processes used by state agencies and large school districts to select textbooks and other instructional materials have long been railed against but only recently studied systematically. And they dramatically impact the nature of current textbooks.

For more than a hundred years educators have expressed concern about the variation in both content and quality of available textbooks,[24] and the issue has been raised periodically over the years.[25] Much of the concern has focused on state adoptions of textbooks in southern and western states—presently in twenty-two states representing close to 50 percent of the dollar market, and representing a substantial increase in sales during the past twenty-five years as the population has moved south and west. The adoption market thus has been growing in size even if no state has moved to statewide adoption since Arkansas established secondary-school adoptions fifteen years ago. But neither has any state abandoned the process.

These states as a whole do influence textbooks—the timing of introductions, as indicated earlier, and the physical specifications. A joint committee of the Association of American Publishers, the National Association of State Textbook Administrators, and the Book Manufacturing Institute jointly agree on standards for paper, bindings, and covers, and most states mandate conforming to these standards. As a result, American children have the most durable textbooks in the world.

A review of studies of adoption procedures, published over the past seventy-five years, will document a gradual liberalization of requirements as almost all states have moved from single adoptions, judged inappropriate by critics for meeting the individual needs of children, to multiple listing of five or more texts from which schools can choose those most appropriate for local use. Publishers call such action by states "granting a hunting license." In other words, book representatives still have to sell to local districts, but normally only from those titles that are listed. (In a few adoption states, schools can use a small percentage of textbook funds to purchase nonlisted materials, a practice which offers flexibility to the schools.)

Statewide listing of textbooks on a regular cycle, every five to eight years, provides children in the states involved with fresh materials and reasonable funding for instructional materials on a regular basis, a strength not always perceived by the critics. Adoption cycles requiring up-to-date textbooks are characteristic of this century's education. Until the Civil War, most states officially directed teachers to use old textbooks as long as possible.[26] Publishers particularly have been aware of abuses in "open territory," or nonlisting regions where funding for instructional materials is often unbudgeted on any regular basis and adoptions can easily be passed over. Many reports of young people using dated social studies or science materials have come from such "open territory" states.

On the other hand, the sunshine laws regulating selection of state textbooks provide an open invitation to textbook critics who wish to complain publicly about the content of books being considered. Most of the widely publicized censorship attempts have occurred in states like California and Texas, which provide for open citizen hearings,[27] although similar objections can emerge in any district.

Another fact about the adoption process, rarely studied by critics until recently, is that procedures followed in large city districts within "open territory" states, like the districts of Detroit, Milwaukee, Baltimore, and others, are remarkably similar to those followed in state adoptions.[28] And the dollars involved in districts as large as Detroit, for example, frequently exceed those involved in the smaller states.

As public criticism of textbooks in use in the schools began to increase in the 1970s, publishers were wont to point out the enormous variety in level of challenge, quality, and content in textbooks made available through the American free enterprise system.[29] But the fact is that as many as ten to fifteen different textbooks are available for selection in the major curricular areas. If inferior textbooks have sometimes been selected, and they have, the problem is clearly with the processes used in selecting textbooks.

Comments of this kind served to direct attention to the adoption processes, which, to no publisher's surprise, turned out to be varied and complex. Not always were selectors informed about new developments in learning and teaching; on occasion they were found to lack familiarity with the basic content of the textbooks they were trying to select. Some committees heard presentations from the publishers represented; others did not. Some were trained for the task of selecting instructional materials; others were not. Some had adequate released time to undertake the task; more did not. Farr and colleagues undertook a systematic study of procedures followed in the reading adoption process in Indiana, and then expanded the research to other states. Almost all adoption procedures that Farr reviewed seemed to lack disciplined, systematic approaches.[30]

Publishers know these conditions, of course, and that is one reason why they listen so carefully to teacher reactions. Research is important and so are the recommendations of curriculum leaders, but only when these are acceptable to teachers. The history of publishing abounds with the wreckage of programs built to satisfy national experts and not modified for use by classroom teachers. Many of the glorious curriculum projects of the 1960s and 1970s, developed under federal funding with strong support from academic specialists in universities, learned this lesson too late. Clearly, the way to ensure stronger textbooks is to develop a stronger cadre of teachers knowledgeable in subject matter and the teaching and learning of subject matter. Such teachers would insist on purchasing the strongest books available.

Because of the extensive interest in reading, much of research on selection of textbooks in the reading area has been conducted by specialists in the teaching of the subject. There is no reason to believe that similar practices do not govern adoptions in science, mathematics, social studies, and language arts, but the profession remains open to replication of the studies of the selection process in other fields. The Indiana findings with respect to reading have been replicated in other states,[31] have been summarized and interpreted in various journals,[32] and have even served as the focus for a national conference of the National Association of State Boards of Education.[33] Subsequent studies, including two of procedures in Texas, report the growing importance of the initial proclamation or call for adoption when it is very specific,[34] as well as concern with text organization and pedagogical soundness. However, despite this overall concern with pedagogy, few investigators find selectors concerned with the research base of a program or with results of publishers' field tests or with market studies. Again and again, researchers find that selectors consider textbooks from reputable publishing houses to be of "equal quality." Hence, qualitative discriminations are not always made.[35] But, again, the emphasis in these recent investigations has been almost too exclusively on reading. Given the amount of activity in this area, it is helpful to note that the Center for the Study of Reading at the University of Illinois, Urbana, has recently developed and tested new guidelines for the processes to be used in selecting readers. The Center reports that such guidelines are having a healthy impact on selection practices.[36]

Prospects for the Future

Many of the changes that publishers are called upon to make really should be addressed to adopting agencies, since it will be these agencies, not the publishers, who write the specifications. If school districts, for example, demand that content textbooks or readers show a specific readability level to qualify for a listing, a publisher will ignore such a mandated requirement only at risk. Acknowledging this fact is not to deny the responsibility of publishers to produce the best possible textbooks under present conditions, and to work with schools, authors, and specialists in curriculum development to strengthen the standards by which quality publications are judged.

Among developments needed to assure continual improvement of textbooks, the following seem particularly useful:

1. Greater attention should be given to instructional quality in evaluating and thus in developing textbooks. Both the design of

instruction and the soundness and adequacy of the content must be considered as carefully as the attractiveness of a textbook or its freedom from objectionable features.

2. Preservice and in-service teacher education must help teachers learn how to evaluate textbooks, and selection committees must include specialists in subject matter and its teaching. It is ridiculous to hold a director of mathematics education responsible for the quality of the curriculum in mathematics if he has not had a strong voice in the selection of instructional materials.

3. Authors must assume greater responsibility for the quality of programs that bear their names and be held accountable for that quality by the profession, much as university professors are for their scholarly efforts. This means, among other things, serious reviews of textbooks by academic colleagues.

4. Earlier publisher involvement is needed in national and state school improvement projects, so that (a) publishers are informed sufficiently early of priority needs, (b) new materials can be made available on time, and (c) developers and reformers have access to publishers' extensive insights into current classroom conditions.

5. Increased school funding for textbook purposes is needed to ensure an adequate up-to-date supply of both basal and supplementary instructional materials and to give schools the flexibility to change instructional materials as the learning needs of children change.

6. Publishers need to reconsider marketing and sales practices which seem, at the least, to divert attention from the instructional quality of textbooks. An overemphasis on customer entertainment and excessive "give-away" programs sometimes appears to encourage favorable reactions. In the long run, the cost of these "freebies" is born by the school district through increased prices on the basic text. More stress needs to be placed on instructional concerns.

A Final Word

The American textbook industry, which already provides our teachers with a greater choice in quality textbooks than any nation in the world, is not likely to change overnight. Changes that do occur will almost certainly be evolutionary, not revolutionary, and driven by the free enterprise market.

We can anticipate that textbooks will remain the "bed rock" tool for instruction, since they have demonstrated their convenience and cost effectiveness. Nonprint visual, auditory, and computerized supplements may augment the basic text but seem unlikely to replace it. The quality of the American textbook seems likely to improve in the face of continued criticism and social pressure. And procedures for selection already are being strengthened as a result of current criticism.

A great deal of change via mergers and acquisitions has occurred in the educational publishing industry in recent years. Though one might argue that these conditions have reached their limit, a major shakeout of the industry is likely in the coming years. Important international publishers with deep pockets have a strong commitment to enter and expand in the world's largest market. Major information and media companies in the United States not currently in publishing may decide to enter the field, creating conditions similar to what happened in the 1960s.

If historic trends continue, schools will also see from time to time the rise of new, specialist publishers committed to the development of alternative instructional materials. The inflexibility of larger publishers and their reluctance to experiment have created conditions likely to nourish the growth of new publishing ventures. Such developments have been characteristic throughout the history of publishing and seem no less likely to be on the agenda for its future.

FOOTNOTES

1. Association of American Publishers, *Annual Industry Statistics* (Washington, DC: Association of American Publishers, 1988); *Who's Who in Educational Publishing* Wellesley, MA: Brown Publishing Co., 1988).

2. Association of American Publishers, *Annual Industry Statistics* (Washington, DC: Association of American Publishers, 1987).

3. Ibid. (Adoption states are listed in this volume, p. 173, note 3.)

4. Association of American Publishers, *Annual Industry Statistics*, 1988.

5. Ibid.

6. James R. Squire, "Publishers, Social Pressures, and Textbooks," in *The Textbook in American Society*, ed. John Y. Cole and Thomas G. Sticht (Washington, DC: Library of Congress, 1981).

7. Institutional Tracking Service, *Reading/Language Arts* (White Plains, NY: Institutional Tracking Service, 1979); EPIE Institute, *Report on a National Study of the Nature and Quality of Instructional Materials Most Used by Teachers*, EPIE Report No. 76 (New York: EPIE Institute, 1978); P. Kenneth Komoski, "The Realities of Choosing and Using Instructional Materials," *Educational Leadership* 36 (October 1978): 46-50.

8. Richard Venezky, "The American Reading Script and Its Nineteenth Century Origins" (Annual Marilyn Sadow Lecture, University of Chicago, April, 1988); Arthur Woodward, "Taking Teaching Out of Teaching and Reading Out of Learning

to Read: A Historical Study of Reading Textbook Teacher's Guides, 1920-1980" (Paper presented at the Annual Meeting of the American Educational Research Association, Chicago, April 1985); George E. Graham, Jr., "A Present and Historical Analysis of Basal Reading Series" (Doct. diss., University of Virginia, 1978).

9. William S. Gray, *Reading* (Newark, DE: International Reading Association, 1984); Nila B. Smith, *American Reading Instruction* (Newark, DE: International Reading Association, 1986; originally published in 1934, revised periodically by the author until 1985, and subsequently by collaborators); Richard Venezky, "The History of Reading Research," in *Handbook of Reading Research*, ed. P. David Pearson (New York: Longman, 1983).

10. Ruth M. Elson, *Guardians of Tradition: American Schoolbooks of the Nineteenth Century* (Lincoln, NB: University of Nebraska Press, 1972).

11. Smith, *American Reading Instruction*.

12. Charles Carpenter, *History of American Schoolbooks* (Philadelphia: University of Pennsylvania Press, 1963), p. 151.

13. Ibid.

14. Venezky, "The History of Reading Research."

15. Smith, *American Reading Instruction*.

16. John D. Nietz, *The Evaluation of the American Secondary School Texts* (Rutland, VT: Charles E. Tuttle, 1966).

17. Gerry Bohning, "The McGuffey Eclectic Readers: 1836-1986," *Reading Teacher* 40 (December 1986): 263-89.

18. Ibid.

19. Squire, "Publishers, Social Pressures, and Textbooks."

20. James R. Squire, "Studies of Textbooks: Are We Asking the Right Questions?" in *Contributing to Educational Change: Perspectives on Research and Practice*, ed. Philip W. Jackson (Berkeley, CA: McCutchan Publishing Corp., 1988), pp. 127-69.

21. Thomas M. Duffy and Robert Waller, *Designing Usable Texts* (Orlando, FL: Academic Press, 1985).

22. Dolores Durkin, *What Classroom Observations Reveal about Reading Comprehension Instruction*, Technical Report No. 106 (Urbana, IL: Center for the Study of Reading, University of Illinois, 1978).

23. John Y. Cole and Thomas G. Sticht, eds., *The Textbook in American Society* (Washington, DC: Library of Congress, 1981).

24. Frank A. Jensen, "Current Practices in Selecting Textbooks for the Elementary Schools," in *The Textbook in American Education*, ed. Guy M. Whipple, Thirtieth Yearbook of the National Society for the Study of Education, Part II (Bloomington, IL: Public School Publishing Co., 1931); Clyde J. Tidwell, *State Control of Textbooks*, Teachers College Contributions to Education, No. 299 (New York: Bureau of Publications, Teachers College Press, 1928).

25. Association of American Publishers and National Education Association, *Selecting Instructional Materials for Purchase*, Report of a Joint Committee (Washington, DC: National Education Association, 1972); Lewis W. Burnett, "State Textbook Policies," *Phi Delta Kappan* 33 (1952): 257-61; idem, "Textbook Provisions in the Several States," *Journal of Education Research* 43 (January 1950): 357-66; Raymond English, "The Politics of Textbook Adoption," *Phi Delta Kappan* 62 (1980): 275-78; Frank A. Jensen, *Current Procedures in Selecting Textbooks* (Philadelphia: J. B. Lippincott, 1931); Sherry Keith, *Politics of Textbook Selection*, Research Report No. 81-AT (Palo Alto, CA: Institute for Research on Educational Finance and Governance, Stanford University, 1981); P. Kenneth Komoski, "The Realities of Choosing and

Using Instructional Materials"; Charles R. Maxwell, *The Selection of Textbooks* (Boston: Houghton Mifflin Co., 1921, 1930); R. H. Robbins, "Choosing the Right Basic Reader," *Curriculum Review* 19 (1980): 395-99; Clyde Jesse Tidwell, *State Control of Textbooks* (New York: Columbia University Press, 1928).

26. Carpenter, *History of American Schoolbooks*, p. 17.

27. Edward B. Jenkinson, *Censors in the Classroom: The Mind Benders* (Carbondale, IL: Southern Illinois University Press, 1979).

28. Ruth Wernersbach, "Textbook Adoption Procedures in Public Schools of Large Urban Districts" (Doct. diss., University of Cincinnati, 1987).

29. Squire, "Publishers, Social Pressures, and Textbooks"; *Book Research Quarterly* 1 (Summer 1985): 4-81.

30. Roger Farr, M. C. Courtland, P. Harris, J. Tarr, and L. Treece, *A Case Study of the Indiana State Reading Adoption Process* (Bloomington, IN: Indiana University Press, 1983); Deborah A. Powell, "Selection of Reading Textbooks at the District Level: Is This a Rational Process?" *Book Research Quarterly* 1 (Fall 1985): 23-35; Squire, "Studies of Textbooks"; Michael Tully and Roger Farr, "Textbook Adoption: Insight, Impact, and Potential," *Book Research Quarterly* 1 (Summer 1985): 4-11.

31. Peter Winograd and Jean Osborn, "How Adoption of Reading Textbooks Works in Kentucky: Some Problems and Some Solutions," *Book Research Quarterly* 1 (Fall 1985): 3-22.

32. *Book Research Quarterly* 1 (Summer 1985): 4-81; Harriet T. Bernstein, "The New Politics of Textbook Adoption," *Phi Delta Kappan* 66 (March 1985): 463-66.

33. Caroline B. Cody, *A Policymaker's Guide to Textbook Selection* (Alexandria, VA: National Association of State Boards of Education, 1986).

34. John D. Marshall, "Better Textbooks, Better Criteria: The Role of Research in Directing Educational Efforts for Reform" (Paper presented at the Annual Meeting of the American Educational Research Association, Washington, DC, 1987) ERIC ED 285 251.

35. Robert Follett, "The School Textbook Adoption Process," *Book Research Quarterly* 1 (Summer 1985): 19-22.

36. Jean Osborn, Beau F. Jones, and Marcy Stein, "The Case for Improving Textbooks," *Educational Leadership* 42 (April 1985): 9-16.

Section Three
TEXTBOOKS AND SOCIETY

CHAPTER IX

The Politics of Textbook Publishing, Adoption, and Use

CAROLINE CODY

Present-day Americans are ambivalent about the degree to which politics should mix with education and public schools, so they may be offended when politics influence what their children read in school. The three-hundred-year-old system of education in the United States, however, clearly commits the important policy decisions about schools and about school books to the political system. Politics affect what money is spent for textbooks, which textbooks are selected and which are censored, and, therefore, which books are published, bought, and read. If we take a cynical definition of politics, "the art of who gets their way," it is clear that Americans speak out, organize, lobby, and vote to get their way about schools and textbooks. It is important to understand that the system is designed to facilitate that process.

Two basic tenets of our American educational system are critical to understanding the politics of textbooks: local control of schools and lay control of what children will learn. The history of American schools reminds us that when schools were established in communities throughout the country, buildings, teachers, firewood, and books were the responsibility of the families who gathered together to create the school. Community leaders made the decisions about schools, and families provided what books they could. When those community schools were formed into state systems of schools and state funding was provided, the major decisions were left to local school boards, although state codes and constitutions assigned some policymaking to the state legislatures and some decisions were assigned to state boards made up of citizens. In spite of federal and state inroads into educational policymaking since the 1960s, the important decisions about schools and about textbooks continue to be made at the local level where community politics are most intimate and most divisive and where the final decision-making body is a local school board accountable to the community.

That history also explains the important role of school boards in determining curriculum and their responsibility for the selection and use of instructional materials. School boards delegate many of their responsibilities to professionals in their employ: curriculum seldom originates with board members and professionals do dominate the textbook selection process. But clearly those responsibilities are only delegated and the final decisions about what children will learn and will read resides with school boards.[1] Recent court decisions have affirmed that responsibility (*Kuhmeirer v. Haxelwood School District*, 56 U.S.L.W. 4079 [1988]; *Smith v. Board of School Commissioners of Mobile County*, 827 F2nd 684 [1987]; *Mozert v. Hawkins County Board of Education*, 827 F2nd 1058 [1987]).

Local, lay control of schools and of what children will or will not read is so basic a principle that few politicians will challenge it directly. Within this tradition, however, the politics of textbooks are played out on the national, state, and local levels with unique complexity. In no other sector of the educational system does politics interact so intimately with professional prerogatives, parental rights, and a national market system.

Textbooks and Politics

There are several reasons why textbooks have been at political issue throughout our country's history. First, the history of funding for textbooks has led many Americans to believe that their selection and purchase provides a rich opportunity for graft and misuse of taxpayers' money. Great political effort has been exerted to design a system that would ensure that neither publishers nor politicians could manipulate the use of textbook funds to their advantage and that funds set aside for textbooks would be wisely spent.

Second, waves of dissatisfaction with public schools and resulting school reform movements have historically returned to textbooks as a mechanism to change and control what teachers do in classrooms. In periods when teachers have been seen as inadequate or when local districts have been perceived to be intransigent, standardization in the books they use has been used to attempt to improve and standardize instruction. For those Americans who have never had experience with classrooms other than those in which the textbook was both the curriculum and the basis for pedagogy, the use of textbooks in this way is an obvious solution to their dissatisfactions.

Third, and most important for this discussion, because textbooks have been the proxy for curriculum in the minds of most Americans, the controversies over textbooks are most often attempts on the part of one group or another or of several groups to gain control of what children will learn and, by an extension that seems self-evident to many Americans, what children will grow up believing.

These issues, for the most part, have been played out at the state and local levels. Federal concern is recent and has occurred as a part of larger efforts inspired by the large national issues that have dominated the national scene since the second world war: national defense, equal rights, and economic development.

FEDERAL POLITICS

When federal government interest in textbook issues developed during the 1980s, there was little precedent for federal action related to textbooks. During the Sputnik era, national defense had inspired concern for new curriculums in mathematics, science, and the social sciences. The National Defense Education Act projects had developed a few new textbooks, but few would claim that they carried a federal stamp of approval.[2] Later, civil rights pressures resulted in federal legislation requiring that school districts examine their policies and procedures relative to the civil rights of employees and students. Title IX of the Civil Rights Act required the establishment of local committees to examine instructional materials. The legislation, however, carefully limited the powers of these committees to an advisory status, should they find any inequities. Both of these instances illustrate the carefulness with which national politicians have avoided any semblance of a challenge to state and local control of curriculum or a move toward a "national curriculum."

A political process important to the politics of textbooks in the 1980s had begun, however, at the national level with the promises of President Lyndon Johnson's Right to Read program. Citizens at the national, state, and local levels—parents, politicians, and educators alike—were challenged by the idea that every child should and could learn to read. That concept and the federal funds to support it challenged school districts to do what American schools had not set out to do before.

As educators, policymakers, and politicians began to struggle to fulfill the promises inherent in Johnson's optimism and commitment, federal research efforts providing new ideas about reading became important and provided the impetus for national action dealing with textbooks. In the late 1970s, research, much of which was funded by the National Institute of Education, began to reveal that all reading problems did not reside with the reader; some reading difficulties could be traced to problems in the way in which books were written and edited.[3] That research became important to policymakers heavily embroiled in fulfilling political commitments to bring about improved reading achievement in their jurisdictions.

The research about reading and books was presented at the hearings of Secretary Terrel Bell's Commission on Excellence in Education. In 1981, Bell was attempting to bring educational issues to the attention of an administration that had proposed the elimination of his department.[4] In its report, *A Nation at Risk*, the commission included problems with textbooks in the list of factors which were contributing to a "rising tide of mediocrity" in American education and threatening the economic security of the nation.[5]

Bell himself felt strongly about rigor in the textbooks and other issues in the report. In a speech about the commission's report to the American Association of School Administrators, he used the phrase, "dumbed down" to describe problems with textbooks. It was a theme that would recur whenever textbook issues were discussed.

It became clear to a group of state and national leaders that, although federal efforts to improve books were not likely, national efforts would be needed to impact the complicated national market. A group of state educational leaders, education association directors, and others met under the sponsorship of the governor of Florida to address the issues of textbook quality and to look at ways in which states might cooperate to ensure improvement in the books from which they had to choose.[6] The issue of textbook quality and of national effort had been raised by politicians in a political setting.

Later that year, Secretary Bell used his discretionary fund to support the Council of Chief State School Officers and the National Association of State Boards of Education in conducting a project to follow up on the Florida meeting and on the *A Nation at Risk* report. The project was designed to educate state policymakers to the issues of textbook quality and to encourage action in and among the states to bring about changes in textbooks.

Changes in the administration of the Department of Education in 1984 and the appointment of William Bennett as Secretary brought changes in the federal approach to improving books. From the beginning of his administration, Bennett's approach to educational change was not to work within the structure of the educational system with projects such as the one funded by Bell, but to bring problems to the attention of the public through what came to be known as his "bully pulpit." Funding for the state political efforts was discontinued, and grants were made to researchers whose research agenda centered on descriptions of the problems with books. Using such studies as evidence that change was needed, Secretary Bennett shared with the American people his vision of what schools could be like through various publications of the Department of Education and through widely covered speeches describing what an ideal school might be like—what curriculum would be offered and what books students would be required to read.[7]

Secretaries Bell and Bennett can be credited with creating a national public debate that goes beyond the themes that children should read and focuses on the content they should read and on the quality of the textbooks which present that content. At the national level, national reports and the federal research agenda, along with the pulpit from which to publicize the findings, have been effective political tools in bringing the issues to the attention of citizens and state and local politicians.

STATE POLITICS

To a large extent, the national debate, acknowledging state responsibility for education, challenged the states to address the problems coming up in the research about textbooks. Within the American tradition, states vary in the degree to which policies and procedures for dealing with textbook issues reside with the state. In about half the states, the state-level political system has not taken a strong role in policymaking relative to textbooks. Legislatures and state boards commonly will have enacted legislation or policy that requires particular topics be taught in schools. Most states have a policy that exhorts schools to use only books which fairly represent minorities and women in their content. Many state legislatures, boards, and courts have had to deal with students who chose to opt out of school or out of a class because their families were offended by materials that students were required to read. These policies, as well as those establishing testing programs, have had important secondary effects on textbooks, but, for the most part, textbooks have not been the subject of direct political action at the state level in these states, most of which are in the northeastern and central parts of the country.

In the remaining states, however, the state political system has played an important role in affecting textbook policies. The politics of textbook funding, selection, and purchase is played out within each state's political tradition and colored by the unique relationships between state and local jurisdictions. For the most part, political interest in the process in these states grows out of the fact that state-level tax revenues are committed to provide free textbooks. Historically, in many of the states which now have earmarked state-level funding for textbooks, funding grew out of populist concern that children were not able to attend school because their parents could not afford to provide textbooks.

For instance, the issue of free textbooks was an important theme of the Huey P. Long legislative program in Louisiana in the 1930s. Governor Long made a commitment to free textbooks as a way of ensuring "every child his rightful place in school."[8] In Louisiana, however, political concerns required that free books go to children in parochial schools as well as those in public schools. Long's "child benefit theory," which was affirmed by the U.S. Supreme Court, established a precedent that now underpins the use of state funds to supply books to students in nonpublic schools in twenty states.

Issues surrounding state funding for free textbooks have led states to establish policies controlling the administration of those funds. Power over funding provides an opportunity for legislatures and state boards to take action to see that textbooks paid for by state funds support state goals for schooling. Not only is protection from graft likely to be an issue in these states; policymakers are more likely to raise the control of teaching and of the curriculum as textbook issues. In any case, those states with state-level funding have been most likely to establish policies and procedures that constrain local action relative to textbooks.

These states, which are often referred to as the "adoption states," are for the most part in the southern and western regions of the country. In most of these states, earmarked funding is provided for textbooks, and the state requires that state funds must be spent on books from a list approved by the state. There are exceptions: in some states with an adoption list, earmarked funding is not provided; one state provides earmarked funding, but does not restrict the local selection of books to a state-approved list. Most adoption states provide an approved list for both elementary and secondary schools. In many adoption states, there are loophole mechanisms that permit local districts to circumvent the process and spend state funds on books not on the approved list.[9]

In the adoption states, a statewide committee for a subject area is formed, most commonly on a cycle of five or six years. The committee is appointed by the state board, the state commissioner of education, or the governor, or some combination thereof. Members often represent regions of the state and may represent levels of the educational bureaucracy—teachers, principals, subject matter specialists, etc. Some states include lay citizens on the committees, but committees in all adoption states are dominated by classroom teachers. Commonly appointees serve only one cycle. Historically, these procedures were established to prevent state politicians, administrators, or members of the committees from controlling the choices of vendors.

The committees, which are commonly staffed by professionals from the state department of education, either review the books themselves or appoint representatives to do the reviews. Criteria for the review may come from boards or from legislation or the committee may develop its own criteria. Most commonly, the reviewers hear presentations from publishers as a part of the review process; however, the participation of publishers is highly regulated in most adoption states. States have developed bonding and other requirements for publishers and extensive constraints on what they can and cannot do during the process of selection to ensure that they do not have undue influence and that they will provide the services and books that they promise in the bid process.

In most adoption states, the state committee recommends to the state board a list of approved books and the state board makes the final adoption. The number of books that can be recommended varies; some states permit approval of an unlimited number. A list of five or six books is most common; no state adopts a single book. During the recent decade, several states have acted to extend the list and thereby to increase local options.

Mechanisms other than state committees are used to compile a state-approved list. In two adoption states, a state list is compiled based on evaluations and field tests done in local districts. One state legislature recently enacted an alternative route designed to get a particularly controversial book on the list: when a number of local districts chose to use the book, it would automatically be put on the state list.

Provisions for community involvement are included in the process in most states. Nine states require that lay citizens serve on the committee. One state has a social content review board, dominated by citizens, which must clear books before they reach the selection committee. Many jurisdictions require that, before books can be adopted, those under consideraton must be available for public review and that public hearings must be held to permit citizens to express their opinions.

To many critics, state adoption mechanisms, because they are at the same time centralized and subject to political influence, have a negative effect on the quality of textbooks available.[10] It is true that the large states and their politics control large amounts of the earmarked funds for textbooks and therefore have a great deal of influence on what is published. Because publishers choose to publish only books that respond to large markets, smaller states, nonadoption states, and other jurisdictions have to choose from among books developed for large purchasers, whatever their politics.

The various state systems are designed to deal with the content of schooling, the control of instruction, and the protection of public funds. Policymakers often develop the criteria for the selection, constraints are put on publishers' behavior in the selection process, and teachers rather than state administrators review the books. There is an assumption that citizens should have influence on what their children will read and learn and, finally, that elected officials accountable to the public shall make the final decisions about textbooks.

It is in the nature of such a political process that differences of opinion occur and, often with textbooks, feelings run strong. Controversies most often occur when boards or committees refuse to respond to the pressures of special interest groups. More often than not, when boards or committees give in to special interest group pressures, there is little notice. When a controversy does arise, however, it attracts the attention of the media because they often have a sensitivity to textbook issues and to any efforts to control what is read. Although there have been several well-covered state-level controversies involving special interest groups and court decisions during the 1980s, state officials report that contention at the state level over the selection of textbooks did not increase during the last decade.[11]

LOCAL ACTION

It is at the local level that the issues have become more contentious during recent decades.[12] In both adoption and nonadoption states, the actual buying decisions are made at the local level. In adoption states, the statutes most often require that local committees, which often parallel state committees in makeup, review books and make recommendations for adoption by local school boards. Lay participation procedures also parallel those at the state level. In nonadoption states, committees are often formed; increasingly, however, local boards choose to permit teachers to vote as to which textbooks will be used in schools. In a few cases, books are chosen at the school level, although most often decisions are at the district level and multiple adoptions are common (that is, several books may be approved for use in the district).[13]

Political action can influence the process at the local level in several ways. Citizens with strong points of view may be assigned to selection committees and, in the process, their strong feelings may sway committee decisions. Citizens may take advantage of the public hearing process to present their point of view to the selection committee or they may exert pressures on members of the school board during the final approval process. In extreme cases, citizens may organize to sponsor a candidate for the school board who will represent their point of view. And in a few cases, small groups of citizens, through the presentation of their strongly felt points of view, often using textbook citations taken out of context, have excited an entire community to political action.

Once purchased, textbooks are not immune from political action. Increased complaints about textbooks in use have occurred since the 1970s.[14] Although state and local school districts find it difficult to remove textbooks from use as a result of political action by a citizen or group of citizens, a point of view once registered can often influence future selections since politicians seek to avoid divisive controversies and know that aspiring politicians can use book controversies to bring attention to themselves.

Since textbooks are actually bought at the local level, local controversies have a great influence on what is published as well as on future selection processes. In deciding what to publish, publishers collect information about what is wanted at the local level from their sales people. When controversies arise, publishers have little defense. They often cannot depend on other segments of the community—even educators—to defend books chosen or under consideration. Defenders of books seldom know about the controversies, and policies often prevent any defense other than that presented by publishers; therefore, any controversy threatens sales. Thus, political pressure can have an effect on textbooks in two ways: citizens can influence policy and procedures and the actual books chosen and used, and they can indirectly influence what publishers, in their efforts to sell books and avoid controversy, choose to put into the next edition of the book.

Publishers also, however, play their own kind of politics in the process at all its levels. The American Association of Publishers (AAP) represents the industry and stays knowledgeable about developments in education. The AAP representative is in Washington when new testing policy is discussed, the organization has hosted meetings with researchers who study textbook issues, and it sponsors research in the field. Publishers go where educators are and sponsor receptions for meetings of the Big City Superintendents or the Council of Chief State School Officers, presenting themselves as partners in the education enterprise. Publishers also court teachers at the meetings of the International Reading Association and other professional organizations: they pay for receptions and provide speakers gratis from among their stable of authors. Publishers stay well-informed about new standards for books coming out of California, about the Alabama governor's recommendation to double the budget for textbooks, and about the controversy in North Carolina over state officials receiving favors from publishers. They use the knowledge that comes from such interaction with educators to establish their credibility and to stay ahead of their markets.

Political Points of View

Americans representing many points of view have been and are interested in what students will read in school. In the 1980s, actions by the federal government, by state policymakers, and by local policymakers were influenced by pressures from a variety of points of view or what might be called political positions. In some cases, long-standing groups representing the broad concerns of special interest groups may be involved or groups may be organized to exert pressure on a particular issue; in other cases, political pressures are exerted by individuals or by informal groups loosely organized for this purpose or by citizens who are not organized at all but are motivated by a common cause.

One point of view was particularly well voiced during the administration of President Ronald Reagan. The classicists or "mandarins," as Fitzgerald labeled them,[15] were outspoken in the many discussions of textbooks during the 1980s. "Excellence" became a code word for a point of view that holds to the values of the classical education. Advocates of this position were the first to abhor "dumbed down" textbooks and to disregard the pressures that had led books to become more readable to a large portion of the nation's schoolchildren. They were enthusiastic supporters of the positions espoused in *A Nation at Risk*. This point of view resounded in the exhortations of William Bennett, whose pronouncements from his Department of Education pulpit articulated many of the themes of the classicists and their vision for improved textbooks: increased rigor, increased emphasis on American history and traditional Western literature, and inclusion of explicit teaching of traditional American values. Groups such as the Council on Basic Education (CBE) have also been leaders in expressing a classical concern about textbooks. A series of CBE publications expressed concern about the lack of rigor and the pedestrian/utilitarian style of 1970s books. In general, the classicists have brought new attention to the content of textbooks and directed attention away from the pedagogical features of textbooks.

One example of concerns such as these occurred during the adoption of English literature books in 1983 in the State of Virginia. In Fairfax County, a college English professor served on the review committee for the literature books and in the process, discovered that the version of *Romeo and Juliet* in the books she was reviewing was not the original Shakespeare version. Scenes had been cut and language changed. She expressed her shock to a like-minded Virginia state board member who upon hearing of the problem took action to ask the Virginia State Department of Education Board to determine if such expurgations were common. Publishers responded to the Virginia survey that, yes, some literature selections are commonly adjusted or edited. Sex and dirty words were not the only justification; some pieces had been adjusted for being boring or just too long. Some publishers acknowledged in the student book that the versions in the book were not the original versions; other books provided that information in the teacher's edition. In some books, however, there was no acknowledgement that students were not reading the literature as it had been written by its author. The publicity about the precensorship of classical works found sympathetic ears among the media and, as a result, their point received wide attention. For instance, the Romeo and Juliet story was the subject of a Sunday Doonesbury cartoon.[16]

A Nation at Risk provides an example of another point of view which had been successful in its impact on textbooks. The report was only one of the many reports on the state of education that tied educational improvement to the economic interests of the country. Since the 1940s, representatives of the business community in the country have involved themselves in what children read in American schools. During the 1940s, the National Association of Manufacturers had made themselves felt in their opposition to social studies books that described "problems" associated with the American economic system. Poverty, for instance, was dealt with as a result of the free enterprise system. Within several years, the offending textbook program disappeared from American schools to be replaced by books that touted the free enterprise system.[17]

During that period, policymakers in a number of states enacted into law the requirement that the strengths of the free enterprise system must be taught and that textbooks chosen should support students' learning of those strengths. Political pressures from people with this concern are strong and continuing. For instance, the Council for Economic Education, a national organization, lobbies for inclusion of their curriculum in schools and provides materials that support their position. In addition, teachers have available to them a wide variety of free materials that espouse the point of view of economic interests and various industries. Only a few school districts have attempted to control the use of these textbook-like materials, which often have a very obvious political and economic point of view.

Political pressures from groups concerned about societal and personal values have had great influence on books. Controversial issues concerning sex roles, affirmative action, religion, parent/child relationships, health, privacy, etc. have had a strong effect on textbooks. From the left and from the right, groups that seek to reform society by controlling what students read have organized, pressured school boards, and taken boards to court.

Values issues have been contentious throughout our country's history, but until minority groups grew strong enough to exert their own political pressure, to elect board members of their persuasion, and until, in some cases, they gained the support of the courts for their point, boards that commonly held the traditional white, Protestant, middle-class point of view held firm.

The civil rights movement and pressures on schools to bring literacy to minority children together created a demand for textbooks that reflected the lives of all the children who would read the books, not just the Dicks and Janes of the suburban neighborhood. Pressures from the minority community throughout the country convinced state and local boards that criteria for the selection of textbooks should include the inclusion of minority role models for readers. Pressures for inclusion of women in other than traditional roles and from other groups also had their impact on the criteria and on publishers. Court decisions on such issues as religion in the schools added to the list of topics that could be controversial in books. Extensive content analysis studies, which have been done on textbooks to determine how often one group or another is included or how often a topic is mentioned, have provided ammunition for political pressure groups from many values points of view.

The success of the movements of the 1960s on book content and the idea that the content of textbooks was open to political pressure was not lost on groups at the conservative end of the values spectrum. Fundamentalist religious groups have used a variety of mechanisms to influence the books used in the public schools. Mel and Norma Gabler's listing of offending materials is circulated throughout the country through the newsletters of the Citizens for Excellence in Education, a fundamentalist organization with 30,000 members. The Gablers' careful cataloging of problems with textbooks has provided support for fundamentalist challenges to books in Texas and in many other states and local districts.[18]

Two court cases brought by groups set important precedents in 1987. In 1983, seven fundamentalist parents brought suit against the Hawkins County, Tennessee, School Board, contending that the district's requirement that their children be taught to read with books which offended their religious beliefs violated their First Amendment rights to "free exercise." In 1986, a federal judge ruled for the families and required the school district to permit the children to opt out of reading classes. Further, the court ordered the school district to pay damages to the parents. In 1987, however, the Appellate Court overturned that decision, stating that students can be required to read and discuss books which might conflict with their beliefs without being compelled to adopt the offending beliefs.[19]

In the other important case, *Smith v. Board of Mobile School Commissioners*, fundamentalist parents brought suit in a federal court contending that Alabama's adopted textbooks were espousing the religion of "secular humanism" and were, therefore, in violation of the "establishment" clause of the First Amendment. Judge Brevard Hand found for the plaintiffs and required that forty-four social studies, history, and home economics books be removed from Alabama classrooms. In March 1987, however, this case was also overturned by the appeals court. In doing so, the court stated that the lack of attention to religion in the books did not constitute "an advancement of secular humanism or an active hostility toward theistic religion."[20]

The Supreme Court of the United States declined to hear the two cases, letting the decisions of the appeals courts stand. These cases were two important setbacks for the fundamentalist groups that had supported the parents in both cases. Making a statement about his disappointment in the lack of support for their point of view in the courts, the head of the Citizens for Excellence in Education volunteered that a new priority would be the election of local school board members who would support their positions.[21]

Complaints from fundamentalist groups explain the increase in complaints at the local level during the past few years. The nature of their complaints has also changed over the years. In the past, their complaints were focused on words and details that were offensive to them, often those listed by the Gablers. More commonly now, however, their complaints focus on the content and themes of the books. They express concerns about "secular humanism," "globalism," "negativism," etc.

Individual parents often make complaints that arise out of value positions. Sexism, cuss words, sexual discussions, concerns about health issues, and other value positions often move parents to complain or to sympathize with group complaints. One of the most common problems with which schools must deal is the recurring complaint by black parents about the use of *Huckleberry Finn*.

Issues such as the *Huckleberry Finn* issue illustrate the political/educational differences that often occur between parents and the community and the education profession and within the educational system between administrators and other staff. Throughout our history, boards of education have commonly delegated responsibility for curriculum and textbooks to the profession. The field of curriculum in education prides itself in knowing what students need to learn and how it can best be taught to them. To many in the profession, the selection of reading materals is a prerogative that grows out of professional knowledge. Controversies over textbooks, therefore, are often characterized by adversarial relationships between teachers and groups of parents, both of whom feel that they know what is best for children.

An example is illustrative. In 1985, a junior high school in Bay County, Florida, received a "Center of Excellence" award from the National Council of Teachers of English for its highly successful reading program. The program, created by the school's English teachers, used junior novels as textbooks and had resulted in enthusiasm for reading as well as higher achievement test scores. However, one novel, which had been chosen as a Library of Congress Children's Book of the Year in 1977, contained language that offended some parents. In the ensuing controversy teachers defended the book, their program, and eventually a long list of classics against sometimes violent complaints by outspoken parents, and, eventually, against removal of the book by the superintendent and the school board. A reporter who covered the case for the local press was threatened and her apartment firebombed; many of the teachers eventually left teaching and the school board left the approval of reading materials in the hands of the superintendent, who agreed with the parents.[22]

Polls taken of parents' opinions about American education seem to indicate an increase in parental interest in being involved in such issues. The 1987 Gallup poll asked opinions about parent involvement in curriculum decisions and in the selection of instructional materials. Forty-five percent of the respondents said that parents should have more say in curriculum decisions; 38 percent called for more involvement in textbook selection; 36 percent said parents should be more involved in library book selection.[23]

Differences within the profession as to prerogatives and power also arise. For instance, it is the administrators in the system—state or local—who are most often held accountable by boards and citizens for what children read and for the achievement of students. Often their jobs are at stake; often they are appointed or elected because they agree to carry out the priorities of the board and the community. All too often, those priorities have implications for the relationship between the administrator and the teaching staff.

For instance, studies of controversies over books show that unless there are formal procedures for dealing with such controversies, the informal processes usually result in the removal of the book by administrators. The Bay County case is extreme but not atypical.[24]

In addition, the legacy of the "right to read politics" of test scores is that administrators often look at textbooks as an important tool for achieving their purposes. One of the tenets of the effective schools movement, a group of ideas that promise higher achievement, is that what is tested is what should be taught. It is no surprise that administrators trained in the principles of this movement would believe that the most important criterion for a textbook would be that it covers the material that will be tested. Administrators often also believe that textbooks present the best pedagogy for teaching the curriculum. It is no surprise that during the 1980s many school administrators made policy decisions such as the following (a) to focus the selection of textbooks on the degree to which the textbook material aligns with the curriculum or with the test; (b) to purchase a single book and/or series thereby assuring that all students are working in the same books throughout the school district; (c) to purchase ancillary materials such as workbooks, film strips, tests, letters to parents, management systems, posters, etc., thereby turning the textbook into a total curriculum. The general goal of such policies is improvement of teaching through standardization. This management use of textbooks has inherent assumptions about teachers and teaching that are believed to be counterproductive by many education experts. Apple has described the impact of such policies as "deskilling the teacher."[25]

During the same period that such policies were being enacted, education critics were already beginning to support the reprofessionalization of teaching. As early as the late 1970s, the Education Research Service reported that about one-third of districts that had negotiated contracts with teacher groups had a clause regarding teacher involvement in textbook selection. In Montgomery County, Maryland, for instance, teachers bargain for an "academic freedom" clause. The American Federation of Teachers has been particularly interested in the textbook selection issue, and at one time proposed that a cadre of teachers receive special training to qualify as book selectors. Professional prerogatives, such as the selection of textbooks, are growing more important during this period of high accountability when the competence of teachers is suspect and when teacher organizations must look for ways to respond to teachers' needs for increased power. Teachers, administrators, parents, and other citizens all want to be more involved with textbooks.

Conclusion

It becomes increasingly clear that more and more pressure groups are interested in influencing the character of textbooks and, thereby, the education of America's children. It is also true that it is very difficult for the political scene to deal with issues of quality since politics deals with issues of power and preference. The problems associated with textbooks are unique in any case. Accommodation comes easy; it is easy for legislators to legislate additional topics to be included in the curriculum and in the books just as it is easy for controversial books to disappear from the shelves.

Under pressures from teacher groups and from conflicting community groups, it is easy to let teachers vote for their preferred books. It is also easy for boards to give in to special interest groups and agree not to adopt the books that include *Huckleberry Finn* or globalism or negativism. It is even easier when publishers edit books carefully to be sure that no controversial material ever makes it to the printer.

Behind the scenes, publishers are acting to reduce conflict with the tacit agreement of school boards and other policymakers. At the same time, the political scene seems to become more fractious, and there is less and less agreement about what Americans want their children to read and to learn. In the American system, it is clear that school boards have the responsibility to decide what students should read and should learn. It is also clear that, with so much conflict of interest focused on textbooks, it is easier for school policymakers to avoid the politically painful decisions. Unless school boards take a strong hand in dealing with textbook issues and are willing to decide what students will learn in their schools and, in addition, are willing to design textbook policies which ensure that quality materials are produced, selected, and used to teach that curriculum, they will have reneged on their three-hundred-year-old responsibility to America's school children.

FOOTNOTES

1. National School Boards Association, *The School Board and the Instructional Program*, Research Report 1981-82 (Washington, DC: National School Boards Association, 1982).

2. Sherry Keith, *Politics of Textbook Selection*, Research Report No. 81-AT (Palo Alto, CA: Institute for Research on Educational Finance and Governance, Stanford University, 1981).

3. John Y. Cole and Thomas Sticht, eds., *The Textbook in American Society* (Washington, DC: Library of Congress, 1981); Richard C. Anderson, Jean Osborn,

and Robert J. Tierney, eds., *Learning to Read in American Schools* (Hillsdale, NJ: Erlbaum, 1984).

4. Terrel H. Bell, *The Thirteenth Man: A Reagan Cabinet Memoir* (New York: Free Press, 1988).

5. National Commission on Excellence in Education, *A Nation at Risk: The Imperative for Educational Reform* (Washington, DC: U.S. Department of Education, 1983).

6. Michael Kirst, "Choosing Textbooks," *American Educator* 8 (Summer 1984): 18-23.

7. William J. Bennett, *First Lessons: A Report on Elementary Education in America* (Washington, DC: U. S. Department of Education, 1986).

8. Harnett Kane, *Louisiana Hayride: The American Rehearsal for Dictatorship, 1928-1940* (Gretna, LA: Pelican Publishing Co., 1943, 1971).

9. California State Department of Education, *Survey of Textbook Evaluation and Adoption Processes in Adoption States and in Sample Districts in Nonadoption States* (Sacramento, CA: California State Department of Education, 1984).

10. Raymond English, "The Politics of Textbook Adoption," *Phi Delta Kappan* 62 (December 1980): 272-78; Roger Farr and Michael A. Tulley, "Do Adoption Committees Perpetuate Mediocre Textbooks?" *Phi Delta Kappan* 66 (1985): 467-71; Michael A. Tulley, "A Descriptive Study of the Intents of State-Level Textbook Adoption Processes," *Educational Evaluation and Policy Analysis* 7 (1985): 289-308; Harriet Tyson-Bernstein, *A Conspiracy of Good Intentions: America's Textbook Fiasco* (Washington, DC: Council for Basic Education, 1988).

11. National Association of State Boards of Education, "Survey of Textbook Adoption Procedures in the 22 Adoption States" (Unpublished report, September, 1985).

12. People for the American Way, *Attacks on the Freedom to Learn, 1986-87* (Washington, DC: People for the American Way, 1987).

13. Educational Research Service, Inc., *Procedures for Textbook and Instructional Materials Selection* (Arlington, VA: Educational Research Service, 1976).

14. People for the American Way, *Attacks on the Freedom to Learn*; Association of American Publishers, American Library Association, and Association for Supervision and Curriculum Development, *Limiting What Students Shall Read* (Washington, DC: Association of American Publishers, 1981).

15. Frances Fitzgerald, *America Revised: History Schoolbooks in the Twentieth Century* (New York: Vintage Books, 1979).

16. Gary Trudeau, "Doonesbury," *Washington Post*, 31 March 1985.

17. Fitzgerald, *America Revised*.

18. David Bollier, *Liberty and Justice for SOME: Defending a Free Society from the Radical Right's Holy War on Democracy* (New York: Frederick Ungor Publishing Co., 1982).

19. "The Court's Decision: The Ruling in *Mozert v. Hawkins County Public Schools*," *Education Week*, 5 November 1986; "A Courtroom Clash over Textbooks," *Time Magazine*, 27 October 1986.

20. "The Court's Decision: Excerpts from the Ruling in *Smith v. School Commissioners*," *Education Week*, 11 March 1987; "Religious Bias," *Time Magazine*, 16 March 1987.

21. People for the American Way, *Attacks on the Freedom to Learn*.

22. Peter Carlson, "A Chilling Case of Censorship," *Washington Post Magazine*, 4 January 1987.

23. Alex M. Gallup and David L. Clark, "The 19th Annual Gallup Poll of the Public's Attitudes toward the Schools," *Phi Delta Kappan* 69 (September 1987): 21.

24. Association of American Publishers et al., *Limiting What Students Shall Read.*

25. Michael W. Apple, *Teachers and Texts: A Political Economy of Class and Gender Relations in Education* (New York: Routledge and Kegan Paul, 1986).

CHAPTER X

Textbooks: Consensus and Controversy

ARTHUR WOODWARD AND DAVID L. ELLIOTT

Textbooks are a ubiquitous aspect of American schooling and they play a major role in shaping day-to-day classroom instruction. Several characteristics of contemporary elementary/secondary textbooks and the way they are used make them a topic of special concern. In the first place, more than at any other time in history, today's textbooks are published as integral parts of rather complete instructional programs that contain not only carefully selected and sequenced subject matter content but also detailed plans for teaching and learning activities, booklets or sheets containing learning exercises, achievement tests, and often supplementary print materials. Secondly, many teachers have come to depend heavily upon textbooks and textbook programs as their main curriculum guide and source of lesson plans, especially teachers at the elementary school level who are responsible for five or more subject areas. Thirdly, most textbook programs in the basic school subjects are developed and published to be distributed to a national market, although there are some publishers who cater to regional or special groups.

Given their status as virtual national curricula in the basic subjects of the curriculum, we should expect that textbooks (and the programs of which they are part) would be collectively supported by a widespread consensus across all the communities in which they are used. Because subject experts as well as teachers are involved in their development, we should expect that the content of the textbooks in each subject area has been selected from the most up-to-date and valid knowledge for each contributing knowledge discipline. Because publishers carry out nationwide market research in the course of producing each textbook program, and because the policies guiding their selection are set by state and local school boards and professional staffs, we should expect that textbook content would be consistent with the educational goals and the values and beliefs of parents and others in the communities that the schools serve.

In this chapter we argue that the kind of consensus described in the preceding paragraph, one that would make it feasible to publish single textbook programs to be marketed across the entire nation while maintaining high standards of instructional quality, does not exist. There appears to be, however, a consensus based on the "lowest common denominator" textbook user, a consensus that leads to the publication and selection of nationally marketed textbooks that are seriously flawed in their presentation of subject matter content. To explain this situation, we present examples of how market forces have influenced the textbook treatment of general science, biology, religion, and women and minority groups—examples that show some of the reasons why consensus on high-quality textbooks is hard to obtain. Then we review some of the approaches that have been used in recent years to try to improve textbook quality. We end with a discussion of the possible future consequences of this situation for the role of textbooks in the schools.

The Marketplace Consensus on Textbooks and Schooling

School programs have been under attack from a number of quarters for at least the past two or three decades, and textbooks have taken a good deal of criticism. Cody notes that when a national consensus about society and its political and social values begins to break down, much of the fallout of that breakdown hits the schools.[1] And when governing bodies such as school boards are incapable of recreating or representing local consensus regarding priorities and approaches in school programs, textbooks often become the lightning rods for much of what is perceived to be wrong with both the schools and society at large. This is in part because day-to-day classroom activities are hidden from public view and therefore hard to criticize directly, while textbooks are very accessible manifestations of what goes on (or is thought to go on) in schools.

Despite all the criticism and the lack of general agreement regarding educational priorities and approaches, there appears to be a national consensus regarding textbooks, one that is created by publishers through analyses of the textbook market, with special attention to the standards set by state and local policymakers, to the campaigns of single-issue pressure groups, and to the opinions of classroom teachers who are the main textbook users.

In constructing this "textbook marketplace consensus," publishers analyze state and large school district curricula, the curriculum recommendations of professional associations, the opinions of teachers and school administrators, and other information that comes to them as a result of their market research. The main objective of this type of consensus building is to determine the instructional design mix (the scope and sequence of subject matter content and skills, teaching-learning approaches, and other features) that when put together in a textbook program will be purchased by as many school districts in the country as possible.

There is ample evidence that this marketplace consensus exists.[2] Most school constituencies—teachers, administrators, parents, and other adults in communities—appear to find textbooks quite acceptable. In a recent survey of teachers, Rogers found that they liked their textbooks,[3] and a survey conducted a decade earlier found that teachers not only used textbooks to structure their classroom teaching but would recommend the materials they were using to other teachers as well as continuing to use them themselves.[4] According to Crismore, parents have great confidence in textbooks and expect that their children should use them and bring them home.[5]

That textbooks are criticized for their poor design and cursory coverage of subject matter content (among other things) can in large measure be attributed to the factors noted above. To the extent the state of the textbook reflects the state of the curriculum, the fact that these market forces involve a good deal of user satisfaction is, we think, a sad commentary on education in America. We turn now to some case studies that are representative of the problems inherent in permitting textbook market forces to drive the curriculum of our schools.

The Case of Science Textbooks

The case of science textbooks is instructive, for here we can see the effects both of market forces and of pressures from special interest groups. On the one hand, market pressures have resulted in encyclopedic texts that purport to fulfill every curriculum content coverage requirement—Hurd has called biology textbooks "the most beautifully illustrated dictionaries we have."[6] On the other hand, pressure from religious fundamentalists and other groups has resulted in the omission or drastic modification of "sensitive" topics such as the theory of evolution, human reproduction, and a whole range of ethical and environmental issues related to science and technology.

As early as 1950, researchers were expressing concern about the way in which science textbooks were becoming compendia of scientific terms as more and more content was added to keep them "up-to-date."[7] More recently, Hurd, Robinson, McConnell, and Ross studied science textbooks for grades six through nine and found that they contained as many as 2,500 new and unfamiliar words—double what would be expected in foreign language texts for the same grade range.[8] Similarly, Brandwein found that a typical high school chemistry "course" (read "textbook") contained 10,000 terms—more than the total vocabulary students are expected to master during four years of high school instruction in the French language.[9] Yager analyzed twenty-five K-12 science texts and found that "terminology is a central feature in most" of them.[10] For example, one sixth-grade text contained 3,400 specialized or technical words, a middle/junior high school text, 4,600; and a high school volume, 9,900.

Of course, the problem with science textbooks involves more than vocabulary. After examining college freshman and secondary level chemistry textbooks, Pauling concluded that they included tremendous amounts of material, and put heavy emphasis on atomic physics and molecular structure.[11] These topics were treated from a theoretical, not a descriptive point of view. He noted:

Descriptive chemistry is generally covered in both college and secondary textbooks beyond page 350. This is far more information than any student could be expected to learn and to understand in one year. Moreover, much of it is presented at so advanced a level—yet at the same time so superficially—that I think it could hardly be understood by a beginning student (p. 26).

Pauling recommended that chemistry textbooks be reduced to half their current size, that confusing aspects of chemistry (such as orbital theory) be omitted, and that emphasis be placed on the descriptive rather than the theoretical aspects of chemistry.

Pauling's conclusions were echoed by Gabel, who tracked the changes in Holt's *Modern Chemistry* over a twenty-year period, focusing on chapters dealing with atomic theory, periodic law, and chemical bonding.[12] She found that, while the length of the textbook declined from 661 pages in 1958 to 628 pages in 1978, little content was deleted while much was added. Gabel found that by 1978 there had been a 40 percent increase in the number of pages devoted to theoretical chemistry, with an accompanying increase in abstraction and reliance on formulas that were presented without any written descriptive introduction.

Perhaps the most damning are the findings of a number of researchers regarding the failure of science textbooks to expose students adequately to the processes of scientific inquiry.[13] In their analysis of nine elementary science series published around the early 1980s, Elliott and Nagel found that each one:

emphasizes topic coverage, memorization of facts and generalizations presented in the text, and (most disturbingly) carrying out cook-book-style hands-on activities with predetermined results. Unfortunately, little attention is given to applying science concepts and skills to daily life. . . . In short, the emphasis is on the products of science rather than on its nature and processes. Little attention is given to the fundamental canons and methods of scientific inquiry, the attitude of objectivity, or the sometimes tedious pursuit of all leads—inevitably leading to deadends—in scientific investigations.[14]

In a review of a recently published life science textbook, Anderson found that "in many typical cases, one or two question-rhetoric-question sequences are followed by an activity."[15] Many of these activities are common in high school courses and are indeed activities, rather than investigations involving the manipulation of variables.

The Case of Evolution in High School Biology Textbooks

The treatment of evolution in high school biology textbooks during this century provides an interesting example of how pressures exerted by special interest groups can influence the selection and presentation of textbook content. These pressures have led publishers to omit or drastically curtail the presentation of a topic that is crucial to the understanding of modern biology and should, when following accepted subject matter conventions, be given extensive treatment in any biology textbook.

For most of this century, the topic of evolution—and its perennial counterweight, creationism—have been the subject of persistent controversy and pressure and antievolution pressure has had a profound effect on high school biology textbooks.[16] Although some textbooks included an extensive discussion of the topic, most textbooks—and certainly the most widely adopted ones—took pains to exclude or limit any discussion of it. Indeed, studies have shown that textbooks that were originally published with an adequate treatment of evolution drastically changed in succeeding editions—and thereafter proved to be popular and widely used.[17]

Then, with the publication of three Biological Science Curriculum Study (BSCS) high school textbook programs, products of the era of federally funded curriculum projects with their extensive treatments of evolution, renewed hope was given to those interested in high-quality science instruction. Although BSCS materials were initially subjected to antievolution pressure, Grobman optimistically pointed to the repeal of laws prohibiting the teaching of evolution in every state except Mississippi and to the fact that a number of non-BSCS authors were already "discussing evolution in a far more direct way than had been customary before."[18] He was joined in his optimism by Grabiner and Miller who concluded that "major historical changes had occurred all militating in favor of the approval of the BSCS books in Texas: the new public interest in improving high school science teaching; the large body of legal precedents limiting religious influence in schools; and the increasing urbanization and educational level of the people of the South."[19]

This celebration was, however, a bit premature. During the more than twenty years following the publication of the first BSCS textbooks, the fervent interest in reforming school programs died down. That interest had prompted federal funding and made possible the teaming of scholars and educators that led to the "new" mathematics, science, and social studies programs. But the heady days when the supporters of BSCS were able to defy the state of Texas seemed long gone. The earlier optimism seemed hopelessly naive after the appearance of press reports of numerous instances of attempts to ban evolution from biology instruction and to ensure that textbooks excluded evolution and included creationism. Indeed, after analyzing high school biology textbooks, Skoog found that the extensive treatment of evolution in the BSCS textbooks "did not survive the 1970s as the emphasis on selected topics concerned with evolution was drastically reduced or eliminated in some textbooks" and "word changes . . . resulted in many statements becoming less definite, more cautious, and thus less controversial than those appearing in earlier editions."[20]

In response to persistent claims that publishers of biology textbooks were succumbing to creationist pressure and that textbooks were excluding evolution, Woodward and Elliott analyzed fifteen editions of high school biology textbooks published in the early 1980s, including recent revisions of BSCS programs.[21] They found four patterns of publisher response to the treatment of evolution: two publishers avoided evolution and Darwin and emphasized alternative explanations of human development; three favored a "balanced" approach and took pains to describe both evolutionist and creationist interpretations of development; a third group of four chose to present a full description of evolution without covering human evolution; and the last group of six publishers presented uncompromising descriptions of all aspects of evolution.

These widely varying ways of handling the highly controversial topic of evolution reveal a good deal about how publishing companies can shape their textbooks in order to sell them to different parts of the school market. In the early 1980s, educators did have a choice when it came to selecting biology textbooks—at least with respect to how those books dealt with evolution. Yet, while this finding is heartening, the actual approach some publishers have taken in dealing with evolution raises serious questions about how they deal with any controversial content.

The Case of Religion in Textbooks

With the publication of research by Bryan, by Vitz, and by Davis, a great gap in textbook content was revealed, especially in those dealing with history and the social studies.[22] Topics dealing with religion were found to be excluded from both U.S. history textbooks and from the literary content of reading series. As Bryan reports from his study of twenty high school history texts:

There is a remarkable consensus to the effect that, after 1700, Christianity has no historical presence in America. . . . Even within this (prior) period, the textbooks have some astonishing gaps. . . . None discusses the role of Anglican Christianity in the Middle and Southern colonies. . . . It is as if Christian religious influences stopped at the border between Connecticut and New York.[23]

Even where religion was covered, Bryan found that it was grossly simplified and disconnected. These history text findings were confirmed by Davis in a People for the American Way study and by Vitz, who replicated and extended the study to representative basal reading series and to elementary school texts.[24] In his examination of high school history texts, Vitz found that:

None of these books had any serious coverage of conservative Protestantism in the last 100 years. A few books mentioned the Scopes trial. . . . There was not one book that recognized the major historical importance of the Holiness-Pentecostal movement, of the split between liberal and conservative Protestantism in the early twentieth century, the Bible Colleges, the Bible Belt, etc. As a result, not one of these books provides any basis for understanding what today is known as the religious right.[25]

Elementary social studies texts did not fare any better. Vitz found that forty grade 1-4 textbooks "introduced children to life in America without any reference in word or image to contemporary Protestantism."[26] In the basal readers, he found only a few references and images that had to do with religion. Indeed, basal text stories omitted any reference to active Protestantism, but did refer to Catholic, Jewish, and Mennonite "minority" religions. He also found that sometimes stories referred to characters praying, but failed to mention how or to whom they prayed.

The caution with which publishers deal with religion is well illustrated in the case of "Molly Pilgrim," a story written by Barbara Cohen and selected by Harcourt Brace Jovanovich for inclusion in its basal reading series. As Cohen relates it, while the editors of the basal series found the story excellent, they requested that references to Jews, Sukkoth, God, and the Bible be excised, even though these concepts were at the very core of the story.[27] According to Cohen's report, the editors felt that these terms were liable to attract negative attention and become reasons why various individuals or groups would object to the textbook.

The Case of the Representation of Minorities and Women

Many studies have been conducted on the inclusion of women and minorities in textbooks.[28] For the most part, these studies have shown that specific groups have received either little or distorted coverage in elementary-secondary textbooks. For example, in an extensive review of the literature on the representation of minorities, Grant and Grant found that, prior to the early 1960s, these groups were almost nonexistent in textbooks.[29]

Similar findings have been made in regard to the inclusion of girls and women. Typical of the studies in this area is Trecker's findings in a study of U.S. history texts that "texts omit many women of importance, while simultaneously minimizing the legal, social, and cultural disabilities which they faced."[30] Moreover, authors mainly describe male leaders while tending to depict women in passive roles.

In response to the political pressures that resulted in new textbook standards being instituted by state education authorities, publishers began to change their textbooks. By the mid-1960s, many more non-Caucasians appeared in narrative and illustration, although at first they were rarely depicted as decision makers or in positions of authority. In a study of U.S. history texts, Garcia and Tanner reported that the black experience was dealt with more extensively and with more verisimilitude than previously.[31] Scott showed similar increases in the representation of female main characters in basal readers between 1976 and 1978 so that they were portrayed almost as often as male main characters.[32] In addition, women were being portrayed in nontraditional roles.

However, not all is fair and equitable, despite the greater political clout of the fairness and equity advocates. The portrayal of women, Hispanics, Afro-Americans, and American Indians has been elevated to new levels of tokenism. The ways in which the market has responded to the legitimate claims of underrepresented groups has resulted more in additional photographs, misleading name changes,[33] and narrative "vignettes" than in meaningful portrayal of their role in society. Vitz also documented a bit of what might be called "bending too far over backwards" in the underrepresentation of white male role models (e.g., businessmen), "stay at home" mothers, and nuclear families.[34]

We have argued thus far that the combination of market forces and pressure groups has had a devastating effect on the instructional quality of textbooks. Generally speaking, most textbooks in any subject area cannot be said to reflect fully and honestly the knowledge disciplines they represent. More specifically, the efforts of special interest groups, whether they are religious sects or conservative political associations, have resulted in distortion or elimination of certain topics.

We believe, however, that the main responsibility for this situation lies not with the textbook publishers but with those who select and use the textbooks that are published and with the structure of the textbook market as it exists today. As in any commercial enterprise, publishers respond to the laws of supply and demand. Each publisher determines what the market is, decides what part of that market to sell to, and publishes textbooks accordingly. Thus, in textbook publishing, market economics is given higher priority than scholarship.

Ways of Influencing the Textbook Marketplace

All this leads to the conclusion that a demand for a superior product must be created in order to make it possible to produce quality textbooks and to sell them successfully in a national market. Assuming that this is the case, it may be instructive to look at some recent attempts to create such a demand.

First, it is important to remember that during the period of the late 1960s and early 1970s, there was a massive federal educational reform effort under which the National Science Foundation supported curriculum projects that produced inquiry-oriented science programs. A number of the major textbook companies published the products of these projects in the form of textbook programs such as PSSC Physics, BSCS Biology, and ChemStudy, plus a handful of elementary school kit-oriented programs such as Science Curriculum Improvement Study (SCIS), Science—A Process Approach (S-APA), and Elementary Science Study (ESS). That these programs do not dominate the school science scene is due to the fact that most schools no longer buy them (if schools ever did); these programs were the victims of market forces, not publisher recalcitrance. Those publishers who took the "high road," as some did in publishing BSCS textbooks, did so because they knew that a significant group of users would buy such materials; most of the new secondary social studies and elementary school science and social studies materials found no such market.

A second way to try to raise the quality of textbook programs is for state and local policymaking bodies to set and implement higher standards for textbook adoption. A good example of such an approach is to be found in California, which, as an adoption state, has for some years been following five-year cycles of curriculum development, each of which begins with the revision of the framework or course of study in a particular subject area and ends with the adoption of a new set of K-8 textbooks. During the 1980s, the California State Department of Education announced its intent to initiate curriculum reform by using this cyclic process to attempt to force drastic revisions in the textbooks used within the state.[35]

This new policy took effect with the 1985 K-8 science textbook adoption but it was implemented without giving the publishers enough lead time to develop completely revised programs. The result was, as Elliott and Nagel have shown, that the treatment of basic science in the adopted programs was inadequate,[36] although the State

Board of Education did try (with some success) to get the publishers to include fuller treatments of the topics of evolution and human reproduction.[37]

The second subject area to come under the new California policy was K-8 mathematics. Although this time the new Mathematics Framework and supplements[38] had been distributed early enough to allow publishers ample time for making major revisions, had they wished to do so, the results were not significantly better than they had been in the previous science adoption. In fact, the one elementary mathematics program that came closest to meeting the new standards was not recommended for adoption and had to be added to the list by the State Board of Education.[39]

Thus it is that significant textbook—and thus school program— reform in both science and mathematics has not yet taken place. Those responsible for writing the new curriculum frameworks put forward new policies and tougher standards. A different group made up of those responsible for choosing the textbooks to be adopted in California opted for textbooks that pretty much maintained the status quo. This latter group, which encompasses many local and regional teacher committees and includes the state's Curriculum Commission, is representative of the national textbook market, the very educators that publishers contact in carrying out their prepublication market surveys. The group that enacted the new policy, on the other hand, is evidently made up of many of the same people who have been critical of school programs and textbooks all along. The textbook marketplace operated as it usually does, with user demand effectively overriding official policy.

A third way to influence the textbook market is by the action of special interest groups. For many people, the efforts of the Gablers to change the contents of the textbooks adopted in Texas (and therefore to influence the textbooks used throughout the nation) is a notorious example of how to exert influence.[40] While the views expressed by the Gablers may seem extreme and the charges they made against textbook content either silly or baseless, such agitation is part of the process of achieving a new consensus or equilibrium in the textbook market. The efforts of the Gablers spawned People for the American Way,[41] a group that has been extremely successful in countering the worst excesses of the Gablers by initiating a debate about education and citizenship and thereby creating a climate that resulted in changes in textbook policies in Texas.

A fourth way to influence the textbook market is through a

broader social movement. Such was the case with the civil rights agitation of the 1960s and similar pushes that followed for fairer treatment of women, the handicapped, and the aged. Beginning in the late 1960s, "fairness," or the more adequate representation of members of minority groups and women, became a prominent issue in the textbook industry and a strong consumer demand emerged. As indicated above, more female and non-Caucasian characters began to appear in textbook illustrations and, to a lesser extent, in the text narrative. In some states textbook standards regarding fair representation were more rigorous than those covering other aspects of content and teaching approaches. For example, whereas California educators could adopt science and mathematics textbooks that failed to meet state standards regarding the portrayal of mainstream science and mathematical problems, no such leeway was permitted in regard to "fairness." Textbooks that do not pass an initial "legal compliance" screening cannot even be considered for adoption, whatever other educational merits they may possess. Thus it was that the marketplace responded to legitimate claims for better representation. Unfortunately, this same marketplace was also willing to accept a new level of tokenism, or "mentioning," since, as indicated earlier, the depiction of women or groups such as Afro-Americans or Hispanic-Americans that was added was mostly in the form of more photographs and other visuals rather than any meaningful portrayal of their roles in history or present-day society.

Conclusion

Analyses of textbook quality, described in this chapter and elsewhere in this volume, indicate that basic subject areas are inadequately presented, that outmoded and inaccurate ideas persist, that higher levels of cognitive functioning are mainly excluded, and that most potentially controversial topics are simply ignored. Nonetheless, studies of textbook use and the degree of teacher dependency upon them indicate that textbook programs are a major factor in shaping instructional programs around the nation. However, in spite of national concern over the poor quality of American education, recent efforts to improve textbooks and reform the curriculum have resulted neither in significant improvements in textbooks nor in the widespread use of other types of curriculum-shaping materials.

In the preceding pages we have presented what we consider to be one of the main reasons for this stagnation of curriculum development. It appears that the American schooling enterprise has become so routinized and set in its ways that it can successfully resist even the most concerted reform efforts. At least one way of accounting for the resilience of the current textbook marketplace is to hypothesize that the current structure and functioning of the schooling enterprise have become so familiar and comfortable for all who are involved in it— students, teachers, administrators, policymakers, parents, and others— that they are reluctant to change. The programs in hand, from the presentation of separate subjects in textbooks to the achievement tests that indicate how well everyone has done, are preferred to new and unfamiliar programs from someone's curriculum project. And avoiding topics that might stir up community controversy or dissent contributes to the comfort and makes it easier for all concerned to concentrate on the basics.

However, we also believe that American education is not monolithic and that there are many teachers across the nation who would use different kinds of instructional materials if they were readily available. There does not need to be a conflict between the economics of the textbook marketplace and the commercial publication of a variety of high-quality textbooks and nontextbook programs. Much of the current situation appears to be rooted in the overwhelming emphasis put on slick and expensive textbook programs that are produced for a national market and are considered to be obsolete after four or five years.

One alternative worth consideration is segmental and regional textbooks that would differ in content and format from those published for national distribution. Since such textbooks would be sold to a smaller market, they would necessarily have to be produced less expensively, omitting glossy and colorful design, and less often. Of course, content relevant to a national audience could still be published in basic textbooks that are accompanied by regional and local supplements. In addition, a good deal more use could be made of classroom sets of tradebooks, of library collections, and (in the not too distant future) of a wide variety of information and learning activities accessed via electronic databases.

There need not be a disequilibrium between scholarship, community needs, and the instructional materials marketplace. It is possible for textbook authors to deal with controversial topics in ways that neither sacrifice scholarship and content validity nor abuse community sensibilities. One way to do this is to include presentations of competing sides of issues in special sections at the ends of textbook units, thus making it possible to inform students about such issues without taking sides. In the case of the treatment of the theory of evolution, for example, the views of creationists could be presented in a section on social issues while at the same time being identified as being in the realm of public policy or religious belief rather than as scientific research.

If the current interest in raising the professional caliber and status of teachers leads to any significant developments over the next decade or so, the textbook program may lose its role as definer of the curriculum. One way to move this process along would be to support teachers in the cooperative development of both local materials and approaches to supplement and enrich textbook fare and local instructional programs that would replace textbooks in certain subject areas at selected grade levels.

FOOTNOTES

1. Caroline Cody, "Can We Have the Freedom to Read in American Schools?" *Ethics in Education* 8 (November 1988): 3.

2. Educational Products Information Exchange Institute, *Report on a National Study of the Nature and Quality of Instructional Materials Most Used by Teachers and Learners*, Report No. 77 (New York: EPIE Institute, 1977); Archie LaPointe, "The State of Instruction in Reading and Writing in U.S. Elementary Schools," *Phi Delta Kappan* 68 (1986): 135-38; Gail McCutcheon, "How Do Elementary School Teachers Plan? The Nature of Planning and Influences on It," *Elementary School Journal* 81 (1981): 4-23; Robert E. Stake and Jack A. Easley, Jr., *Case Studies in Science Education*, Vol. II: *Design, Overview, and Findings* (Champaign: Center for Instructional Research and Curriculum Evaluation, University of Illinois, 1978), pp. 13: 59-61.

3. Vincent Rogers, "School Texts: The Outlook of Teachers," *Education Week*, 3 August 1988.

4. EPIE Institute, *Report on a National Study of the Nature and Quality of Instructional Materials*.

5. Avon Crismore, "Students' and Teachers' Perceptions and Use of Sixth Grade Social Studies Textbooks in Champaign Middle Schools: A Case Study" (Unpublished report, Champaign, IL, 1981). ERIC ED 232 952.

6. Paul Hurd, quoted in Robert Rothman, "Panelists Flay Biology Curriculum as Outmoded, Filled with Factlets," *Education Week*, 19 October 1988.

7. A 1950 Master's thesis by Julian N. Toltness at the University of North Dakota found that four high school chemistry texts contained from 761 to 856 terms. See *Phi Delta Kappan* 33 (1952): 287.

8. Paul D. Hurd, James T. Robinson, Mary C. McConnell, and Norris M. Ross, Jr., *The Status of Middle School and Junior High School Science*, Vol. 1 and *Summary Report*; Vol. II, *Technical Report* (Louisville, CO: Center for Educational Research and Evaluation, Biological Science Curriculum Study, 1981).

9. Paul Brandwein, cited in Robert E. Yager, "The Importance of Terminology in Teaching K-12 Science," *Journal of Research in Science Teaching* 29 (1983): 577-88.

10. Ibid.

160   TEXTBOOKS: CONSENSUS AND CONTROVERSY

11. Linus Pauling, "Throwing the Book at Elementary Chemistry," *Science Teacher* 50 (September 1983): 25-29.

12. Dorothy L. Gabel, "What High School Chemistry Texts Do Well and What They Do Poorly," *Journal of Chemical Education* 60 (1983): 893-95.

13. See Robert E. Yager, "Let Kids Experience Science, and Watch the Crisis in Education Subside," *American School Board Journal* 170 (1983): 26-27; John S. Rigden, "The Art of Great Science," *Phi Delta Kappan* 64 (1983): 613-17; David L. Elliott and Kathleen C. Nagel, "School Science and the Pursuit of Knowledge—Deadends and All," *Science and Children* 24, no. 8 (1987): 9-12; and Wayne A. Moyer and William V. Mayer, *As Texas Goes, So Goes the Nation: A Report on Textbook Selection in Texas* (Washington, DC: People for the American Way, 1985).

14. Elliott and Nagel, "School Science and the Pursuit of Knowledge," pp. 9-10.

15. Hans O. Anderson, "What's Missing in Science," *Bookwatch* 1 (May 1988): 2.

16. Otto B. Christy, *The Development of the Teaching of General Biology in Secondary Schools*, Peabody Contribution to Education No. 201 (Nashville, TN: George Peabody College for Teachers, 1937). Rita Ciolli, "The Textbook Wars," *Newsday Magazine*, 18 December 1983; Dorothy Nelkin, *The Creation Controversy: Science or Scripture in the Schools* (New York: W. W. Norton, 1982).

17. J. I. Cretzinger, "An Analysis of Principles or Generalities Appearing in Biological Textbooks Used in the Secondary Schools of the United States from 1800 to 1933," *Science Education* 5 (1941): 310-13; Judith V. Grabiner and Peter D. Miller, "Effects of the Scopes Trial," *Science* 185 (1974): 832-37; and Cornelius J. Troost, "Evolution in Biological Education Prior to 1960," *Science Education* 50 (1968): 300-301.

18. Arnold B. Grobman, "The Changing Classroom: The Role of the Biological Sciences Curriculum Study," *BSCS Bulletin* 4 (1969): 203-19.

19. Grabiner and Miller, "Effects of the Scopes Trial," p. 836.

20. Gerald Skoog, "Coverage of Evolution in Secondary School Biology Textbooks: 1900-1982" (Paper presented at the Annual Meeting of the American Biology Teachers Association, 1982).

21. Arthur Woodward and David L. Elliott, "Evolution and Creationism in High School Textbooks," *American Biology Teacher* 49 (March 1987): 164-70.

22. Robert Bryan, *History, Pseudo-history, Anti-history: How Public School Textbooks Treat Religion* (Washington, DC: Learn, Inc., 1984); Paul C. Vitz, "Religion and Traditional Values in Public School Textbooks: An Empirical Study," in *Equity in Values Education: Do the Values Education Aspects of Public School Curricula Deal Fairly with Diverse Belief Systems?*, Section 1, Part 2, NIE-G84-0012 (New York: New York University, 1985) ERIC ED 260 019; and O. L. Davis, Jr., Gerald Ponder, Lynn M. Burlbaw, M. Garza-Lubeck, and A. Moss, *Looking at History: A Review of Major U.S. History Textbooks* (Washington, DC: People for the American Way, 1986).

23. Bryan, *History, Pseudo-history, Anti-history*, p. 3.

24. Davis et al., *Looking at History*; Paul C. Vitz, "Religion and Traditional Values in Public School Textbooks"; idem, *Censorship: Evidence of Bias in Our Children's Textbooks* (Ann Arbor, MI: Servant Press, 1986).

25. Vitz, *Censorship: Evidence of Bias in Our Children's Textbooks*.

26. Paul C. Vitz, "Teaching about Religion: The Disturbing Challenge," *Curriculum Review* 26 (1987): 60-61.

27. Barbara Cohen, "Censoring the Sources," *School Library Journal* 32, no. 7 (1986): 97-99.

28. Arthur Woodward, David L. Elliott, and Kathleen C. Nagel, *Textbooks in School and Society: An Annotated Bibliography and Guide to Research* (New York: Garland Publishing Co., 1988), pp. 91-96.

29. Carl A. Grant and Gloria W. Grant, "The Multicultural Evaluation of Some Second and Third Grade Textbook Readers—A Survey Analysis," *Journal of Negro Education* 50 (1981): 63-74.

30. Janice L. Trecker, "Women in U.S. History High School Textbooks," *Social Education* 35 (1971): 249-60.

31. Jesus Garcia and Daniel E. Tanner, "The Portrayal of Black Americans in U.S. History Textbooks," *Social Studies* 76 (1985): 200-204.

32. Kathryn P. Scott, "Whatever Happened to Dick and Jane? Sexism in Texts Reexamined," *Peabody Journal of Education* 58 (1981): 135-40.

33. Gail McCutcheon, Diana Kyle, and Robert Skovira, "Characters in Basal Readers: Does 'Equal' Now Mean 'Same'?" *Reading Teacher* 32 (1979): 438-41.

34. Vitz, *Censorship: Evidence of Bias in Our Children's Textbooks*.

35. See, for example, California State Department of Education, "Standards for Mathematics Textbooks," in *Mathematics Framework for California Public Schools, Kindergarten through Grade Twelve* (Sacramento: California State Department of Education, 1985).

36. Elliott and Nagel, "School Science and the Pursuit of Knowledge."

37. Arthur Woodward, "On Teacher and Textbook Publishing: Political Issues Obscure Questions of Pedagogy," *Education Week*, 21 January 1987.

38. California State Department of Education, *Mathematics Framework for California Public Schools*.

39. During the 1986 mathematics adoption, the textbook series that most nearly met the standards was not recommended by the selection panels and was added to the list by action of the State Board of Education. On the previous mathematics adoption, the standards were not upheld even this much. See M. Blouke Carus, "California and Textbook Reform: Too Little Too Late, Too Much Too Soon" (Paper presented at the Annual Meeting of the American Educational Research Association, Washington, DC, 1987) ERIC ED 276 128; and David L. Elliott, "Selection Standards vs. Actual Adoptions: A California Textbook Example" (Paper presented at the Annual Meeting of the American Educational Research Association, Chicago, 1985).

40. See Robert P. Doyle, "Censorship and the Challenge to Intellectual Freedom," *National Elementary School Principal* 61, no. 3 (1982): 8-11; and Mel Gabler and Norma Gabler, "Mind Control through Textbooks," *Phi Delta Kappan* 64 (1982): 96.

41. See Barbara Parker and S. Weiss, *Protecting the Freedom to Learn* (Washington, DC: People for the American Way, 1983).

CHAPTER XI

Textbook Evaluation and Selection

MICHAEL TULLEY AND ROGER FARR

Historical Perspectives

State and local level textbook adoption policies and processes emerged in response to the needs of professional educators and to the demands created by an evolving system of public education in the United States. By 1850, graded, group instruction necessitated uniformity of textbooks and, as a result, many states formed policies that governed the "adoption" of textbooks for use in local school districts. Eventually, a need was perceived in many states for uniformity or consistency across larger geographic and political boundaries than the local district, and by the late 1800s legislation establishing state-level adoption policies and procedures was established.[1]

The perception that state-level adoption was needed at this time was based largely on the belief that as population mobility occurred across districts, parents were forced to buy new textbooks because different books were used from school district to school district within the same state. State legislators felt that by adopting common textbooks for use in schools throughout the state they could help parents with the financial burden of having to buy different textbooks when a family moved from one school district to another. By 1915, approximately half the states had developed some form of state-level control over textbook selection procedures.[2] The number of states maintaining these state-level processes has remained relatively stable for several decades; there are presently twenty-two "adoption" states, and twenty-eight that are classified as "open" or nonadoption states.[3]

Despite the fact that it seems relatively easy to divide states into adoption and nonadoption states, that division is, in many ways, an oversimplification of the actual situation. For example, some states only adopt textbooks at the elementary level and leave the selection of textbooks at the secondary level up to each school district or individual school. The number of textbooks included on each state's list also differs significantly. Some states decide to have an adoption list of only five or seven textbooks regardless of the number of textbooks that are submitted. Others include every textbook that meets basic evaluation criteria, which often means that the lists are virtually unlimited. States also differ in major ways in the processes they use to review textbooks. Some spend as much as a year or more trying out textbooks, having the texts reviewed by a variety of committees, and holding open forums to discuss the submitted textbooks. Other states establish fairly small committees that complete their work in a relatively short time period. Some states establish committees that are representative of various political constituencies while others select committees based on the qualifications of the reviewers. Florida, for example, has established a mandatory training program for textbook adoption committee members.

State and local textbook adoption policies have followed definite geographic patterns: the New England and North Atlantic states have consistently maintained local selection processes, as have the majority of the northern and midwestern states. Nearly all southern states, in contrast, have developed and maintained state-level adoption processes.[4] A widely accepted theory concerning the significance of these patterns is that these differences reflect regional traditions and styles of governance that have been extended to education.

Until the last several years, the literature in the area of textbook adoption was fairly limited. The early literature includes discussions of the advantages and disadvantages of free textbooks and debates about the value of state adoptions. There are also occasional summaries documenting the states that conduct statewide adoption and those that do not. These summary studies provide only minimal descriptions of the specific adoption processes used in the various states, and are usually limited to a summary of questionnaires and surveys.

These early questionnaire and survey studies were primarily descriptions of the state- and/or local-level policies in place in particular states, at a given time.[5] While these contributions do little to increase our understanding about the specific manner in which adoption procedures operate, they do at least make it possible to trace the chronological movement of individual states either toward, or away from, state-level control of textbook selection.

The earliest available tabulation of adoption policies appeared in 1891,[6] when it was reported that as early as 1883, ten states had already implemented state control of textbook selection. By 1905, that number had risen to twenty-three states, and to twenty-five states by 1925.[7] However, intervening events or forces that may have led to the increasing number of centralized processes are not described. In the absence of definitive explanations, it can only be assumed that authorities in these states subscribed to prevailing beliefs pertaining to the relative advantages and disadvantages of state versus local control of textbooks.

Throughout the first half of this century, most of the professional literature related to textbook adoption was preoccupied with the ongoing debate over the advantages and disadvantages of state versus local school district selection of textbooks. Among the recurring arguments in favor of state-level adoption were the uniformity of curriculum that was assumed to be the result of common textbook adoption and use, the reduction of textbook costs resulting from contractual control and volume purchasing, and the periodic review and updating of curriculum which, it was felt, would result from selecting new textbooks in prescribed adoption "cycles," or periods of usage. Equally logical and compelling counterarguments and positions in favor of local-level processes appear in the literature as well.[8]

The search for explanations for the development of textbook adoption processes must consider the free textbook movement, which was basically the struggle to provide textbooks paid for by local taxes rather than by the parents of each school child. Although the free textbook movement and state textbook policies evolved somewhat independently, the goal in each case is the same: the selection of single textbooks across an entire school district, and preferably across an entire state.[9] The most obvious and attractive vehicle for achieving that uniformity, in both instances, was centralized administration of textbook selection.

From its inception, the free textbook movement was heralded as an important and advantageous educational development.[10] By the mid-1880s, when the first statewide free textbook legislation was enacted in Massachusetts, nineteen of the nation's largest cities had similar policies in place,[11] and by 1915, fifteen states and most metropolitan areas had free textbook laws.[12]

Arguments in favor of free textbooks, even if only tangentially related to the issue of textbook adoption, may be instructive in that they help to illuminate the educational and political contexts from which both movements arose. The arguments, if not voiced from an entirely egalitarian posture, are at least practical in their recognition of, and concessions to, fiscal realities. Briefly, the more noteworthy of the arguments were that free textbooks should logically accompany free and compulsory education, that they made possible a change in textbooks when deemed necessary without placing an undue financial burden on parents, that volume purchases and reuse lowered textbook costs, and that free textbook legislation would make textbook and curricular uniformity possible.[13]

By 1950, debates concerning both movements no longer received much attention, and for a period of approximately twenty-five years only a handful of articles related to textbook adoption appeared in the professional literature. When the subject of textbook adoption began once again to capture the interest of researchers in the mid-1970s, the focus of textbook inquiry had shifted from descriptive summaries of types of adoption processes to more in-depth analyses of how these processes were being carried out.[14]

This recent interest in textbook adoption stems from the general criticisms of education that reached a crescendo with the publication of *A Nation at Risk*.[15] Criticisms of education included the claim that since textbooks dominated classroom instruction and were relied on to such an extent by classroom teachers, the textbooks should be examined as one of the potential culprits in the decline in educational achievement. When researchers and educational critics declared that the textbooks were inadequate, attention shifted to the procedures for adopting textbooks.[16]

Current Practices

Given the importance of the textbooks in American education, it is surprising that so little is known about the ways in which state- and local-level adoption processes are conducted, and that educators have only recently directed their energies toward inquiries in this area. As suggested above, the tendency to divide the fifty states into two distinct groups—the twenty-two adoption and the twenty-eight nonadoption states—suggests that practices within either group are more similar than is certainly the case; adoption processes within either group are not uniform. Nevertheless, it is possible to identify some broad similarities and differences between the adoption and the nonadoption states.

Chief among the differences is, of course, the two-tiered evaluation and selection process that exists in all adoption states, and which yields a restricted or approved list of textbooks from which local districts must select.[17] But even here practices vary considerably. Some adoption states list as few as five textbooks while others include on their approved lists all those texts that match prescribed adoption or curricular criteria. A second difference is the influence on textbook development and content that state-level adoption processes make possible. This so-called "California" or "Texas effect" is generally accepted as valid by publishers, as well as by educational administrators at both the state and local levels.[18]

The editorial offices of all major textbook publishers have lists of the major adoption states that indicate when those states will be adopting textbooks in each subject area. Also posted are the criteria those states have submitted to publishers telling them what they want the textbooks to include. These criteria are often in the form of curriculum objectives, and they sometimes include prohibitions as to what should not be included in the texts. Publishers often time their new publications to match the schedules of these adopting states. For example, if Texas is adopting reading textbooks in a particular year, many of the reading textbook publishers will be ready with new books (and new copyright dates) just in time for the Texas adoption. The companies will also develop attractive brochures to show how their books meet the curriculum objectives Texas has established. Thus, not only is the content of the textbooks significantly influenced by the adoption states, particularly the major adoption states including Texas, California, and Florida, but so is the timing of the publication of new textbooks tied to the adoption cycles of these states.[19]

Among the recent investigations is a study that attempted to describe state-level adoption in terms of the intents or advantages that legislatures or Departments of Education were attempting to achieve through their respective centralized adoption processes.[20] The handful of purposes identified in that study generated hypotheses, examined in a second study, that attempted to determine whether these perceived advantages actually exist. The second study revealed that, at least in terms of textbook costs, periods of usage, and consistency or control of curricula, local districts in the nonadoption states do not appear to be at any particular disadvantage due to an absence of state-level control of adoption. Thus, considerable doubt has been cast on the value and validity of centralized, state-level processes.[21]

It is not likely that the debate over the relative advantages and disadvantages of state- versus local-level textbook adoption will be resolved, at least in the near future, largely because there continue to be strong proponents on each side of the issue. There have been only slight modifications in state-level policies in the past several decades.

Thus, it seems most reasonable to assume that existing state-level structures and mechanisms for the selection of textbooks will likely continue in these twenty-two states.

It should be obvious that textbook adoption policies and processes vary considerably, especially at the local level. The number of local districts in the U.S. alone is sufficient to support this assertion. Even if adoption occurs at the district level, there are thousands of potentially different adoption procedures and processes. Moreover, many decisions are made within districts, at the building, grade, or even individual classroom levels, which probably multiplies this number significantly. Despite this diversity, studies have demonstrated that one commonality within all the adoption processes is the significance of the textbook adoption committee, which is essentially the decision-making body that determines which textbooks make their way into classrooms. These committees are typically composed of teachers, administrators, and sometimes parents.

Researchers are beginning to discover those factors and interactions that lie at the center of committee functions and decisions. Two recent and insightful studies attempted to look beneath the organization of adoption committees, to the activities and decisions engaged in by individual committee members.[22] Both studies were conducted within Indiana (one of the twenty-two adoption states). One study focused on the state-level adoption of reading textbooks, while the other focused on the processes used by local committees in adopting reading textbooks. Although there is little basis for generalizing the findings of either study to other states or districts (or even to other subject areas), these two inquiries nonetheless provide a glimpse into the dynamics that characterize and influence textbook adoption committees.

In the state-level study researchers directed attention toward individuals who had served as reviewers or advisors to the textbook commission (the adopting authority). These reviewers were primarily responsible for examining and recommending textbooks to commissioners. Among the most interesting findings were that many reviewers—most of whom were also classroom teachers—felt that they had not been provided with adequate directions and that they did not have sufficient time to examine the textbooks adequately. They also reported that evaluations were based more upon global or general impressions than upon the specific strengths and weaknesses of textbooks.

The second study demonstrated that these same problems exist at the local level. The study also identified five factors that local reviewers considered to be important persuasions when evaluating and selecting textbooks: the physical appearance of the textbooks, data gained from pilot tryouts, local philosophies pertaining to subject matter pedagogy, the relative influence of publishers, and formal and informal political and interpersonal relationships.

One of the more disconcerting discoveries pertains to the selection criteria employed during the textbook review process. Some type of evaluation instrument is a part of virtually all textbook selection procedures, and most adoption committees use predetermined criteria, typically in checklist form. Many state and local districts develop their own checklists, but in many instances criteria are derived from instruments available from publishing companies, state Departments of Education, or professional organizations.

The criticisms that can be leveled at the content and application of these instruments are numerous.[23] For example, the number of criteria on some instruments is overwhelming, and many checklists require only that reviewers determine the presence, rather than the quality of various features. Criteria are usually not ranked by priority, but instead equal weight is given to all features, leaving reviewers to establish their own priorities. Districts and committees generally *do not* set standards that help reviewers agree on good and poor examples of various features of textbooks. Most of the studies have found that reviewers *do not* have adequate time to review the books. Thus, the common procedure is to form overall evaluations or opinions by "browsing through" or using the "flip test." After a general impression is formed from the flip test, the reviewer completes the criteria sheet so that the check marks for the specific criteria match the reviewer's general evaluation. Thus, specific criteria are cast aside and general impressions are used to evaluate the books.

Recommendations for Further Inquiry

The most basic issue that needs further study is whether textbooks actually influence the quality of education. Textbooks are dominant influences in many classrooms and thus they seem to determine content—and they also seem to determine teaching practices. There are, however, no studies showing that textbooks are a major factor in determining the quality of education.

It seems that more careful study needs to be given to the role of textbooks. What role can and should textbooks play in classrooms? What aspects of textbooks are most important? As long as educators continue to assume that the textbook is the curriculum, teachers will be powerless to exert change. Schools and teachers have allowed textbooks to dominate. If textbooks were seen as adjuncts to a curriculum, as aids to a teacher, and not as a total curriculum, perhaps they could be viewed from a more rational perspective.

Ultimately, the purpose of any investigation in the area of textbook adoption should be to point to specific areas in which adoption policies and processes can be improved. Because so little research has been conducted in this area, virtually every dimension of these processes might be considered a legitimate target for further inquiry. But the selection of textbooks is too critical to the educational enterprise to plunge into modification or reform on the basis of conclusions derived from investigations conducted in a hasty or haphazard manner. Inquiry should proceed, therefore, in an orderly progression, guided by conceptual frameworks that allow for hypotheses to be generated and tested in the contexts in which adoption policies and processes have been shaped and implemented.

With these caveats in mind, four broad areas appear to be of immediate concern. The most relevant need is to understand more fully how methods employed during the review and selection of textbooks can be made more reliable and valid. It follows that if adoption processes are improved, the quality and appropriateness of decisions made during those processes will also be enhanced. Second, educators must better understand the complex political dynamics of adoption processes, including the manner and extent to which those dynamics affect textbook-related decision making. Examples of these factors include relationships between committee members and administrators, the role of parents or special interest groups, the proper role and relative influence of publishers' representatives, communication among committee members, and the manner in which individuals are chosen to serve on adoption committees.

Researchers have largely ignored events and activities that either precede or follow the selection of a particular textbook. Included in this third area of concern are factors such as how districts, schools, or even individuals organize and prepare for an adoption, and how they introduce new textbooks into the classroom. In some states, the adoption of new textbooks becomes the adoption of a new curriculum. The preparation of tests, learning objectives, and teacher training programs are all developed to coincide with the adoption of new textbooks. It is no wonder that when the adoption of textbooks becomes such an all-encompassing event the textbooks take on great importance. There are also many school districts in which the adoption of textbooks is seen as the end of a series of curriculum improvement activities. The new books are shipped to classrooms and administrators believe the curriculum has been revised. There is no question that how textbooks are used is vastly more important than which particular textbooks are used. The selection of new materials should not be seen as the end of curriculum improvement, but should instead be just one activity in an ongoing school improvement program.

Lastly, researchers must continue their attempts to identify the levels at which the most effective textbook adoption decisions can be made. We need to know whether textbook selection is a task more effectively conducted when individual classroom teachers are wholly responsible for decisions, or whether better, more informed decisions are made by grade-, building-, or district-level committees.

Recommendations for Practice

Given the dearth of information pertaining to textbook adoption, it can easily be argued that recommendations aimed at changing adoption processes, at either the state or local level are premature, built upon an unstable foundation, and of limited generalizability. The recommendations discussed below are subject to these limitations. Yet, we believe that they are the most obvious and logical suggestions for improving practices. Thorough consideration should be given to the applicability of each to particular adoption situations. These recommendations are most useful, perhaps, as backdrops against which to orchestrate more intensive, context-specific examinations of textbook adoption practices in each state or local school district.

1. *Textbook review and adoption should be conducted at the local district level rather than at the state level.* The few investigations conducted at the state level have at least aimed at the heart of the issue: Do state-level adoption processes provide local school districts with distinct advantages that they would otherwise not enjoy? More importantly, do "better" textbooks, however defined, find their way more readily into classrooms in these states than in the nonadoption states? Unfortunately, all indications are that maintaining elaborate state-level mechanisms provide no clearly identifiable advantage. Rather,

these processes might be viewed as artifacts of political and professional considerations that are no longer relevant to current educational realities.

The greatest value of textbook adoption may be that it causes educators to review the curriculum periodically. Such reviews are valuable in-service sessions. The discussions as to what a school district is attempting to accomplish, and how best it can be accomplished, can be an important impetus to school improvement.

Teachers and administrators should be the ones who select the tools they feel will be most useful to them. The freedom to select textbooks that are most useful to each district or each classroom teacher may also result in a greater feeling of responsibility and ownership over the curriculum.

Furthermore, there is no evidence that local districts lack either the expertise or the desire to select their own textbooks. Implementing this recommendation would save a considerable amount of money by eliminating state-level adoption committees in twenty-two states across a variety of curriculum areas.

2. *Individuals responsible for the selection of textbooks should receive thorough training in review and evaluation procedures.* Most textbook adoption studies have concluded that classroom teachers typically do not receive training in textbook evaluation. Virtually no preservice preparation in this area is included in present preservice teacher education programs, and much of what teachers do know about textbook evaluation appears to be the result of trial and error or previous experience, rather than any systematic development of knowledge and expertise. Further, individuals selected to serve on textbook adoption committees should be those most competent in a particular subject area, and those who understand and have kept up with issues and research in the teaching of the subject in which books are being reviewed. It is not just experienced teachers who should serve on textbook adoption committees; knowledge of content and pedagogy should be paramount in selecting committee members.

Training sessions should include the examination and review of specific examples of good and bad textbook features. Training that emphasizes the need to identify specific strong and weak features and to support these decisions is necessary. Training sessions should also be opportunities for evaluators to get to know other members of the review committee and to become comfortable with disagreement.

Many school districts use all-teacher votes in selecting textbooks. While such a procedure, on the surface, seems to be a good democratic practice that allows all teachers a voice in selecting materials, the procedure is actually quite flawed. Most teachers who vote have not adequately reviewed the books, they are not sure of the criteria to be used, and they have no training in examining textbooks. If all teachers are to vote, then they should be given training in how to examine textbooks and they should be given the time to review all of the books carefully. Selecting textbooks should not be a popularity poll; it is a professional activity that demands time and effort.

3. *More specific criteria are needed to guide textbook reviews.* An adoption committee's most important initial task should be the identification of criteria to be used in evaluating textbooks. This should begin with a review of the school curriculum and a thorough discussion of what is to be expected from the textbook. Perhaps the greatest problem with textbooks is that they are viewed as the total curriculum in some school districts. Textbooks are tools to be used in implementing a curriculum. Educators need to understand that textbooks are of minor importancce when contrasted with the influence of a teacher.

Committee members should decide, on the basis of school district philosophies and goals, as well as their own beliefs about effective teaching, which factors constitute a "good" textbook in a particular subject area. The tendency to produce long lists of factors to be reviewed should be avoided. There are too many factors to be studied in most adoption evaluations. The existence of long lists usually results in superficial evaluations because of the overwhelming number of factors that reviewers are supposed to evaluate. In addition, when the lists are long it is almost certain that less important and more important factors will take on equal importance.

Probably no more than twenty factors ought to be considered in any textbook review. These should be the factors that committee members feel are the most important in selecting a textbook. These should also be factors on which textbooks are most apt to differ. There are many features of textbooks which committee members know will not differ significantly from textbook to textbook. Armed with this knowledge, the textbook committee can reduce the list to those factors on which books may differ.

Once the review criteria are identified, individuals must agree on the meaning of each factor. One effective way to accomplish this is to identify specific examples of criteria from various textbooks. Bad examples as well as good examples are useful as standards against which each textbook can be evaluated. Committee discussions of these examples are almost certain to increase the reliability and validity of the evaluation process.

After the good and bad examples are selected, and there is agreement that these are indeed good and bad examples, then the committee members should try out their examples with a small sample of textbooks. As a group activity, these sample textbooks can be reviewed and the committee members can decide whether a particular textbook is most like the good example or the bad example. This should be done for each feature that the committee has identified as being essential for the textbook to be selected rather than for the overall quality of the textbook. A rating scale can be devised from this procedure. If a sample textbook is most like the good example, it can be given a score of 5; if it is most like the bad example, it can be given a 1. A score of 3 would indicate an evaluation about halfway between the good and bad standard.

4. *Tryouts of criteria and evaluation procedures are needed.* Procedures and instruments used to evaluate textbooks should be tested before an actual evaluation takes place. Committee members should test all evaluation procedures, preferably with a representative textbook, or with some previously considered text that the district has not used. Revisions in evaluation will almost certainly be necessary, as members discuss the problems (and successes) encountered. Procedures developed in this manner, regardless of how simple or complex, will be of greater reliability and validity than those implemented without the benefit of a tryout.

It is especially important that the tryout phase include opportunities for committee members to discuss differences in the results of the trial evaluation. It is not necessary that all committee members come to the same conclusion about a particular feature of a textbook. It is important, however, that committee members know why they disagree. During the tryout and practice phase, committee members should be asked to defend particular evaluations. It is not enough merely to evaluate; the evaluation must be explained and defended.

5. *Adoption committees must be provided adequate time to conduct thorough evaluations of textbooks.* Many of the recommendations discussed here will likely create the need for more time than is presently allocated for textbook evaluation. Whatever time is required is justifiable, however, given the importance of this task. Educators should be given released time from other responsibilities to engage in adoption related activities. To expect teachers to review textbooks

during lunch hours, planning periods, or on weekends is not only an unprofessional approach, but will also lead to hurried, haphazard, and incomplete reviews.

There are a number of things that can be done to use time more efficiently. One technique that can save considerable time is to identify a small number of criteria that are at the very top of the priority list for the textbook to be selected. This may be three or four factors from the original list of twenty. This "short criteria list" can then be used to cut a long list of potential textbooks to a much smaller list. The decision can be made that any of the texts that do not achieve a good review on these most important criteria will not be included for further study.

In addition, it is not necessary to examine carefully every occurrence of a particular type of lesson. For example, in the review of a reading textbook, the committee may decide that how vocabulary is taught is one of the factors to be reviewed. After the committee has decided what good and poor vocabulary lessons look like, a sample of 10 percent of all the vocabulary lessons can be studied carefully. These lessons should be selected randomly from all the vocabulary lessons in a book. It is much better to study a few lessons carefully than to review all of the lessons superficially.

A typical committee pattern is to have the sixth-grade teachers review the sixth-grade books, the seventh-grade teachers the seventh-grade books, and so on. While teachers want to review the books they may be using in their classrooms, it is usually much better to have teachers select a feature such as the teaching of vocabulary and examine that feature across grade levels. The articulation and development of instruction across grades is more important to student learning than how well a teacher likes a particular book at a particular grade level. In actual practice, it may be possible to have some committee members work across grade levels on various factors while others review all of the factors at one grade level.

6. *Controlled pilot studies are needed to compare programs.* Full-year pilot studies by one teacher with one textbook series are not useful evaluations. Most often those teachers who pilot particular programs become advocates of those programs. There is no specific evidence as to why this seems to be true. However, a number of researchers have reported the phenomenon. Publishers are also aware of this and often try to get the most influential teacher in a school district to pilot their textbooks. Publishers know that if these influential teachers come to like the textbook, they will have an important ally in the adoption process.

Rather than full-year tryouts, there should be short-term tryouts in which a teacher tries out an instructional unit from each of three competing programs. This takes less time and allows the teacher to make a comparison, something that is lacking when a teacher pilots only one program.

These comparative tryouts should be focused on specific factors. The teacher carrying out the pilot should be asked to report on the pilot tryouts first in terms of the specific criteria and then in terms of general features. Tryout teachers should not be selected from only the best teachers, but should include a range of teachers in terms of both experience and background. Tryouts should also be conducted in classrooms that represent the full range of abilities and backgrounds of students who will be expected to use the textbooks.

Comparative tryouts should be conducted by mixing the programs across teachers and across grade levels. For example, if four programs have been selected for tryout, then all programs should be compared to all other programs even though any single teacher will only try out three programs. This means that teacher *one* may try out programs A, B, and C while teacher *two* would try out programs A, C, and D and teacher *three* would try out programs B, C, and D, and so on.

Comparative tryouts are perhaps the most important aspect of a textbook adoption. Tryouts provide opportunities for teachers to find out which aspects of a textbook help them achieve their goals. Tryouts also provide an opportunity for a more careful examination of a textbook. Tryouts are similar to taking a car for a drive before making a purchase. Most car buyers want to see how a car drives before buying. Car buyers usually feel that merely looking at a car on a lot or in a showroom is an inadequate evaluation.

7. *Publishers' contact with reviewers must be designed to determine specific information.* Adoption committees need to consider how much and what type of contact to have with publishers' representatives. To assume that an adversarial relationship exists between publishing companies and educators is not rational. Nor is the argument that educational publishers should be subjected to any more—or any less— stringent regulation than other commercial enterprises with which public schools are involved.

Strict guidelines governing interactions between representatives of publishing companies and committee members, advocated by some educators, and in place in some instances, may be unnecessary. They may also be counterproductive. It would be naive to discount the potentially powerful influence that publishing companies can exert upon adoption committees. Yet, it is also true that publishers and their representatives can be a valuable resource to adoption committees. Well focused, timely presentations can save time, and can also clarify questions that arise before, during, and after review. Eliminating or restricting interactions with publishers, in an attempt to insulate educators from routine marketplace influences, is a superfluous, overly cautious, and pessimistic approach, especially if such controls exist at the expense of educators' access to the resources that publishers make available. In all likelihood, whatever influence does exist is exaggerated by the manner in which districts conduct textbook evaluations. It is easy to understand how committee members might be influenced by salespersons and presentations, particularly if these contacts occur during a time-consuming, pressure-filled process characterized more by a lack of time and expertise than by adequate resources.

FOOTNOTES

1. Charles R. Maxwell, *The Selection of Textbooks* (Boston: Houghton Mifflin, 1921).

2. Nelson B. Henry, "Value of State Textbook Adoptions Is Debatable," *Nation's Schools* 12 (December 1933): 19-24.

3. Lewis W. Burnett, "State Textbook Policies," *Phi Delta Kappan* 33 (January 1952): 257-61. In 1985, Squire listed the following as adoption states: Alabama, Arizona, Arkansas, California, Florida, Georgia, Idaho, Indiana, Kentucky, Louisiana, Mississippi, Nevada, New Mexico, North Carolina, Oklahoma, Oregon, South Carolina, Tennessee, Texas, Utah, Virginia, and West Virginia. See James R. Squire, "Textbooks to the Forefront," *Book Research Quarterly* 1 (Summer 1985): 12.

4. Raymond English, "The Politics of Textbook Adoption," *Phi Delta Kappan* 62 (December 1980): 275-78.

5. Association of American Publishers and National Education Association, *Instructional Materials Selection and Purchase*, rev. ed. (Washington, DC: National Education Association, 1976).

6. E. J. Townsend, "The Textbook Question," *Education* 11 (May 1891): 556-65.

7. C. J. Tidwell, *State Control of Textbooks* (New York: Columbia University Press, 1928).

8. Michael A. Tulley, "A Descriptive Study of the Intents of Selected State-Level Textbook Adoption Processes," *Educational Evaluation and Policy Analysis* 7 (1985): 289-308.

9. Michael A. Tulley and Roger C. Farr, "The Purpose of State-Level Textbook Adoption: What Does the Legislation Reveal?" *Journal of Research and Development in Education* 18 (Winter 1985): 1-16.

10. William L. Marshall, *Should Public Schools Furnish Textbooks Free to All Pupils?* (Chicago: Illinois State Teachers Association, 1898).

11. A. C. Monahan, *Free Textbooks and State Uniformity*, U.S. Bureau of Education Bulletin No. 36 (Washington, DC: U.S. Department of Education, 1915).

12. Predictions made early in the century that free textbook legislation would spread were accurate. By 1950, thirty-four states had mandatory, and fourteen had permissive, free textbook legislation. Thus, free textbooks were available to the vast majority of students in the United States. Free textbooks provided one of the strongest arguments to support state selection of textbooks. William R. Hood, *Free Textbooks for Public Schools*, U.S. Bureau of Education Bulletin No. 50 (Washington, DC: U.S. Bureau of Education, 1924).

13. V. R. Durrance, "Public Textbook Selection in the Forty-Eight States," *Phi Delta Kappan* 33 (January 1952): 262-65.

14. Roger C. Farr and Michael A. Tulley, "Do Adoption Committees Perpetuate Mediocre Textbooks?" *Phi Delta Kappan* 66 (March 1985): 467-71; Harriet T. Bernstein, "The New Politics of Textbook Adoption," *Phi Delta Kappan* 66 (March 1985): 463-66.

15. National Commission on Excellence in Education, *A Nation at Risk: The Imperative for Educational Reform* (Washington, DC: U.S. Department of Education, 1983).

16. Harriet Tyson-Bernstein, *A Conspiracy of Good Intentions: America's Textbook Fiasco* (Washington, DC: Council for Basic Education, 1988).

17. The restrictions as to whether a school district may actually select for use a textbook that is not on the state's approved list vary widely. Most often, a school district can ask for a waiver to use a book that is not on the list. The granting of the waiver is sometimes accompanied with the caveat that state funds may not be used to purchase the books. In these cases, if the district decides to purchase the books, local funds must be used. In reality, few districts vary from the approved state lists because of the extra cost, the increased paper work to receive the waiver, and the assumption that the state lists must contain the best of the available textbooks and they must match the state curriculum better than textbooks not included on the list.

18. Sherry Keith, *Politics of Textbook Selection*, Report No. 81-AT (Palo Alto, CA: Institute for Research on Educational Finance and Governance, Stanford University, 1981).

19. Mike Bowler, "Textbook Publishers Try to Please All, But First They Woo the Heart of Texas," *Reading Teacher* 31 (February 1978): 514-18; Barbara Crane, "The 'California Effect' on Textbook Adoptions," *Educational Leadership* 32 (January 1975): 283-85.

20. Michael A. Tulley and Roger Farr, "Textbook Adoption: Insight, Impact, and Potential," *Book Research Quarterly* 1 (Summer 1985): 4-11.

21. Roger Farr, Michael Tulley, and Larry Rayford, "Selecting Basal Readers: A Comparison of School Districts in Adoption and Nonadoption States," *Journal of Research and Development in Education* 20 (Summer 1987): 59-72.

22. Roger Farr, Mary C. Courtland, Phil Harris, Jetta Tarr, and Linda Treece, *A Case Study of the Indiana State Reading Textbook Adoption Process* (Bloomington, IN: Center for Reading and Language Studies, 1983); Deborah Powell, "Retrospective Case Studies of Individual and Group Decision Making in District-Level Elementary Reading Textbook Selection" (Doct. diss., Indiana University, 1986).

23. Sherry Keith, "Choosing Textbooks: A Study of Instructional Materials Selection Processes for Public Education," *Book Research Quarterly* 1 (Summer 1985): 24-37.

CHAPTER XII

Textbook Use and Teacher Professionalism

ARTHUR WOODWARD AND DAVID L. ELLIOTT

The heavy use of, and in many cases teacher dependence on, textbooks suggests a relationship between the quality of textbooks, effective teaching, and student achievement. Given the central role played by textbooks in schooling, one would expect that they would be a focus of debate about how to improve schooling. However, since the publication of *A Nation at Risk*[1] the focus of school reform has been primarily on the poor performance of students, the low expectations of student achievement, and the school curricula. Textbook quality has not been considered *crucial* in the reform process. Thus, there has been no acknowledgment that textbooks represent an important link between institutional change, teacher professionalism, and improved student success.

Present research evidence indicates that textbooks are widely used, yet most are poorly written and conceived and emphasize lower-order facts and skills rather than higher-order cognitive activities. There is also a body of evidence indicating that teachers feel compelled to follow these materials, flawed though they may be, and policies and practices supporting the use of textbooks are in effect in most school districts across the country. Moreover, when complaints are made about the poor quality of textbook programs, the publishers are quick to point out that they are producing textbooks that sell—those that their market research and sales records indicate most teachers and administrators want.

Textbook Use

Research evidence indicates that textbooks are ubiquitous and widely used in classrooms. As early as 1913, Cubberley noted the important role that textbooks played in instruction.[2] Since then, many studies have confirmed the dominance of the textbook in the classroom. Indeed, a wide range of studies—from the Educational Products Information Exchange Institute's (EPIE) large survey of teachers to Cahen, Filby, McCutcheon, and Kyle's qualitative study of an elementary school[3]—indicate that despite the variation in textbook use one might expect depending on subject, grade, and expertise[4], textbooks are extensively used in schools. In a survey of several thousand teachers, EPIE found that textbooks and other commercially produced instructional materials were the basis for 67 percent of classroom instruction and another 22 percent of classroom instruction was based on nonprint materials.[5] Thus, 89 percent of instructional time was structured around some sort of instructional material. These findings are supported by other less extensive studies. For example, in a survey of 100 senior high school American history classes, Gross found that 79 percent followed one text closely. Gross noted:

For good or for bad, textbooks remain the heart of most United States history courses taught in the senior high schools today. Textbooks also serve to determine the form of course organization through both the content and numbers of units or chapters, as well as by virtue of their approach. . . . As a result, . . . command of textbook content remains a major end in itself.[6]

A report of research on arithmetic texts used in fifty elementary classes noted a high dependence on texts and their use to structure instruction.[7] Bagley's survey of 539 lessons in thirty states also found high reliance on textbooks in high schools.[8] In a survey of 1580 elementary school teachers and 141 elementary school principals, Barton and Wilder found that 98 percent of first-grade teachers and 92 to 94 percent of second- and third-grade teachers used basals on "all or most of the days of the year."[9] Eighty-five percent of elementary principals in the sample considered basal materials "absolutely essential" or "very important." Interestingly, 96 percent of teachers from "better schools" (a term not defined in the article) also thought basals "absolutely essential" or "very important" for teaching reading.

Turner's survey of 339 teachers found that 85 percent of them used basal readers, and that 56 percent of districts represented by the teacher sample required basals to be followed strictly.[10] Weiss found that 90 percent of science and mathematics classes at each grade used textbooks.[11]

Cahen, Filby, McCutcheon, and Kyle's observational study of an elementary school found excessive dependence on reading and mathematics textbooks.[12] The authors noted:

[T]eachers adhered closely to texts in mathematics and reading, even though they recognized difficulties associated with them. . . . Because stories were independent of the skills presented in the reading program, the teachers might have used stories from other sources or skipped those stories. . . . But they didn't. Rather, they adhered to the text virtually verbatim. Texts were not adapted to accommodate the needs or interests peculiar to the Pine Springs children (p. 114).

In a study of the planning activities of twelve teachers, McCutcheon found that the suggestions in mathematics and reading textbooks were the source for 85 to 95 percent of instructional activities in these subject lessons.[13] In a later study of textbook use in an Ohio elementary school, McCutcheon found that nine of ten teachers used the teacher's guide extensively and with few modifications.[14] When teachers modified suggestions in the teacher's guide, the changes consisted of reordering questions, inserting relevant local examples, omitting material considered redundant or too difficult, and omitting activities requiring manipulations, group work, or divergent thinking.

It seems very clear from the studies cited above that textbooks are widely available and heavily used in schools. In some cases teachers absolutely depend on their textbooks and teacher's guides, following them very closely. However, the term dependence should not indicate that teachers necessarily follow lesson plans word for word (even though there may be "scripts" in the teacher's guide) or take every instructional suggestion as gospel (although some teachers may do so). Indeed, to follow a lesson or unit plan ad seriatim may simply be impossible, especially with basal programs, given the time constraints under which teachers work.

Dependence on textbooks as opposed to use of textbooks is an issue at the core of professional practice. If teachers follow closely the scope and sequence of their textbooks, subscribe to the instructional design and approach implicit in that sequence, and rely on lesson plans without significant adjustment or the use of supplementary materials and activities, then it is fair to say that teaching is determined by and dependent on the textbook.

It is important to note that not all teachers are dependent on textbooks. Studies by Stodolsky and by Freeman and Porter suggest that use of textbooks varies quite widely.[15] Some teachers are completely independent, others dependent. Some teachers reorder the sequence of topics, eliminate activities, and so forth. These authors suggest that, in general, teachers tend to teach the core elements of the textbook and the teacher's guide. In other words, teachers will teach the most important core topics, skills, or content.

Given that use does vary, why do some teachers depend on textbooks, others use them selectively, and still others not use textbooks at all? Bagley suggested that experience may be a factor in the degree of textbook use.[16] In his survey of 539 lessons he obtained a "snap shot" of instruction across thirty states. Lessons were varied—some teachers were engaged in project activities, for example—but of those using textbooks he found that 27.3 percent of first-year teachers used the textbook during recitations, 16 percent of teachers with two to five years of experience did likewise, and only 11.7 percent of teachers with over five years of experience used textbooks during recitations. The EPIE research also suggests the effect of experience: a strong relationship was found between teacher experience (number of years teaching) and teachers' perceptions of how well students performed with the materials.[17]

Subject matter expertise is another factor that seems to influence how and what teachers teach. A number of studies, although not primarily concerned with textbooks, indicate that the degree of subject matter knowledge affects teaching. In reporting Hashweh's dissertation on planning by science teachers, Carlsen notes that "high knowledge" teachers planned to ask about material not covered in the text and required students to synthesize material, while "low knowledge" teachers used questions that simply had students recall information found in the textbook.[18] In a study of eleven seventh-grade science classes, Mitman, Mergendoller, and St. Clair found that less reliance on the textbook "seemed associated with higher levels of teacher substantive knowledge and self-confidence, and, to a lesser extent, their dissatisfaction with the 'instructional caliber of texts'."[19]

The amount of time allocated to certain subjects and the nature of the instructional materials may also explain different textbook use. McCutcheon suggests that social studies was allocated relatively little instructional time compared to reading and mathematics.[20] Teachers therefore could not follow the social studies textbook as closely as they did in the two core elementary school subjects. Rather, they were forced to create lessons and select materials and assignments from disparate sources. Lack of time may also explain Weiss's findings that

63 percent of K-6 teachers only "covered" 75+ percent of their science textbooks compared to 89 percent of their mathematics text.[21]

There are a number of possible ways of explaining why teachers use textbooks. As Olson has noted, the written word carries with it an authority that makes it very difficult to dispense with weighty tomes that appear to be so comprehensive and so well designed.[22] Indeed, as Barton and Wilder note, many teachers believe that the contents of texts are based on scientific principles, and administrators, according to Shannon, hold similar opinions.[23] Teachers also think textbooks provide a high level of content expertise that they themselves do not possess and that texts are clear and well organized.[24]

The expectations by parents that their children should use textbooks, the cultural support for using these materials, the seemingly high quality design of textbooks, and their apparent congruence with local curricula, reinforce and support the use of textbooks. Given these factors, it is not surprising that many teachers are well satisfied with their textbooks. Indeed, the National Assessment of Educational Progress (NAEP) for reading found that 90 percent of teachers were satisfied with their instructional materials.[25] The EPIE Institute report of 600 teachers reveals that 80 percent would recommend, without reservation, the material they were using to a teacher with a similar class and that they would willingly use their texts again.[26]

Before discussing the implications of teacher reliance on textbooks, let us explore just how good textbooks are.

The Quality of Textbooks

There is, of course, nothing wrong with using, relying on, or even depending on textbooks if they are of as high quality as many assume them to be. However, as briefly described below, considerable research casts doubt on the quality of textbooks as *instructional* materials. If teachers rely on these materials to any degree, if administrators mandate their use, or if testing systems are closely aligned to textbook content, then it is the textbook, not the teacher that drives instruction.

At both the elementary and secondary levels textbooks have been harshly criticized. The weak treatment of U.S. history in high school history texts has been severely criticized by Cheney, Gagnon, and Sewall.[27] Woodward has found numerous problems with illustrations in textbooks.[28] For example, in the case of high school civics texts, the amount of text is dramatically reduced once front and back matter and illustrations have been taken into account. Photographs and other illustrations take up to 30 percent of the content pages, which themselves represent 80 percent of the complete textbook. Woodward found many illustrations served no discernible instructional purpose, a finding supported by Hunter, Crismore, and Pearson.[29]

Studies by Kantor, Anderson, and Armbruster and by Armbruster and Anderson found texts to be badly written, rambling, inconsistent, disconnected, and "inconsiderate."[30] They concluded that students would have difficulty making sense out of the text prose. Social studies textbooks have been criticized for their avoidance of controversy, their emphasis on superficial coverage of topics, and the inclusion of dated and dubious facts and opinions.[31] Science textbooks have been similarly criticized, both for their reluctance to emphasize science exploration and problem solving and their failure to include evolution.[32]

The Image of the Teacher

As noted above, a number of reasons explain why teachers might rely on textbooks and be quite confident that they are using good quality materials. Most publishers strive to supply materials that will make the task of the teacher as easy as it can be—e.g., by placing minimum responsibility on the teacher for the selection, organization, or planning of activities. In return, they expect the text to be used the way the author intended, since the author is assumed to be better at organizing the course in detail, determining precise instructional language, and supplying key resources.[33]

Even the most capable authors of nationally marketed texts cannot anticipate all the contingencies of local use. As Cronbach points out, a textbook author cannot fully provide for individual differences or capitalize on opportunities in a particular locality. "Education is complex: society is changing, communities have different problems, individual learners have quite different readiness patterns and rates of learning."[34] Thus, the ideal teacher would be one "who has the time, motivation, knowledge, and stamina to study his pupils as individuals, to draw on the whole sweep of the culture around him, to plan each day's work in the light of that day's uniqueness." Since few teachers approach the ideal, most require at least some degree of help from other resources such as textbooks.

However, there is a serious problem in the overreliance on textbooks, as Eisner has indicated. Although a textbook may meet "real needs growing out of a situation that perhaps demands too much from teachers," the "reliance on the textbook and the workbook cultivates a form of pedagogical dependency on the part of teachers. . . . It inadvertently fosters stock curricula responses."[35]

The teacher who is overdependent on the textbook will, year after year, allow textbooks and workbooks the major say in the selection of concepts to be taught, the facts and learning activities to be used, and the timing of instruction. Herrick describes what he calls a "Level III" teacher as one who is

concerned about the interests, questions, and problems of children only incidentally as they can be brought into [or used to enliven] the discussion of textbook materials. The teacher is interested primarily in the speed with which children can pass through the material and the degree to which they can understand it. His evaluations are usually in terms of the facts covered by the text and seldom in terms of the concept to be understood, its relationships to other important ideas, and their import for the problems these children face in their living. The next steps in the curriculum are determined by the next page, next chapter, or some such subdivision of the content to be covered.[36]

In contrast, Herrick's "Level I" teacher, who might be called the true professional, approaches the ideal implied above in that he or she selects the concepts and skills to be taught from the design of the curriculum in the various subject fields and works with students and community resources in planning learning experiences and the use of instructional materials. Such a teacher need not be an expert on all subjects, but should be able (and have the time) to judge among materials published by professional authors and responsible publishers.

Which of these fits the most widely held image of teachers, Level I or Level III? We suspect it is the latter. The "bottom line" appears to be that teachers as a group are considered to be ill-trained and poorly motivated—just average. Not surprisingly, given this dismal image of the teacher, the textbook is seen by scholars, publishers, and school administrators as the insurance policy against inadequate teaching. Thus, in response to public pressure to bring about better student achievement by raising standards, school policymakers and administrators inexorably turn to textbooks and tests in order to demonstrate that things are indeed improving and that teachers are doing their jobs.

The combination of textbook prescriptions and pressure to have students do well on standardized achievement tests results in school systems that trap teachers of all levels of competence into having to rely on textbooks, which they probably had no part in selecting, to prepare students for tests designed to tap learnings that are, if anything, more narrow and restricted than the contents of the textbook programs.

One consequence of a system thus devised is that it works against recruiting and retaining creative teachers—those capable of tailoring their instructional interventions to the characteristics of their students and of taking their students into aspects of the several subject areas and their interrelations that are only hinted at in current textbooks. Such people either become frustrated as a result of the restrictive nature of the system, are promoted to supervisors or administrators, or they leave the system. While some better trained and more experienced teachers will rise above their circumstances and make some improvement on any teaching pattern suggested to them, "one of the stubborn facts of American education is the lack of training, lack of support, and indeed lack of professional morale of large numbers of teachers."[37]

The Case of Reading Basals

Nowhere is the encouragement of teacher dependence on textbooks clearer than in elementary school subjects, especially reading. A popular fifth-grade reading basal teacher's guide[38] shows clearly the low regard in which teachers are held. Several reading lessons are constructed around the story of "The Prison of the Jars." However, before the teacher ventures to have students read the story, it is starkly summarized in three brief paragraphs. Then "basic words" are introduced, accompanied by a detailed lesson plan.

Write the Basic vocabulary on the chalkboard. Have volunteers read and define the words, providing help as necessary. Explain that "*noble*" can be used as an adjective to describe aristocratic actions. You may wish to point out that "*reign*" has the same vowel sound and spelling as "*neighbor*," and that the "*g*" in reign does not stand for a sound. "*Reign*" can be a noun or a verb but in this selection is used as a noun (p. 243).

Teachers following this teacher's guide then ask pupils the following questions:

What is a synonym for *murder*? (*slay*)
What does *reign* have to do with a queen? (*It tells how long she rules.*)

What word is a synonym for *traditions*? (*customs*)
Who were the people most likely to be the king's friends? (*nobles*)
What is another way to say "tried to find"? (*sought*) (p. 243)

"Enrichment words" and "independent writing activities" follow. Finally, the teacher and the students get to the story. However, the teacher is instructed to "set reading purpose," after which comes guided reading. As students read the story the teacher is provided with questions to ask students and with answers to those questions. (In the example given here, L means literal, MI means main idea, CE means cause/effect, DC means drawing conclusions.)

Page 176. Who was Chang Li? (*L-MI. The wise ruler of the kingdom.*)
Page 177. What did the dream tell Chang Li about the demons? (*L-MI. The demons hid during the day but could be known by a red spot.*)
Why was Chang Li frightened? (*CE, DC. He knew the demons in his dream would bring evil.*) (p. 244).

Once the story is completed a detailed plan is provided for the discussion section of the lesson. The lesson plan covers "discuss purpose," "summarize selection," "apply ideas," "focus on comprehension." The road map for the discussion is quite clear:

Discuss Purpose. Ask what steps Chang Li took to save his kingdom once he learned of the danger the demons posed. (*He sought the advice of his nobles. He followed the advice of Whang, the court seer. He recognized that the stones with red spots were the demons. He sealed the demons in jars. He locked the jars in the temple.*) Then help pupils evaluate the actions of Tsin-yin by asking them to explain why he ordered the temple doors to be opened. (*He wanted to show the wisdom of the new ways.*) Allow pupils to discuss what lesson might be learned from the story. (*That new ways are not always better than old ways, that a situation must be studied carefully before a great change is made.*) Conclude the discussion by pointing out that when Chang Li was the ruler, his ways were the new ways. Pupils should be aware that the conflict between old and new has no easy resolution (p. 248).

For the "focus on comprehension" section, five questions are listed along with answers. The lesson then moves into the section on "developing reading skills" where pupils are cycled through a variety of worksheets.

While it is, of course, possible to depart from the lesson plan, in a sense the plan's very comprehensiveness forces commitment. Once a teacher begins to follow the lesson plan, it may be very difficult to depart from it. This reliance is exacerbated by a testing and management system that tracks student progress through criterion-referenced tests and elaborate record-keeping devices.

In reference to basal texts in reading, Duffy, Roehler, and Putnam state: "instead of being given considerable latitude in how to use the basal textbook, as was formerly the case, many teachers are now expected to follow specific directions and procedures regarding its use."[39]

... and Teacher's Guides

Research by Woodward indicates that teacher's guides have changed, as have the images of the teacher they portray.[40] Two reading series published since the 1920s were analyzed. In the early manuals, suggestions were very general. The 1923 Series A guide contained a number of lesson objectives from which the teacher could choose, such as rapid silent reading or making an outline. The guide contained various suggestions for obtaining outside resources to stir pupils' interest in the unit story theme. By the 1930s, as the reading programs began to emphasize the use of interest themes, the guides discussed the kinds of strategies and activities that could be used to introduce the basal themes and stories. In the case of a unit on travel and communication, general objectives were listed and ongoing projects suggested, such as finding out about modern explorers (this was the period of great exploits by explorers and aviators). All suggestions to the teacher were quite general. It was expected that pupils would silently read through each story and read it again and answer a number of questions. Apart from occasional model lesson plans that delved quite deeply into the method of teaching a story, the teacher's guide simply contained lesson objectives such as "to satisfy curiosity." It was assumed that the teacher could and would construct an appropriate lesson.

Basals published in the 1950s continued to follow the pattern established by prior materials. However, in the case of Series A (1956), teachers were to interrupt the silent reading of each story three times to ask specific questions about events and characters in the story. Both Series A and B provided complete study skill and comprehension exercises after each story.

The 1960s teacher's guides reflected the move to greater and greater "support" of the teacher, with the introduction of scripts that the teacher was supposed to read verbatim in introducing a story or assignment, and a general prescriptive approach throughout. By the 1970s, the manuals were more scripted and more comprehensive in the kinds of suggestions and activities they included. Each story was usually preceded by an "overview" and followed by a number of exercises and workbook activities. In the case of Series A (1976), a rigid time schedule was laid out in which thirty-six skill sequences were to take four days each, seventeen bonus selections a total of twenty-three days, and four checkpoint sections a total of eight days.

In the case of the modern reading basal, it is notable that, in contrast to earlier materials, the role of the teacher is that of a manager of lessons, questions, and activities. Because recently published basals and teacher's guides attempt to meet every eventuality and need, teachers are given little discretion as to what can happen in a lesson. Also, because these materials are based on a philosophy of reading that emphasizes the sequential acquisition of hundreds of skills within the framework of a management system that determines pupil placement and assignments, it is not surprising that the teacher's role is that of an administrator of a preplanned lesson. Discretion and judgment, essential elements of teaching and professionalism, are skills that have little place in such a reading lesson.

Lest we think that the kind of contemporary teacher's guides are a phenomenon limited to reading, let us consider elementary social studies. In a fifth-grade social studies textbook by Jarolimek, King, Dennis, and Potter,[41] the lesson plan accompanying the chapter on the "Growth of the English Colonies" shows many of the characteristics of the reading basal guide.

Introducing the Lesson
1. As they read, have students make a list of the colonies that made up each geographic group of colonies: the New England colonies, the middle colonies, and the southern colonies.
2. Ask the class to note the main reason or reasons each colony was founded and to note the date or approximate date the first settlement was made in each (p. 70).

Then the teacher's guide describes teaching the lesson in detail and provides answers to questions teachers are to ask:

Teaching the Lesson
Making a Chart: Draw a chart on the chalkboard with the following vertical column heads: Name of Colony, When Settled. . . . Label the chart "The New England Colonies." As students read pages 70-72, ask them to provide the information for you to fill in the chart.

Making Comparisons: How did the Puritans differ from the Pilgrims in their attitude toward the Church of England? (The Puritans wanted to stay within the Church of England, but they wanted the Church practices purified; the Pilgrims did not want to belong to the Church of England.)

Recognizing Cause and Effect: Why did the Puritans leave Salem to build the new community of Boston? (Because many of the colonists had grown ill from the damp air of Salem.) What other colony have you read about that is environmentally unhealthy? (Jamestown) (p. 71).

The lesson plan also included the following items: Participating in Discussion, Recalling Details, Making Inferences (" 'What do you think Williams's attitude toward the Indians was?' Students should infer that Williams recognized Indians as people with rights."), Locating Places on a Map (" 'Where was Rhode Island in relation to Massachusetts?' South"), and Making Comparisons.

The above example of teaching activities for a chapter may sound quite reasonable, if somewhat lacking in imagination and reference to detail that makes history exciting. Unfortunately, these "lesson plans" become less than impressive when one finds that the answers accompanying activities and so forth are simply mirror images of what is in the pupil's textbook.

Conclusion

Although not all teachers depend on textbooks, the fact that textbooks are so widely available in schools, are used in many classrooms by many teachers, and for all intents and purposes define the curriculum, we must be concerned that textbook use (or overuse) is inimical to professional teaching. We think that the characteristics of Level I teaching described earlier are those that many readers would enthusiastically hope describes all teachers. They would quickly translate Level I characteristics to the teacher or teachers they had— those who seemed able to inspire in students a love of learning and of subject. But, not all teachers are Level I teachers and apart from the exception, it is probably the case that teachers must learn to become superior teachers, just as medical doctors must learn to become superior diagnosticians. The aim of every teacher, then, must be to aspire to professionalism and superiority.

If the attainment of Level I teaching is a process involving hard work, reflection, and experience, it follows that the degree of textbook use, decision making, and so forth will vary. For example, student teachers and beginning teachers are likely to need the teacher's guide and textbook more than someone who has developed skills of class-room management and content organization.[42] Indeed, the identification of trade books and other supplementary materials and the development of lesson plans based on them (which implies movement toward more sophisticated practice) is simply an impossible task for the beginning teacher.

While dependence on textbooks by neophytes is understandable, less justifiable is the heavy use of textbooks by more experienced teachers. This is especially distressing given the poor quality of many instructional materials.

Unfortunately, there is much evidence that teachers, as a whole, find little wrong with textbooks. Perhaps they are captivated by the graphics. The fact remains that a perusal of an elementary social studies textbook, for example, is disquieting, for it will quickly become clear that below the surface, the "story" is confusing and inadequate.

The experience of the curriculum reform movement of the 1960s and 1970s and the reluctance of teachers to accept innovative materials is a cautionary lesson for those who think that it is possible rapidly to change schools, curricula, and practice. Given existing social and organizational structure, it seems that teachers are conditioned to look askance at innovation. Indeed, Crismore found that teachers eagerly and with some relief abandoned a resource-based, middle-school social studies program in favor of a traditional textbook approach.[43] Ironically, it is openness and a willingness to innovate that are at the very heart of professionalism.

The recent efforts to remake teaching into a professional activity are signs that it may be possible to create a social system that encourages and rewards growth, initiative, innovation, and the attainment of professional status. The introduction of career ladders, mentor teacher programs, building-based planning, and the like are promising initiatives. Without such initiatives there seems little prospect of creating an incentive structure that encourages decision making and independence and, as importantly, gives teachers the perspective to judge textbooks in terms of professional practice and instructional goals.

FOOTNOTES

1. National Commission on Excellence in Education, *A Nation at Risk: The Imperative for Educational Reform* (Washington, DC: U. S. Government Printing Office, 1983.

2. Ellwood P. Cubberley, "Textbooks," in *Cyclopedia of Education*, ed. Paul Monroe (New York: Macmillan, 1913).

3. Leonard S. Cahen, Nicola Filby, Gail McCutcheon, and Diane W. Kyle, *Class Size and Instruction* (New York: Longman, 1983); Educational Products Information Exchange Institute (EPIE), *Report on a National Study of the Nature and Quality of Instructional Materials Most Used by Teachers and Learners*, No. 76 (New York: EPIE Institute, 1977).

4. Donald J. Freeman and Andrew C. Porter, "Does the Content of Classroom Instruction Match the Content of Textbooks?" (Paper presented at the Annual Meeting of the American Educational Research Association, New Orleans, 1988); Susan S. Stodolsky, "Is Teaching Really by the Book?" in *From Socrates to Software: The Teacher as Text and the Text as Teacher*, ed. Philip W. Jackson and Sophie Haroutunian-Gordon, Eighty-eighth Yearbook of the National Society for the Study of Education, Part 1 (Chicago: University of Chicago Press, 1988), pp. 159-84.

5. Educational Product Information Exchange Institute, *Report on a National Study of the Nature and Quality of Instructional Materials.*

6. Richard E. Gross, "American History Teachers Look at the Book," *Phi Delta Kappan* 33 (1952): 290.

7. "Use of Arithemtic Texts," *Phi Delta Kappan* 33 (1952): 282.

8. William C. Bagley, "The Textbook and Methods of Instruction," in *The Textbook in American Education*, ed. Guy M. Whipple, Thirtieth Yearbook of the National Society for the Study of Education, Part 2 (Bloomington, IL: Public School Publishing Company, 1931), pp. 7-26.

9. Allen H. Barton and David E. Wilder, "Research and Practice in the Teaching of Reading: A Progress Report," in *Innovation in Education*, ed. Matthew B. Miles (New York: Teachers College, Columbia University, 1966).

10. Rebecca R. Turner, "How the Basals Stack Up," *Learning* 17 (1988): 62-64.

11. Iris R. Weiss, *Report of the 1985-86 National Survey of Science and Mathematics Education* (Research Triangle Park, NC: National Science Foundation, 1987).

12. Cahen, Filby, McCutcheon, and Kyle, *Class Size and Instruction.*

13. Gail McCutcheon, "Elementary School Teachers' Planning for Social Studies and Other Subjects," *Theory and Research in Social Education* 9 (1981): 45-66.

14. Gail McCutcheon, "How Do Elementary School Teachers Plan? The Nature of Planning and Influences on It," *Elementary School Journal* 81 (1980): 4-23.

15. Freeman and Porter, "Does the Content of Classroom Instruction Match the Content of Textbooks?"; Stodolsky, "Is Teaching Really by the Book?"

16. Bagley, "The Textbook and Methods of Instruction."

17. Educational Products Information Exchange Institute, *Report on a National Study of the Nature and Quality of Instructional Materials.*

18. William S. Carlsen, "Why Do You Ask? The Effect of Science Teacher Subject-Matter Knowledge on Teacher Questioning and Classroom Discourse" (Paper presented at the Annual Meeting of the American Educational Research Association, Washington, DC, 1987.

19. Alexis L. Mitman, John R. Mergendoller, and George St. Clair, "The Role of Textbooks in Middle Grade Science Teaching" (Paper presented at the Annual Meeting of the American Educational Research Association, Washington, DC, 1987), p. 28.

20. McCutcheon, "Elementary School Teachers' Planning."

21. Weiss, *Report of the 1985-86 National Survey of Science and Mathematics Education.*

22. David R. Olson, "On the Language and Authority of Textbooks," *Journal of Communication* 30 (1960): 186-96.

23. Barton and Wilder, "Research and Practice in the Teaching of Reading"; Patrick Shannon, "The Use of Commercial Reading Materials in American Elementary Schools," *Reading Research Quarterly* 19 (1983): 68-85; idem, "A Retrospective Look at Teachers' Reliance on Reading Materials," *Language Arts* 59 (1982): 844-53.

24. Elliot W. Eisner, "Why the Textbook Influences Curriculum," *Curriculum Review* 26 (1987): 11-13; Weiss, *Report of the 1985-86 National Survey of Science and Mathematics Education.*

25. Archie LaPointe, "The State of Instruction in Reading and Writing in U. S. Elementary Schools," *Phi Delta Kappan* 68 (1986): 135-38.

26. Educational Products Information Exchange Institute, *Report on a National Study of the Nature and Quality of Instructional Materials.*

27. Lynne V. Cheney, *American Memory* (Washington, DC: National Endowment for the Humanities, 1987); Paul Gagnon, "Democracy's Jewish and Christian Roots," *American Educator* 11 (1987): 22-23; idem, "Democracy's Untold Story," *American Educator* 11 (1987): 19-26, 46; Gilbert T. Sewall, "American History Textbooks: Where Do We Go from Here?" *Phi Delta Kappan* 69 (1988): 552-58.

27. Arthur Woodward, "Photographs in Textbooks: More Than Pretty Pictures?" (Paper presented at the Annual Meeting of the American Educational Research Association, San Francisco, 1986); idem, "Textbooks: Less Than Meets the Eye," *Journal of Curriculum Studies* 19 (1987): 511-26; idem, "Stress on Visuals Weakens Texts," *Education Week,* 9 March 1988.

29. Barbara Hunter, Avon Crismore, and P. David Pearson, "Visual Displays in Basal Readers and Social Studies Textbooks," in *The Psychology of Illustration,* Vol. 2, *Instructional Issues,* ed. Harvey A. Houghton and Dale M. Willows (New York: Springer-Verlag, 1987).

30. Bonnie B. Armbruster and Thomas H. Anderson, "Structures of Explanation in History Textbooks, or So What if Governor Stanford Missed the Spike and Hit the Rail?" *Journal of Curriculum Studies* 16 (1984): 181-94; R. N. Kantor, Thomas H. Anderson, and Bonnie B. Armbruster, "How Inconsiderate Are Children's Textbooks?" *Journal of Curriculum Studies* 15 (1983): 61-72.

31. David L. Elliott, Kathleen Carter Nagel, and Arthur Woodward, "Do Textbooks Belong in Elementary Social Studies?" *Educational Leadership* 42 (1985): 22-25; Jane Newitt, "The Pedagogy of Fear and Guilt: How Textbooks Treat the World Economy," *Social Education* 48 (1984): 47-48; Paul C. Vitz, *Censorship: Evidence of Bias in Our Children's Textbooks* (Ann Arbor, MI: Servant Press, 1986; idem, "Religion and Traditional Values in Public School Textbooks: An Empirical Study," in Paul C. Vitz, *Equity in Values Education: Do the Values Education Aspects of Public School Curricula Deal Fairly with Diverse Belief Systems?*, Section 1, Part 2, NIE-G84-0012 (New York: New York University, 1985); Arthur Woodward, David L. Elliott, and Kathleen Carter Nagel, "Beyond Textbooks in Elementary Social Studies," *Social Education* 50 (January 1986): 50-53.

32. David L. Elliott, Kathleen Carter Nagel, and Arthur Woodward, "Scientific Illiteracy in Elementary School Science Textbooks," *Journal of Curriculum Studies* 19 (1986): 73-76; Gerald Skoog, "The Topic of Evolution in Secondary School Biology Textbooks, 1900-1977," *American Biology Teacher* 49 (1987): 621-40. Arthur Woodward and David L. Elliott, "Evolution and Creationism in High School Textbooks," *American Biology Teacher* 49 (1987): 164, 166-70.

33. Eisner, "Why the Textbook Influences Curriculum."

34. Lee J. Cronbach, "The Text in Use," in *Text Materials in Modern Education,* ed. Lee J. Cronbach (Urbana: University of Illinois Press, 1955), p. 193.

35. Eisner, "Why the Textbook Influences Curriculum."

36. Virgil E. Herrick, "The Concept of Curriculum Design," in *Toward Improved Curriculum Theory*, ed. Virgil E. Herrick and Ralph W. Tyler, Supplementary Education Monographs, No. 71 (Chicago: University of Chicago Press, 1950).

37. Cronbach, "The Text in Use," p. 193.

38. Theodore Clymer, Roselmina Indrisano, Dale D. Johnson, P. David Pearson, and Richard L. Venezky, *Ride the Sunrise* (Lexington, MA: Ginn and Co., 1985).

39. Gerald G. Duffy, Laura R. Roehler, and Joyce Putnam, "Putting the Teacher in Control: Basal Reading Textbooks and Instructional Decision Making," *Elementary School Journal* 87, no. 2 (1987): 357-66.

40. Arthur Woodward, "Taking Teaching Out of Teaching and Reading Out of Learning to Read: A Historical Study of Reading Teacher's Guides, 1920-1980," *Book Research Quarterly* 2 (1986): 53-73; idem, "Overprogrammed Materials: Taking the Teacher Out of Teaching," *American Educator* 10 (1986): 26-31.

41. John Jarolimek, Allen Y. King, Ida Dennis, and Florence Potter, *The United States* (New York: Macmillan, 1987).

42. Deborah L. Ball and Sharon Feiman-Nemser, "Using Textbooks and Teacher's Guides: A Dilemma for Beginning Teachers and Teacher Educators," *Curriculum Inquiry* 18 (1988): 401-423.

43. Avon Crismore, "Students' and Teachers' Perceptions and Use of Sixth Grade Social Studies Textbooks in Champaign Middle Schools" (December 1981). ERIC ED 232-952.

Section Four
CURRICULUM AND INSTRUCTIONAL MATERIALS IN THE FUTURE

CHAPTER XIII

Alternative Technologies as Textbooks and the Social Imperatives of Educational Change

STEPHEN T. KERR

Most adults have in their heads an image of a textbook: a familiar friend or antagonist from school days past, a bit worn around the edges (covered with a ubiquitous hard paper cover that gradually collected notes and doodles as the year progressed); a sullen companion of late nights spent mastering material for an exam; an object of half-bored classroom activity, when working problems. The textbook was the teacher's amanuensis, an affirmation through its symbolic link with the world of knowledge of the teacher's authority and the student's responsibility in class, and a kind of continuing reminder (in days when homework was common) of the duties of studenthood. But the images are probably not powerful ones, as the textbook itself (at least in the image of those who used it) is not often viewed as an influential participant in the culture of the school.

Might textbooks become more powerful for students and teachers? Might they become not only the passive containers for the accumulated wisdom of society and its teachers, but also active stimulants of students' thought and of teachers' instructional activity? These hopes—perennial ones when new media of instruction have come upon the scene—have been raised again in recent years by the advent of such new methods of packaging and delivering instructional materials as video tape, videodisc, microcomputers, CD-ROM (Compact Disc-Read Only Memory), and telecommunication networks.

194

The vision presented by proponents of these new approaches is attractive: students work at their own pace, in environments where progress and evaluation are nonjudgmental and hence nonthreatening; interest and motivation are piqued by novel methods of presentation (graphics, color, animation), and by elements of fantasy, challenge, and creativity inherent in the media themselves; achievement rises because the materials themselves give rapid, frequent, and exact feedback on a student's work; thinking skills and the ability to handle "higher-order" cognitive tasks also improve. In their most developed form, materials become not mere collections of organized information, but true learning tools: they incorporate content, but also provide instructional helpmates that enable the learner to analyze and pose questions, retrieve information, organize it to solve problems, and check results rapidly. They also allow the student to self-diagnose learning difficulties. As familiarity with the tool grows, the student progressively becomes master of both tool and content.

In this chapter I review the origins of these ways of thinking about technologically enhanced alternative materials in American schooling. I then examine new alternatives that have recently become available (especially computers and related technologies), and the usefulness and capabilities of these materials as "textbooks." I conclude with a look at possible futures, and the likelihood of further incorporation of electronic text materials into classrooms of the twenty-first century, given probable continuities and changes in schools.

Alternative Materials as Textbooks: A Heritage of Problems

During the years of this century, American teachers have witnessed a parade of new technologies for instruction: photographs, motion picture film, sound recordings, filmstrips, slides and overhead transparencies, television and television recordings in several formats (including cassettes and videodiscs), programmed instruction, and, most recently, computer-assisted and computer-managed instruction. Some of these formats merged and created new blends: sound filmstrips, super-8 film cartridges, sound-slide presentations, materials under computer control but harnessing the storage capacity of optical media (videodisc, CD-ROM, and CD-I [Compact Disc-Interactive]).

In each case, large claims were made initially for the value of the new approaches in meeting student needs and providing important new instructional capabilities. These predictions were invariably followed by modest changes—the development of software that was often disappointing in terms of its quality and novelty, mild interest by a smaller number of teachers than originally thought, smaller (or more frequently no) gains in student achievement or thinking ability, and (importantly for our work here) the continued dominance of traditional textbooks as the preferred classroom material for most classroom teachers.

Why has this been so? Why have American educators been so entranced with the new, yet so bound by traditional patterns where real teaching practice is concerned? The answers are important as we seek to understand the impact new forms of technology may have on traditional textbooks.

WHAT IS AVAILABLE IN SCHOOLS

In material terms, the spread of traditional audio-visual means of instruction has been a success story for American education. Statistics show that the average elementary school now has one overhead projector for each classroom, almost as many cassette players or recorders, at least one film projector and/or video tape player, and probably at least one computer.[1]

How much and how well these devices are used depends in part on the adequacy of school and district software collections. In some cases those collections will be highly controlled, with materials flowing to and from the classroom from a central office; in other cases, individual schools manage a large part of the collection that is used. In any event, the quantity of material available is not likely to be very large. Many alternative media (e.g., videotapes) are thought to be expensive in comparison with textbooks, and use is thus routinely restricted to whole-class instruction. Districts typically allocate only a small portion of the total instructional materials budget (itself never more than a few percent of annual total expenditures) for software acquisition. This makes the development and dissemination of alternative materials effectively a "nonmarket" for educational publishers. Most will only create nontextbook products to support product lines of traditional texts.

PATTERNS OF USE

There are relatively few statistics on teachers' actual use of alternative instructional materials. Part of the reason lies in the fact that they have never become an integral enough part of classroom life to warrant close attention by educational researchers. In one attempt to reckon the extent of use of film, radio, and television, Cuban concluded that only about 1 percent of class time was spent using such materials (compared with up to 90 percent dominated by use of traditional textbooks).[2]

But such media have found a niche, if not a large one. Televised instructional programs are used more intensively at the lower grade levels than in secondary schools, primarily due to the popularity of such programs as "Sesame Street."[3] Audio materials (e.g., Language Master cards) and filmstrips also have a larger place at the elementary level. Overhead transparencies, perhaps the humblest of alternative media in terms of their complexity and sophistication, have nonetheless proven enormously popular. This popularity is anomalous and therefore something we should examine here in more detail.

Invented in the 1930s, the overhead projector did not come into wide use in the United States until the 1960s. At that point, its use spread rapidly.[4] Why did the overhead projector achieve such quick and general success? First, overheads are simple: creating materials and using the hardware requires minimal training and minimal advance preparation. Second, the overhead reinforces existing ways of teaching: the teacher faces the students, may talk to the class, and may switch transparencies or turn off the projector. Third, the overhead has advantages that a chalkboard does not: material may be shown graphically in segments and overlays, revealed progressively, annotated with student comments, and/or revised as the lesson progresses. Finally, the overhead is relatively cheap: for the cost of a single complete computer system, one might reasonably purchase three or four overhead projectors, together with carts and several years' supply of associated consumables (transparencies, marking pens). These advantages are mundane but nonetheless practical.

Other alternative materials have penetrated the educational system less evenly. Language laboratories and interactive audio systems enjoyed brief flurries of popularity in the 1960s and 1970s respectively; films and video have always had eager users among teachers, but the enthusiasm of many of them was often tempered by difficulties in finding and using titles that would support the curriculum. Indeed, more than one observer has noted the restraining influence exerted by the practical problems of arranging for the use of alternative media in schools—problems that include ordering titles long in advance, having special facilities available, spending time previewing materials, learning how to operate hardware effectively, and breaking with established tradition.[5]

Software for alternative instructional systems comes from a variety of sources. There are series of supplementary films, videotapes, and sound recordings produced and distributed by major publishers as accompaniments to traditional texts; and there are similar materials independently produced and marketed by firms specializing in alternative media. Teachers and students may also produce their own materials, but often with considerable difficulty, as anyone might attest who has watched the final screening of films or videotapes from a class devoted to amateur production.

ATTITUDES AND THEIR EFFECTS

Why the relatively spotty use of alternative media in comparison with traditional texts in American schools? Problems of access, cost, and production, as well as the difficulty of matching curriculum to particular materials explain some of the hesitancy of teachers to use alternative media. General uncertainty about the use of technology and lack of exposure to alternatives during teacher training also play a role, especially where newer approaches such as computers and video are concerned.[6] And there is likely something even more pervasive here: an assumption that anything other than a traditional textbook is not really worth using in the classroom. The roots of these attitudinal problems are worth exploring here.

Both teachers and students share an assumption deeply rooted in the origins of alternative media as entertainment, an assumption that using such materials as films, videotapes, or even overly pictorial books is not really education—only entertainment. Teachers are conditioned to believe this from their student teaching experience and from early evaluations by principals and supervisors. Films and other nontext materials are often relegated to the role of providing a respite when a substitute teacher takes over a class or during afternoon hours in elementary schools when children are perceived to need a mental "break" before returning to real work.[7] Many appear to share the attitude of a principal on arriving at a classroom to do an observation and finding the teacher showing a film: "I'll come back when you're teaching."

The attitude appears to be shared by students, if only on an unconscious level. Recent empirical studies of students' attributions of success and failure in learning suggest that print is perceived as a difficult medium from which to learn, while television and film are thought to be comparatively easy.[8] Students consequently tend to assume that if they fail to learn from a textbook, the fault probably lies with the inherent complexity of its content and the way it is presented, rather than in the student's lack of effort or understanding. On the other hand, failing to learn from a film or videotape suggests that the problem is the student's own, since those media are seen as intrinsically simple.

Overcoming this assumption that one can mentally "put one's feet up" when a film is to be shown takes effort on the part of both teachers and students. Asking a series of preliminary questions to focus student attention on specific, instructionally relevant details in a film before showing it has been shown to increase later retention of factual information.[9] Other techniques have also been recommended as ways of increasing students' learning from nonprint materials: reviewing related material from the textbook or earlier lessons, stopping the film or tape in order to ask questions of students, saying there will be a quiz on the material to be covered, having students take notes, etc. Note that most of these approaches serve to place the alternative media in a setting that reminds the student of the instructional, rather than entertainment, purpose of the presentation. Whether this *should* be the case is another question, one that we will have occasion to return to later.

FORMAL FEATURES OF ALTERNATIVE MEDIA

Since it is clear that alternative media have had difficulty finding a strong place in classroom practice, it may be valuable for us to ask which of their formal features (in addition to the assumption of their entertainment role, noted above) contribute to this problem. The discussion here takes us back some twenty years to claims advanced about the importance of using film and video in education.

There was a brief flurry of interest in the idea of "visual literacy" at the time when television and film were seen as the "new media" of education—instructional approaches that would be "more relevant" and thus more able to engage students' interest and attention. The assertions of Marshall McLuhan, John Culkin, John Debes, and others about the inherently more involving nature of film and video were translated by some enthusiasts into claims for the increased instructional potential of these approaches.[10] Programs in visual literacy were started in many schools around the country, and some entire curricula were structured around the notion of teaching students to be both proficient consumers and producers of visual materials.[11]

But these programs ran into several serious difficulties, some practical and others (more importantly) conceptual. Practically it proved impossible to generate the quantity and variety of software needed to support a full curriculum based on visual imagery. And conceptually several things rapidly became clear. Visual literacy was enormously problematic to define. For some it meant the ability to "read," although what was to be read (underlying assumptions, production techniques, or attempts at attitudinal manipulation) was often unclear. Others focused on the ability to "write" (produce) visuals, but to what degree of proficiency? Attempts to be more specific about the nature of visual literacy concluded that there were fundamental differences between printed verbal and pictorial materials that made impossible a general translation of principles from one to the other—the difficulty of specifying negative relationships, for example.[12]

There were additional features of visual materials that made their use difficult as a regular part of the educational program. Such production techniques as use of color and rapid scene cutting were frequently borrowed from commercial film and video, sometimes increasing the affective impact of a piece, but perhaps also lessening its instructional potential. (The critique of the "Sesame Street" series, for example, made this issue a central one.)

Perhaps the most serious problem was the realization that, while it may be desirable for students to think more deeply about the barrage of visually oriented materials they were exposed to on a regular basis, one of the ultimate principles of schooling in any society must be to provide students with fundamental skills in print literacy. This problem is large enough in itself to occupy a good portion of the total curriculum at the elementary level, with no guarantee of success even there.

THE IMPORTANCE OF DESIGN

As initial enthusiasm over the use of alternative media cooled, scholars looked again at a rather disappointing sixty-year heritage of research results. They concluded that, other things being equal, the instructional effect of the medium of presentation itself is negligible. Factors more likely to encourage student learning are the quality of design present in the materials and the completeness with which instructional strategies are specified.[13]

In the case of some video-based and many computer-based materials, considerable care has been devoted to the initial specifications of the product—defining what the program is to do, how it will do it, selecting and organizing content very intentionally to meet those goals, providing a range of student activities designed to enable learners with different levels of preparation and ability to attain those goals, and building in appropriate evaluation instruments to measure students' achievement. It is these designed qualities of the materials, not the fact that they are delivered through one or another technological means, that promote learning. This approach therefore suggests that a teacher working alone or with a traditional text, given sufficient time and preparation, could achieve results similar to those obtained through the use of alternative programs.

One consequence of this realization has been a growing vision of alternative instructional materials and textbooks not as dissimilar, but as sharing many essential features. There has been, for example, increased focus on the application of instructional design principles to traditional textbooks and other text-like materials.[14] At the same time, there has been a search for features that uniquely define alternative materials, in the realization that there necessarily continue to be important underlying differences among approaches. Administrative flexibility and the possibility of addressing a variety of student needs with a single set of materials are clearly among the advantages of using film, video, or computer-based materials. What the other distinctive features of various media are remains a matter of some dispute—edited motion visuals (film, video), for example, can easily compress or expand time through the use of time-lapse or slow-motion photography.[15] But the fundamental cognitive effects of these features are still not well understood. And some teachers see the focus on highly specified and designed materials as inimical to their own efforts in any event.[16]

Several conclusions can be drawn from this review of the fate of earlier alternative instructional materials. First, strong barriers of tradition and other "situational constraints" make the use of such materials impractical for teachers; while the committed are able to overcome these obstacles, there is a pattern that requires effort to break. Second, teacher and student attitudes toward alternative materials also militate against nontext materials; alternatives have been seen as enjoyable, but also therefore as frivolous or unworthy of serious use. Third, in spite of these problems, there are some things that the alternatives can do uniquely well—allow students to work freely at their own pace, for example, and show the world in ways otherwise impossible. Finally, the value of careful design and specification of all types of materials has come to be seen more clearly over the past few years, but this has also left some teachers uncertain about their own role in a classroom in which highly designed (and therefore "teacher-proof") materials predominate.

Computer-Based Alternatives and Textbooks as "Cognitive Technologies"

Computers, together with a range of related technologies for storage, connection, and dissemination (videodisc, CD-ROM and CD-I, local area networks, desktop publishing) have raised for educators once again the possibility of radical change in the type and capability of basic educational materials. Many commentators see in these approaches the possibility of transforming classroom practice in ways that older technologies could not.[17] But given the uncertainties and problems noted above, what real advantages do technologically based alternatives (or additions) to traditional textbooks have for classroom practice? We will examine what new technologies have recently become available and how those materials are being used in schools. Then we will look at what unique capabilities they have and how those might be turned to good instructional effect.

THE CURRENT SCENE: COMPUTERS AND SOFTWARE MULTIPLY

Computers spread rapidly in American schools during the early 1980s. Whereas only 18.2 percent of all K-12 schools had a computer available in 1981, by 1985 fully 86 percent did, and that figure was close to 95 percent at the secondary level.[18] By 1988, the total number of machines had grown to somewhere between 1.2 and 1.7 million.[19] In an interesting contrast to earlier technological changes that were usually mandated from above by central office administrators, the computer onslaught was encouraged by teachers and parents, often to the extent (in the ubiquitous anecdote) of being funded by the proceeds of PTA bake sales.

Purchases of software to run on computers also grew rapidly during this period. By 1987, school districts were spending about $170 million per year on instructional programs for school computers, an amount equal to about $4.00 per student.[20] While this is a substantial figure, it is in fact a minor segment of the overall K-12 market for instructional materials (about $35 per student per year).[21] Software purchased for use on instructional computers increasingly emphasizes "tool uses"—application programs such as word processors and spreadsheets.[22] Some 81 percent of large school districts indicated they planned to spend more on such programs during 1988, while only 25 percent indicated they would spend more on computer-managed programs to provide direct instruction.[23]

Other new technologies have also captured educators' attention. While videodisc and CD-ROM systems are still exotica for most schools, awareness of their potential is spreading. Many districts have acquired laser printers and desktop publishing programs to allow them to format and print school newsletters, documents for school events and ceremonies, and notices that students take home to parents. Individual teachers have made programs such as "Print Shop" (a program that allows simple graphics to be created with a dot-matrix printer) the most popular software titles of the decade. Five such programs were among the ten top-sellers in the mid-1980s.[24] And there is rising interest in educational networks and "utilities" that would allow teachers to communicate with one another across district and state boundaries.

While these developments sound impressive, they must be tempered with the realization that the hardware and software now in place do not allow for an abundance of time using the computer: averages range from about thirty-five minutes per week at the elementary level to ninety minutes at the secondary level,[25] not enough to provide a great range of experiences or the opportunity to cultivate many of the skills intended by the enthusiasts. To increase the computer:student ratio from 1:30 to 1:3, a change many see as desirable for more powerful and pervasive classroom application, would require adding 12 million computers to the installed base at a cost of $4.2 billion.[26]

Problems of hardware incompatibility continue to plague schools and districts, as does uncertainty over whether to stress software to be used on single, free-standing microcomputers, or to opt for networked configurations (sometimes using proprietary hardware) and larger, integrated packages of instructional software. Given the relatively small size of the software market, the number of different school districts with independent instructional and purchasing policies, and the high costs and long lead time required for the development of software, it may be pointless to expect major publishers to take on the task of instructional software development on a large scale.[27]

NEW TECHNOLOGIES: PATTERNS OF USE

Given the spurt of enthusiasm for computer use and the rapid purchase of machines and software, it was perhaps inevitable that questions of how to integrate these new approaches effectively into the everyday life of schools and classrooms were relegated to second place. A series of studies conducted during 1982-83 and 1985-86 by Henry Becker of the Center for the Social Organization of Schools at Johns Hopkins University demonstrated the variation in patterns of use. Initially, computers were used heavily to teach about computers—that is, in courses dealing with "computer literacy" and the fundamentals of computer programming—and also in mathematics classes. Use was also heavier at first at the high school level.[28]

As educators became more sophisticated in their thinking about how computers might mesh with teaching, alternative uses began to proliferate. Computers increasingly came to be used in writing and language arts classes, as well as in other subjects (social studies, science, foreign languages). If teachers' first impressions of the computer's role revolved around notions of computer literacy, they rather quickly came to see an expanded role for computers and software as *tools* to aid students in a variety of ways, but most importantly in writing and in mathematics and science.[29] Nonetheless, the first use of computers in most districts continues to be to teach about computers.[30] Given the likely spread of computers into all aspects of life and improvements in programming environments and tool software, some have characterized this approach as "the drivers' education of the 1990s"—a fundamentally redundant exercise, given social and technological changes.

Other important variations have to do with student sex and socioeconomic status (SES). Males were more likely at first to get access to computers, to use them before and after school for game-playing, and to focus on learning how to program the machines; girls tended to want to use the devices for word-processing. Some districts solved this problem by segregating computer literacy classes by sex, by scheduling machines to allow individuals assured access, or through in-service work with teachers to sensitize them to the potential problem. While there was some concern at first that low-SES students were using computers primarily for drill-and-practice applications while their higher-SES peers had the opportunity to learn programming skills and how to use applications software, these concerns seem to have been addressed by shifted patterns of more egalitarian use over the past few years. Nonetheless, a major study of computer capabilities of third-, seventh-, and eleventh-grade students showed a lower level of computer competence among blacks and Hispanics.[31]

Many teachers are willing at least to explore the new technologies for instruction, although many also have reservations about what technology can and should do in schools.[32] Early studies of how computers came to be used in schools suggested that some teacher "buffs" typically took the lead in modeling use of the new technology.[33] Other important determinants of teachers' use include the base of technical support a district or school offers, the opportunity to participate in selecting programs, and the possibility of earning external (monetary) rewards.[34] Most teachers using computers, however, report no radical changes in their teaching practices attributable directly to the technology.[35]

UNIQUE INSTRUCTIONAL CAPABILITIES AND THEIR EFFECTS

Given the probability that the hardware itself through which instructional materials are delivered does not have powerful effects, are there unique capabilities that the computer-based hardware-software combinations now coming into wide use make available? To what extent, in other words, and in what ways do computers and their cousins offer teachers new ways of encouraging students to learn, and what kinds of learning can the new technologies foster most ably?

Several critical features stand out: the ability to monitor actively student work and offer suggestions for improvement or revision; the possibility both to explore the world in a more diverse and complicated way than before, and to feel personally in control of that exploration; the opportunity to work collaboratively on instructional problems with peers widely separated in physical space; the chance continuously to edit reality, to see intellectual products as inherently mutable; the capability to show information in different ways, and to change easily how information is represented to meet a different set of needs or preferences; and finally, as access becomes easier, the requirement of being able to sift quantities of information for significance and relate it to specific problem-solving tasks. All these warrant our consideration here.

The addition to instructional software of "intelligence" is one of the most attractive possibilities in view today. Intelligent programs of computer-assisted instruction (CAI) monitor student progress in a more flexible and intense way than traditional CAI programs. They may not only respond to student errors by suggesting remedial exercises, but also pose questions to the student to determine the appropriate type of remediation required. They may keep track of a student's right and wrong answers, survey that pattern of responses as it develops, invisibly alter materials presented, and at the same time provide feedback to the teacher.[36]

Intelligent tool or application programs work in other ways. Rather than providing feedback on the correctness of responses, intelligent application software analyzes structure, syntax, and usage in a student's work as it is being created. A useful survey of the growing variety of intelligent programs that can aid in the teaching of writing, for example, coined the term "cognitive technology."[37] Such programs benefit students in that they not only provide analytical guidance on the quality of the work being prepared as it is under way, but they may also model for the student the requisite cognitive processes involved. For example, an outline-generating program might not only allow a student to prepare an overview of a piece of writing before beginning, but also provide a structure that leads to a more complete, effective, and complex written product. Such programs could prompt the student to set goals, evaluate, revise, and so on. Inasmuch as such processes appear to be connected with good and successful writing, making them clear and explicit to students as they work could lead to improved cognitive development in particular task domains. The prospects for such tools in other fields are promising, but as yet largely undeveloped.

Exploring the world is certainly not something that only computers enable students to do. But the variety of explorations permitted by complex simulation programs and databases using videodisc or CD-ROM technology can extend for the average student a range of possibilities that only students in schools with extraordinarily well-equipped libraries and other facilities could have hoped to enjoy a few years ago. It is not merely the scale of exploration that is important here, but also the chance that it offers the student to be in control, to manipulate the world in a direct, personal, and powerful way. When a student works with a simulation program that allows direct manipulation of an entire micro-climate or micro-environment, there is an element of engagement (fantasy, challenge, control, creativity) present that is lacking in less completely stimulating surroundings. Malone calls this "intrinsically motivating instruction"; Laurel calls it "pleasurable engagement"; Carroll and Thomas call it "fun."[38] Designers of software increasingly are trying to provide users with a sense of being directly in control of actions that are taking place under their command.[39]

Collaborative work is an opportunity that both teachers and students in an earlier era simply lacked. Yes, one could correspond, but the delays and uncertainties entailed often made it not worth the time and effort; for students, access to telephones in schools was a rare privilege, not an everyday expectation. Computers linked to either local or wider networks make direct communication with peers feasible and may encourage a wider view of one's place in the world. For teachers, the possibility of working with other teachers and sharing instructional tactics may be an important step in further professionalization of their occupation. For students, it offers the chance to comment jointly on distant friends' work, and perhaps to participate in collaborative projects involving joint collection and analysis of data.

The advent of word processors changed the attitudes of many students toward the work of writing. Now what used to be drudgery (the reworking and rewriting of compositions) has become easy; the focus may go on thoughtful improvement rather than on the mechanics of reproduction. Similar tool programs now offer the possibility of editing numbers (spreadsheets), other data (databases), and even visual images. As all of these applications become more widespread, the notion that there is a single, canonical version of any document may wither away, and all materials may come to be seen as inherently mutable. The advent of desktop publishing and fast laser printers that produce new copies on demand will accelerate this phenomenon. It remains to be seen what this will do to students' views of the worth of traditional texts and printed materials in general.

Together with the ability to edit and modify material comes the ability to represent it in diverse ways. Spreadsheet and database programs already offer the user the possibility of creating alternate "views" of identical information—showing columns of figures as pie charts or bar graphs, for example, or selecting certain items from a particular record in a database to display on-screen at any given time. As interface and display technology become more sophisticated, it is likely that further options will be developed, perhaps under user control or perhaps under intelligent control from within the program itself. These might, for example, allow students who prefer to see data displayed in primarily graphic form enter and work with information in that way; other students might amend the display of a word-processor to show a small "conceptual map" of the ideas being developed and presented in the paper. Further in the future may be the possibility of automatically linking conceptual verbal material to visual representations from large databases on videodisc or CD-ROM.

Finally there is the problem of analysis. If technology can give more rapid access to large quantities of information (a CD-ROM disc can hold the equivalent of 250 books of 250 pages each), it cannot automatically enable the student to see which pieces of that trove of data are significant and which are not. Indeed, the aura of infallibility that surrounds computers and other high technology in many students' (and perhaps teachers') minds could lead to an unthoughtful acceptance of the results of computerized data searches as providing the "right answer." If students now have difficulty in sorting through entries in an encyclopedia and constructing their own interpretation of information presented there (as opposed to merely parroting or paraphrasing the facts), how can we reasonably expect them to take on the much more complex task of sorting through many times that amount of information and making some sense of it?

The answer, of course, is that we cannot expect them to do so—unless we provide them with appropriate frameworks and the training to make sense of data in new forms and new volumes. It is also the case, however, that many students do eventually learn how to use successfully encyclopedias, dictionaries, reference works, and other traditional library resources. How they do that, and what places those works have in their own conception of the educational universe, are not topics that have been much studied; more work will need to be done linking information science and basic school instruction. On a broader plane, the current efforts to raise teachers' and students' "critical thinking skills" may have much to contribute here, inasmuch as the use of large databases both fosters and depends on abilities to think critically, to separate claims from supporting data, to evaluate the quality of data presented in support of arguments, and to judge the appropriateness of the conclusions reached.

THE FUTURE OF COMPUTER-BASED TEXTUAL MATERIALS

These qualities of new alternative instructional media offer some attractive advantages over traditional textbooks. They make it possible for the instructional materials themselves (rather than the teacher) to assess students' work. They offer motivation and guidance, as well as remedial support. They allow students and teachers to work together in new ways, thus overcoming the parochialism of which education has long been accused. They also provide alternative ways of representing reality or of pacing progress through material, thus allowing "individualization" to become a reality. And they allow students the opportunity (and consequently require the skills) to work with problems that demand data in real-world quantities and varieties.

Hypertext offers a useful illustration of the combination of two of these qualities—the encouragement of exploration and the need for analysis. Originally coined by computer visionary Ted Nelson in the early 1970s,[40] the term was used to describe computer-based textual materials in which a reader's progress would not necessarily be sequential (as with printed text), but rather conceptual: a reader might "zoom in" on one section of the material, request a condensed version of another section, look for examples to illustrate the reading, and so on. The concept finally found partial application in Apple's popular "Hypercard" program for the Macintosh. Developers have had problems, however, in specifying sensible design rules for hypertext.[41] It is difficult to define just how and when users ought to be able to branch to alternate sections, what the conceptual links ought to be, and how to signal the various possibilities to the user through the interface.

There are even more radical perspectives on the future of the textbook that stress combinations of computers and video. In such scenarios, students interact effortlessly (i.e., through natural language, writing, drawing, body language, gestures, and expressions) with a range of computer controlled devices that alternatively present information, question and cajole the learner, suggest ways of exploring the subject further, and provide assistance when problems are encountered. George Leonard forcefully articulated such a vision in his *Education and Ecstasy*.[42] These ideas have found some realization in projects at the MIT Media Lab,[43] at Brown University's IRIS (Institute for Research on Information and Scholarship,[44] and through manufacturer-sponsored events such as Apple's "Project 2000" contest to create the "personal computer of the year 2000." (The winning entry, the notebook-sized "Tablet," was created by a team at the University of Illinois).[45]

But even if such materials can be created and disseminated in large numbers, will they find a place in schools, or will they wind up on the shelves of school closets? To answer that question, we need to consider the nature of schools as social environments in which these new alternatives to textbooks will have to function, the conditions they will need to satisfy if they are to find a long-term home there. This requires us to address some important questions regarding the way teachers think about their work, the nature of teachers' professional practice, and how teachers are prepared.

Conditions for Success: The Nature of Schools and Teaching

NEW VIEWS OF HOW CHANGE TAKES PLACE IN EDUCATION

In the literature on innovation in education and the fate of new instructional strategies, teachers have been seen not only as users of educational technology but also as barriers to its use. Teachers' attitudes toward computers, their willingness to change, the extent of their acceptance of technology have all been studied. The assumption among technophiles has often been that only an obstructionist teacher could fail to see the obvious advantages of new approaches. To change was portrayed as the rational course; to resist change was to be irrational.

Educational policymakers are now coming to recognize the flaws in this "rational-empirical" model of change. The history of earlier innovations suggests that there are serious constraints on teachers' use of technology—time and training needed to learn how to operate devices and software; time needed to acquire and set up hardware; time to introduce software to students, and then to monitor and evaluate them; the pressures to match technologically based materials to state- or district-mandated curricula. These may be the real determinants of whether a new practice is used. Powerful traditions— of face-front classroom teaching, of nonformal instruction in families and other out-of-school settings, and of bureaucratic and managerial school organization—have been enormously hard to break not just because they represent the status quo, but also because they are workable solutions to a set of not very satisfactory circumstances.[46]

This realization that introducing new technologies is not easy was part of a larger reconceptualization of how change in education takes place and what sorts of changes are desirable. In studies of change dating from the late 1970s, more emphasis has been placed on "development of an innovation in use,"[47] on "reinvention" (altering a new practice slightly to make it fit local conditions),[48] and on teachers' concerns about new practices (e.g., professional adequacy, "institutional fallout") and their levels of use (from "untested" through "refinement" and "renewal").[49]

EDUCATIONAL CHANGE AND EDUCATIONAL REFORM

These approaches are reflected in the current "second wave" of educational reform proposals. While the "first wave" in the early 1980s[50] concentrated on top-down requirements that schools improve their curricula and toughen instruction in basic subjects, more recent discussion has emphasized teacher-centered professionalism as a precondition for further significant change in education.[51] Joseph McDonald characterized this second wave as the search for "the teacher's voice."[52]

These new views of educational change recognize several important facts about schools. First, schools are parts of society. They make up a complex social institution, and this institution has societal value beyond merely providing students with process skills and factual information (and is therefore unlikely to disappear even if much routine instruction could be delivered via technology). Second, teachers' work is complex and limited in important ways. Teachers' concerns must therefore be considered when change is proposed, and even good teachers may find it difficult to adopt technology. Third, encouraging teachers to change the way they practice requires giving them significant control over the conditions of their work—control over key decisions regarding how instruction is given, what curricular materials are used, how teaching is evaluated and rewarded, how the work of the school is managed and directed, what research is carried out, and what the content of teachers' own initial and continuing professional education should be.

To the extent that these views of change and reform in education are correct, they also must be taken into account when considering particulars of how technology can and should be used in schools. New and better approaches will be needed in the design of software, the development of models of teaching with technology, the creation of computer-based tools to support teachers' work and professional growth, and in improved training and research.

NEEDED IMPROVEMENTS IN SOFTWARE DESIGN

Procedures for designing instructional software have been worked out over the past several years. Called "instructional design" or "instructional systems development," the method focuses on identification of objectives, specification of tasks, design of materials, and testing and revision of an entire instructional system.[53] The changes noted above will require that a better initial job be done in assessing teachers' needs, that their tacit knowledge of student problems and barriers be taken into account, and, importantly, that programs be designed with wide latitude for teacher control and modifiability.[54]

NEEDED MODELS FOR HOW TO USE ALTERNATIVE MATERIALS

Teachers' everyday classroom work involves great uncertainties regarding instructional methods and outcomes.[55] Thus, teachers' models of teaching—mental images of how a classroom should look and feel, ideas about activities, ways of integrating instructional materials with lessons—are often less organized and less goal-oriented than technologists would prefer.[56] The task is therefore to create models of teaching with technology that accept the constraints while they also expand the teacher's idea of what is feasible. Such models should reduce a teacher's burden of unrewarding classroom work (e.g., repetitive tutoring, grading exercises), buttress a teacher's position as guide and mentor for students, and demand minimal extra time for preparation. They should also be introduced and supported by appropriate prior training. Demonstration projects often focus on what can be done under optimal conditions; what is required now are approaches that work for more typical schools and teachers.

NEEDED ASSISTANCE FOR TEACHERS' PROFESSIONAL WORK

The mandate for increased teacher professionalism requires that alternative instructional technologies provide improved capability to manage one's work, to communicate with peers, and to improve practice through research and development. Computer-based tools to do some of these things have already found a wide audience— spreadsheets for grading; word processors for administrative reports, letters to parents, and preparing instructional materials; databases for resources or student work. Efforts have also been made to encourage professional interchange among teachers using bulletin board programs (e.g., Harvard ETC's Computer Conferencing Project).[57] Teacher-oriented computer software to support collaborative development of materials, as well as their evaluation and dissemination are not yet common, but the flurry of interest in tools to aid computer-based collaborative work[58] may lead to more interest in creating such programs for education.

NEEDED CHANGES IN TEACHER TRAINING AND IN RESEARCH

Appropriate training and sufficient time for teachers to become comfortable with technology are critical. When and how to provide that training are still matters of dispute. Until teacher training institutions integrate technology into their own preservice curricula, it is hard to imagine how new teachers can develop an enthusiastic appreciation for teaching with technology. Unfortunately, we are hindered by our current lack of awareness of the ways of working of those teachers who do use alternative media effectively—the meaning of technology in their own day-to-day activity, the "look and feel" of classrooms in which technology has been well integrated, and the internal habits of mind that teaching with technology imposes and encourages.

The Future of the Textbook

If alternative instructional materials must meet such a wide range of preconditions to achieve success, is there any real chance that they will come to have a more central role in classrooms—perhaps parallel to traditional textbooks? Or should we simply resign ourselves to the status quo for the foreseeable future? Technology enthusiasts must begin by admitting that traditional texts present certain key advantages: portability, low cost, an established place in teacher-training programs, well-developed production technology, a structure comprehensible to a large percentage of teachers and students, and most important, a critical role in promoting literacy—a skill that society values highly. If the alternatives to textbooks are to find a permanent place in the school curriculum, they need not necessarily match these advantages, but they must at least present a comparably compelling rationale of their own.

There are exceptionally attractive qualities of the new alternatives that could ultimately make them indispensable. The tasks for developers of such media are complicated, however, by the very qualities and advantages that make their products attractive. As preceding chapters in this volume demonstrate, the textbook, with which we have a five-hundred-year acquaintance, still challenges designers to deal adequately with the complexities of print—text layout; graphics and illustrations; a meta-structure of questions, headings, appendices and indexes; and diverse patterns of use. With computer-based alternatives, many of the conceptual challenges of print-based materials remain, while new complexity is added in the way of intelligent remediation, flexible formatting, animation, and the sheer potential size of programs with varied and numerous subbranches. Given the increased technical challenge of the design effort, it is not surprising that many designers are "seduced by elegance," overcome with the technical possibilities that work in the new media makes possible.

And yet, as the discussion above of change in education and the role of teachers in fostering that change suggests, the principal tasks of educators in improving the system of schooling over the next several years are more likely to focus on the human, social, and organizational side of the equation than on the purely technical. Thus, if technology is to find a long-term place in schools, I believe it must first show its usefulness to teachers in terms that *they* define as important. It must not only be neutrally nonthreatening but also positively helpful (in the sense that it replaces current activities or relieves the teacher of burdens now perceived as unproductive). It must find a home in preservice teacher training, and specifically in a would-be teacher's student-teaching experience. Perhaps most importantly, it must be modifiable by the teacher using it, but at the same time it must unobtrusively present new information, prompts, and suggestions to the teacher in a way that makes the material its own in-service training agent. The latter quality may be the most difficult one for designers to provide.

A MODEL FOR FAILURE: ELECTRONIC PABLUM

Most alternative materials are used at present in support of supplementary activities in classrooms; they either are not of sufficient size and scope, or lack sufficient depth and sophistication, to provide the entire structure of a course of study. Technical and practical restrictions (e.g., computers or other hardware available at any given time for student use) play some role in this, but teachers' own long-standing predilections for textbooks and for the structure that they provide are more central.

Current producers and distributors of software have largely accepted this role. To develop and market entire curricula in several subject areas would be an enormous job, one that no single publisher has yet had the capability to tackle. Besides, changing the nature of teaching and the vision that teachers have of what their instructional materials should provide is probably not part of the role that publishers would willingly define for themselves. The current situation allows those teachers with interest and commitment to become involved in a limited way without necessarily requiring change in teaching styles or conceptions of student activity.

In this direction lies a continued stagnation in the way in-structional materials are conceived, developed, and used in class-rooms. If the capabilities that the new approaches make available are to be used to best advantage, a path must be found that brings these to teachers' attention in a way that is at once subtle and forceful. That path may be to conceive of textbooks as cognitive technologies.

A MODEL FOR SUCCESS:
TEXTBOOKS BECOME COGNITIVE TECHNOLOGIES

The alternative to stagnation is to design materials so that they take advantage of the capabilities of technology while at the same time allow their easier integration into existing curricula and patterns of teaching. This does *not* mean that new computer programs would simply be more "teacher friendly," although that would certainly be a desideratum; it does mean that their capabilities would be used not only to support students' growth and development but also to suggest to teachers themselves how instructional patterns might be altered.

An example may be illustrative. A teacher in a sixth-grade science class is dealing with ecology and the interdependence of living systems. Materials used in support of the unit include videodisc-based illustrations and a related computer program that presents students with a variety of data, simulations, problems, and so on. The program includes elements of artificial intelligence, and so students are questioned, cajoled, and reminded at various points as they work; the program keeps track of these data, and uses them to modify what is presented to each student.

But the program also contains a variety of data and subprograms for the teacher. Some of these are explicitly available and run on command—they provide information on student achievement, time taken to reach certain objectives, whether students stay "on task" as they work, and so on. But other parts of the teacher's program structure collect and provide information in more subtle ways: if students seem to be experiencing recurring conceptual difficulties over time, the program suggests to the teacher ways of overcoming these; if students appear to dawdle over completing certain aspects of the assignment, the program indicates motivating activities; if alternative paths through the material or ways of incorporating new topics are not being explored, the program offers options for structuring the lesson differently. The depth and specificity of these suggestions itself varies, so that new or less confident teachers are not overwhelmed with suggestions each time they use the program, yet more experienced or more committed teachers may access the full range of alternatives as they prefer.

The program also has available a variety of lesson plans and approaches that teachers may examine before beginning a lesson. These indicate ties to preceding parts of the curriculum, and to related topics in other disciplines (the ecology unit is related to units on government and policymaking in social studies, on statistics in mathematics, and on persuasive communication in language arts). In a fairly sophisticated version, the video disc portion of the program provides for the teacher short "snap shots" of how the program looks in action in a number of classrooms in which teachers use quite different approaches. Intelligent parsers allow teachers to modify program objectives or add their own, and then identify the relevant parts of the program that relate to the new goals. Similar sections dealing with evaluation allow teachers to change how students are evaluated—the weight assigned to particular outcomes, the degree of competence required to move from one section of the material to another, and so forth. Records of these changes are kept so teachers can survey past modifications as they ponder new ones.

Through telecommunications, teachers using the same program are able to collect and compare results across schools, districts, states, regions, or nations. Some such comparisons are carried out automatically, with no intervention required by the teacher. (In this case, however, there would clearly need to be some *initial* willingness on the teacher's part to join in such efforts; any other approach would smack of computerized job-monitoring practices that have proven disastrous to employee morale in other areas.) In this way, teachers joining in a computerized teleconference have the opportunity to start a "conversation" from common data about a program or approach they all share in common, rather than starting (as is now typical) from different points. Students share assignments and projects in like fashion.

In this example, the program becomes not merely a vehicle for presentation of information (although it does do this, and does it well). It also takes on roles of organizing the curriculum; of placing both student and teacher within a framework of related and previously covered concepts; of providing the teacher with help and suggestions for alternative approaches that are immediately available, but also out of students' view; and of connecting teachers and students with their peers around topics of common concern. Most importantly, it provides the teacher with assistance in ways that are under the teacher's own control. Rather than being "teacher-proof," the materials themselves encourage teachers to take advantage of the diversity and flexibility inherent in computerized instruction. Since they do this in a context that also tracks student progress and retains records (under teacher direction and control), concerns about accountability are also addressed.

Most important of all, there will need to be developed and put in place (concurrently with the development of the system just described) a social support network to tie the materials directly into the everyday work lives of teachers and students. This will require changes in school and district policies (and rewards) so as to provide for extended training with the system, integration with teacher training programs of local colleges and universities (and time and incentives for their faculty to learn it as well), and conscious attempts by teacher unions and district administrators to change assumptions about classroom practice so as to accommodate the new approaches. Teachers themselves, in other words, would have not only to tolerate the system, but to want actively to incorporate it into their teaching as a part of wider expansion of professional development and collegial responsibilities. Only in this way may such alternatives to traditional textbooks succeed in schools.

The "computer revolution" in education may follow two paths: it may wash over the schools, leaving little change in educational practice. This has been the fate of many earlier "revolutions" in schooling. But schooling is not the ossified system that many imagine; rather, schools have proven to be remarkably (though sometimes minimally) flexible—they modify their practices just enough to swallow up a proposed revolutionary change and make it their own, under their terms. The second path is to work to make the change not revolutionary, but rapidly and dramatically evolutionary. This involves assisting teachers and administrators in larger changes now well under way, changes that involve increasing the teacher's voice in decision making, in self-management and professional development. Technologically based systems of the sort described above could find a ready place in schools under these conditions, and thus provide rapid evolutionary change over time. That would be a worthy goal for the designers and developers of alternative computer-based textbooks of the future.

FOOTNOTES

1. Isabelle Bruder, "*Electronic Learning's* Eighth Annual Survey of the States, 1988," *Electronic Learning* 8 (October 1988). 38-4J; Thomas W. Hope, "AV Media Uses and Expenditures in Education," in *Educational Media Yearbook*, ed. James W. Brown (Littleton, CO: Libraries Unlimited, 1984), pp. 98-103; J. Riccobono, *School Utilization Study: Availability, Use, and Support of Instructional Media* (Washington, DC: Corporation for Public Broadcasting and National Center for Education Statistics, 1985).

2. Larry Cuban, *Teachers and Machines: The Classroom Use of Technology Since 1920* (New York: Teachers College Press, 1986); EPIE (Educational Products Information Exchange Institute), *Report on a National Study of the Nature and the Quality of Instructional Materials Most Used by Teachers and Learners*, EPIE Report No. 76 (New York: EPIE Institute, 1977).

218   ALTERNATIVE   TECHNOLOGIES

3. Riccobono, *School Utilization Study.*

4. For discussion of the spread of overhead projectors, see Eleanor P. Godfrey, *Audiovisual Media in the Public Schools, 1961-64* (Washington, DC: Bureau of Social Science Research, 1965), ERIC ED 003 761; and idem, *The State of Audiovisual Technology, 1961-66,* Monograph No. 3 (Washington, DC: National Education Association, 1967), ERIC ED 018 081.

5. David K. Cohen, "Educational Technology, Policy, and Practice," *Educational Evaluation and Policy Analysis* 9, no. 2 (1987): 153-70; Cuban, *Teachers and Machines*; Stephen T. Kerr, "Pale Screens: Teachers and Electronic Texts," in *From Socrates to Software: The Teacher as Text and the Text as Teacher,* ed. Philip W. Jackson and Sophie Haroutunian-Gordon, Eighty-eighth Yearbook of the National Society for the Study of Education, Part 1 (Chicago: University of Chicago Press, 1989).

6. See, for example, Steven A. Seidman, "A Survey of Schoolteachers' Utilization of Media," *Educational Technology* 26 (October 1986): 19-23.

7. Cuban, *Teachers and Machines.*

8. Gavriel Salomon, "TV is 'Easy' and Print is 'Tough': The Differential Investment of Mental Effort in Learning as a Function of Perceptions and Attributions," *Journal of Educational Psychology* 76 (1984): 647-58.

9. A. A. Lumsdaine, "Instruments and Media of Instruction," in *Handbook of Research on Teaching,* ed. N. L. Gage (Chicago: Rand McNally, 1963), pp. 583-682.

10. H. Marshall McLuhan, *The Gutenberg Galaxy* (Toronto: University of Toronto 1962); idem, *Understanding Media* (New York: McGraw-Hill, 1964); J. M. Culkin, "Film Study in the High School," *Catholic High School Quarterly Bulletin* (October 1965): John L. Debes, ed., *Elements of Visual Literacy,* Publication AT-25 (Rochester, NY: Eastman Kodak Co., 1968).

11. Roger B. Fransecky and Roy Ferguson, "New Ways of Seeing: The Milford Visual Communications Project," *Audiovisual Instruction* 18, no. 4 (1973): 44-49.

12. See, for example, John Berger, *About Looking* (New York: Pantheon, 1980); David R. Olson, ed., *Media and Symbols: The Forms of Expression, Communication, and Education,* Seventy-third Yearbook of the National Society for the Study of Education, Part I (Chicago: University of Chicago Press, 1974); and Gavriel Salomon, *Interaction of Media, Cognition, and Learning* (San Francisco: Jossey-Bass, 1979).

13. Richard Clark, "Reconsidering Research on Learning from Media," *Review of Educational Research* 53, no. 4 (1983): 445-59; Richard Clark and Gavriel Salomon, "Media in Teaching," in *Handbook of Research on Teaching,* ed. Merlin Wittrock, 3d ed. (New York: Macmillan, 1986), pp. 464-78.

14. See Thomas M. Duffy and Robert Waller, eds., *Designing Usable Texts* (Orlando, FL: Academic Press, 1985); James Hartley, *Designing Instructional Text,* 2d ed. (New York: Nichols, 1985); David Jonassen, ed., *Instructional Design for Microcomputer Software* (Hillsdale, NJ: Erlbaum, 1987); Charles Reigeluth, ed., *Instructional Design Theories and Models* (Hillsdale, NJ: Erlbaum, 1984).

15. On the notion of distinctive features, see Clark and Salomon, "Media in Teaching."

16. See, for example, Ted Nunan, *Countering Educational Design* (New York: Nichols, 1983).

17. Robert McClintock, "Into the Starting Gate: On Computing and the Curriculum," *Teachers College Record* 88, no. 2 (1986): 191-215; Seymour Papert, *Mindstorms: Children, Computers, and Powerful Ideas* (New York: Basic Books, 1980): Marc Tucker, "From Drill Sergeant to Intellectual Assistant: Computers in the Schools," *Carnegie Quarterly* 30, no. 3-4 (1985): 1-7.

18. Henry J. Becker, *Instructional Uses of School Computers*, Reports from the 1985 National Survey, Issue No. 1 (Baltimore, MD: Center for the Social Organization of Schools, Johns Hopkins University, 1986), p. 2; Office of Technology Assessment, *Power On! New Tools for Teaching and Learning*, Report No. OTA-SET-379 (Washington, DC: U.S. Congress, Office of Technology Assessment, 1988).

19. Bruder, "*Electronic Learning's* Eighth Annual Survey"; Office of Technology Assessment, *Power On!*

20. Quality Education Data, *Hardware and Software Budgets for School Districts to Increase*, (Boulder, CO: Quality Education Data, Inc., August 2, 1988); Office of Technology Assessment, *Power On!*

21. Office for Technology Assessment, *Power On!*

22. Henry J. Becker, *Instructional Uses of School Computers*, Reports from the 1985 National Study, Issue No. 3 (Baltimore, MD: Center for the Social Organization of Schools, 1986).

23. Quality Education Data, *Technology Plans for 1987-88*, QED Large District Survey (Boulder, CO: Quality Education Data, Inc., June 1987).

24. Sherwood Harris and Lorna B. Harris, *Teacher's Almanac* (New York: Facts-on-File Publications, 1986).

25. Becker, *Instructional Uses of School Computers*, Issue No. 1, p. 5.

26. Charlotte Cox, "Children, Computers, and New Ways of Learning: An Interview with Seymour Papert," *Curriculum Review* 26 (January-February, 1987): 14-18; Office of Technology Assessment, *Power On!*

27. See McClintock, "Into the Starting Gate," and Gail Meister and Henry Levin, *Educational Technology and Computers: Promises, Promises, Always Promises*, Project Report 85-A13 (Stanford, CA: Institute for Research on Educational Finance and Governance, Stanford University, 1985).

28. Henry J. Becker, *School Uses of Microcomputers*, Reports from a National Survey, Issue No. 1 (Baltimore, MD: Center for the Social Organization of Schools, Johns Hopkins University, 1983).

29. Becker, *Instructional Uses of School Computers*, Issue No. 3.

30. Michael Martinez and Nancy A. Mead, *Computer Competence: The First National Assessment* (Princeton, NJ: National Assessment of Educational Progress, Educational Testing Service, 1988).

31. Ibid.

32. Joan Bliss, Peter Chandra, and Margaret Cox, "The Introduction of Computers into a School," *Computer Education* 10, no. 1 (1986): 49-54; M. S. Wiske, P. Zodhiates, B. Wilson, M. Gordon, W. Harvey, L. Krensky, B. Lord, M. Watt, and K. Williams, *How Technology Affects Teaching*, ETC Publication No. TR87-10 (Cambridge, MA: Educational Technology Center, Harvard University, 1988).

33. Karen Schingold, Janet Kane, and Mari Endreweit, "Microcomputer Use in Schools: Developing a Research Agenda," *Harvard Educational Review* 53, no. 4 (1983): 412-32.

34. Cathleen Stasz and John D. Winkler, *District and School Incentives for Teachers' Instructional Uses of Microcomputers*, Report No. Rand-P-7086 (Santa Monica, CA: Rand Corporation, 1985), ERIC ED 268 995; John D. Winkler, "How Effective Teachers Use Microcomputers for Instruction" (Paper presented at the Annual Meeting of the American Educational Research Association, New Orleans, 1984), ERIC ED 264 839.

35. Becker, *Instructional Uses of School Computers*, Issue No. 3, p. 10.

220   ALTERNATIVE TECHNOLOGIES

36. Derek H. Sleeman and John Seeley Brown, eds., *Intelligent Tutoring Systems* (Orlando, FL: Academic Press, 1982); E. Wenger, *Artificial Intelligence and Tutoring Systems* (Los Altos, CA: Morgan Kaufmann, 1987).

37. Roy D. Pea and D. Midian Kurland, "Cognitive Technologies for Writing," in *Review of Research in Education*, Vol. 14, ed. Ernst Rothkopf (Washington, DC: American Educational Research Association, 1987), pp. 277-326.

38. T. W. Malone, "Toward a Theory of Intrinsically Motivating Instruction," *Cognitive Science* 4 (1981): 333-69; Brenda K. Laurel, "Interface as Mimesis," in *User Centered System Design*, ed. Donald A. Norman and Stephen W. Draper (Hillsdale, NJ: Erlbaum, 1986), pp. 67-85; John M. Carroll and John C. Thomas, "Fun," *ACM SIG CHI Bulletin* 19, no. 3 (January 1988): 21-24.

39. Donald A. Norman, *The Psychology of Everyday Things* (New York: Basic Books, 1988); Ben Shneiderman, *Designing the User Interface: Strategies for Effective Human-Computer Interaction* (Reading, MA: Addison-Wesley, 1987); Jocelyn Wishart and David Canter, "Variations in User Involvement with Educational Software," *Computer Education* 12, no. 3 (1988): 365-79.

40. Ted Nelson, *Computer Lib/Dream Machines*, rev. ed. (Redmond, WA: Tempus Books, Microsoft Press, 1987).

41. Frank G. Halasz, "Reflections on Notecards: Seven Issues for the Next Generation of Hypermedia Systems," *Communications of the ACM* 31, no. 7 (July 1988): 836-52; Andries van Dam, "Hypertext '87," *Communications of the ACM* 31, no. 7 (July 1988): 887-95.

42. George B. Leonard, *Education and Ecstasy* (New York: Delacorte, 1968).

43. Stewart Brand, *The Media Lab: Inventing the Future at MIT* (New York: Viking, 1987).

44. See Nicole Yankelovich, Norman Meyrowitz, and Andries van Dam, "Reading and Writing the Electronic Book," *Computer* 18, no. 10 (1985): 15-30.

45. Luke T. Young, Kurth H. Thearling, Steven S. Skiena, Arch D. Robison, Stephen M. Omohundro, Bartlett W. Mel, and Stephen Wolfram, "Tablet: Academic Computing in the Year 2000," *Academic Computing* 7, no. 12 (May/June 1988): 62-65.

46. Cohen, "Educational Technology, Policy, and Practice"; Larry Cuban, *How Teachers Taught: Constancy and Change in American Classrooms, 1890-1980* (New York: Longman, 1984); idem, *Teachers and Machines*; Andy Hargraves, "Experience Counts, Theory Doesn't: How Teachers Talk about Their Work," *Sociology of Education* 57 (1984): 244-54; John Olson, *School Worlds and Microworlds* (New York: Pergamon Press, 1988).

47. Michael Fullan and Alan Pomfret, "Research on Curriculum and Instruction Implementation," *Review of Educational Research* 47, no. 2 (Spring 1977): 335-97.

48. Ronald E. Rice and Everett M. Rogers, "Reinvention in the Innovation Process," *Knowledge* 1, no. 4 (1980): 499-514.

49. Gene E. Hall and Susan Loucks, "Teacher Concerns as a Basis for Facilitating and Personalizing Staff Development," *Teachers College Record* 80, no. 1 (1978): 36-53; A. Michael Huberman and Matthew Miles, *Innovation Up Close: How School Improvement Works* (New York: Plenum, 1984).

50. For example, National Commission on Excellence in Education, *A Nation at Risk: The Imperative for Educational Reform* (Washington, DC: U.S. Government Printing Office, 1983).

51. American Federation of Teachers, *Resource Kit: School Restructuring* (Washington, DC: American Federation of Teachers, 1986-87).

52. Joseph P. McDonald, "The Emergence of the Teacher's Voice," *Teachers College Record* 89, no. 4 (1988): 471-86.

53. See, for example, Robert M. Gagné, ed., *Educational Technology: Foundations* (Hillsdale, NJ: Erlbaum, 1987).

54. For an example, see Nira Hativa, "The Microcomputer as a Classroom Audiovisual Device: The Concept, and Prospects for Adoption," *Computer Education* 10, no. 3 (1986): 359-67.

55. Robert E. Floden and Christopher M. Clark, "Preparing Teachers for Uncertainty," *Teachers College Record* 89, no. 4 (1988): 505-24.

56. See Christopher M. Clark, "Asking the Right Questions about Teacher Preparation: Contributions of Research on Teacher Thinking," *Educational Researcher* 17, no. 2 (1988): 5-12; Penelope Peterson, "Teachers' and Students' Cognitional Knowledge for Classroom Teaching and Learning," *Educational Researcher* 17, no. 5 (1988): 5-14.

57. Educational Technology Center, *Fourth Year Report*, ETC Report No. TR88-5 (Cambridge, MA: Educational Technology Center, Harvard University, 1988).

58. For example, John Seely Brown and Susan Newman, "Issues in Cognitive and Social Ergonomics: From Our House to Bauhaus," *Human-Computer Interaction* 1, no. 4 (1985): 359-91.

CHAPTER XIV

Textbooks, Curriculum, and School Improvement

DAVID L. ELLIOTT AND ARTHUR WOODWARD

The preceding chapters of this Yearbook have described the status of commercially published textbooks as the premier instructional material of American public elementary and secondary schools, how they achieved that status, and some of the problems involved. In this final chapter, we summarize and briefly reflect on what we see as the major themes that have emerged from the preceding chapters and then conclude by presenting what we see as some promising directions for future curriculum development efforts and the role of textbooks in these efforts.

Elementary and High School Textbooks in the 1980s

There are five main conclusions that can be drawn from the contents of the previous chapters.

1. *Commercially published multigrade textbook programs constitute a virtual national curriculum in the basic subjects for public elementary and junior high schools.* Although there are many exceptions, a significant number of teachers depend heavily on textbook programs to structure their day-to-day teaching in at least some of the basic school subjects.

In contrast to the situation sixty years ago, contemporary student textbooks contain not only narrative text but section and chapter exercises and they are accompanied by arrays of workbooks, and worksheets, and (often) supplementary booklets for student use. In addition, teacher's editions of the student textbooks contain background information, detailed teaching plans, and achievement tests. There are, of course, some variations across the offerings of different publishers, but it is hard to make a case for the existence of significantly different alternative approaches in the presentation of reading, mathematics, language arts, science, and social studies in the competing textbook series that are currently on the market. (See chapters 1-3, 8, 10.)

2. *The key decisions regarding the content and instructional formats of these textbook programs are made primarily in a national textbook marketplace in which the chief participants are selector/users and publisher/producers.* Although the marketplace is somewhat influenced by state education policies, educational research findings, periodic educational reform movements, and pressures from special interest groups, the salient characteristics of textbooks are determined by an ongoing negotiation between textbook producers and consumers. The major textbook publishers are parts of profit-seeking companies; the main selectors and users are local teachers and school districts. The market process involves a complex set of interactions between users' adoption procedures and publishers' production and marketing procedures—interactions which are carried out under rules set forth by the legislatures and education departments of the several states. (See chapters 1, 4, 8, 9, 11.)

3. *Most attempts at educational reform over the past sixty years have had relatively minor effects on the American public school curriculum and the textbooks that have persisted as major structurers of school programs.* Neither the pre-World War II reform efforts nor a series of projects mounted starting in the 1950s have had much lasting effect on either the mainstream school curriculum or on textbooks and their key role in the schools. Similarly, most of the products of modern electronic technology, from the radio to computers, have so far achieved only minor supporting roles in classrooms. (See chapters 2, 3, 13.)

4. *Despite the fact that teachers have preferred textbooks over alternative approaches, the instructional quality of elementary and secondary school textbooks has been the target of much negative criticism during recent years.* Chief among the shortcomings researchers have identified are "mentioning," or shallow coverage of a wide range of topics; "inconsiderateness," or poor writing; emphasis on lower-level memorizing of facts and generalizations to the exclusion of problem solving and other higher-order cognitive processes; the avoidance of important topics because some consider them too controversial; and failure to promote adequate understanding of the real nature of the knowledge fields, such as science and history, that are the bases of school subjects. (See chapters 3, 9, 10, 12.)

5. *Finally, it seems evident that many present-day teachers would be hard pressed to maintain basic instructional programs in the basic subject areas without elaborate multigraded textbook programs.* A number of

critics have decried the fact that many teachers depend heavily upon textbooks to provide them with the main content and instructional methods of their teaching. However, without textbook programs, we probably would not be able to sustain the public school system that we have in this country, particularly below the high school grades. The reason for this is that there are not enough teachers who, by themselves, have the education, the ability, and the stamina to design, provide materials for, and implement adequate instructional programs in five or more subject areas.

It has been suggested that the American public school system has performed as successfully as it has since its beginnings in the nineteenth century largely because it has institutionalized procedures that originally made it possible for large numbers of minimally trained classroom practitioners to function effectively, even those who were "poorly trained, uninspired, and uncreative."[1] During the nineteenth century, more highly trained "principal teachers" made out daily lesson plans that enabled minimally trained eighth-grade graduates to carry on instruction in two- or three-room schoolhouses. Over the decades of this century, the system has evolved to where teachers have college degrees and are much better prepared than their earlier counterparts, but many still depend on principal teachers in the form of textbook programs to structure much of their day-to-day teaching. (See chapters 3, 12.)

Failure of Local Initiative

We know the effects of reliance on textbooks: students are shortchanged in learning about important topics and teachers tend to become followers, not initiators of learning plans and strategies. What is surprising is the acquiescence of administrators, curriculum directors, and superintendents of schools in this reliance on textbooks. We would assume that such educational leaders would want to be responsible for curriculum development and implementation in their schools instead of deferring to the authors and editors employed by commercial publishing companies. That this does not happen seems to us a telling indictment of such leaders and their support of the status quo.

The fact that adoption states and school districts from both adoption and nonadoption states find the textbooks they select congruent with their curriculum is somewhat troubling. For it follows that, if textbooks are based on a national consensus, then most, if not all, textbooks will be similar in content scope and sequence to others covering the same subject areas and grade ranges. How then can such textbooks meet curriculum goals and objectives in diverse school districts? Presumably, the curricula of rural Kentucky school districts are very different from those of suburban Chicago or metropolitan Los Angeles.

It seems to us that congruence between such a national curriculum and the requirements of local curricula can only be achieved if the local authorities decide to adopt the national curriculum as their own, or if local teachers adapt the nationally published textbooks they use through extensive supplementation and editing. Of course, when local administrators and teachers peruse competing textbook series in the course of the selection process they will see that the tables of contents name many of the topics and concepts they are looking for as well as currently fashionable terms such as "problem solving" and "higher-order thinking skills." In similar fashion, many local school authorities try to see that textbook topic coverage is well correlated with the topic coverage on the nationally standardized achievement test results that they accept as sufficient indicators of the extent to which local instructional goals and objectives have been attained. But when they look more closely, they should notice significant discrepancies between their local courses of study and what the textbooks and tests really have to offer.

The local curriculum should, of course, provide the philosophy and principles that guide instruction in the several subject areas in the pursuit of local goals and objectives, including the selection and sequencing of content and the development of teaching methods and means for evaluating student progress. When such local curriculum decisions are made and properly implemented, it should be easy to recognize that textbooks are only one of a number of instructional resources that must be used to fulfill goals and objectives; when decisions are not made, the textbook programs in use become the curriculum by default.

A number of researchers have noted that the flurry of local and state-level activity that goes into developing courses of study most typically results in the printing and distribution of curriculum guides that end up on shelves gathering dust. Ritualistically, policymakers and administrators can point to such guides as evidence that their state or district does indeed have a clear philosophy and course of study to guide instruction. They can also point to the "correlations" (usually supplied by a publisher) that purport to demonstrate that the textbooks adopted by a district are congruent with the local curriculum, the assumption being that such congruence means that these textbooks can thus become the curriculum and take the place of the curriculum guides. Hence, the curriculum is a deadening rather than an energizing phenomenon when it comes to teaching and learning and the exercising of teaching and professional leadership responsibility.

Answering the Question (Reprise)

We return now to the discussions of the fundamental problem with textbooks and the schools presented by Westbury and Kerr in the first and thirteenth chapters respectively, beginning with the basic question posed by Westbury: *Does a profit-seeking publishing industry operating in the present context of the American school system and society have the capability to function both as a national curriculum authority and as an effective developer and distributor of school books?* On the basis of the analyses of the various aspects of the Yearbook theme that have been treated in the preceding chapters, *we must conclude that the answer to this question must be in the negative.* Over the past half-century it has not yet been possible for professional educators and policymakers simultaneously to depend heavily on textbook programs to give essential form and substance to the instructional programs of the nation's schools *and* to bring about the sort of basic reforms in school programs that are as urgent today as they seemed at many points in the past.

The root of the problem is not, however, located primarily with the textbooks, their publishers, or the teachers who use them; the fault is, as Westbury and Kerr have both asserted, with the basic structure of the American school system and the way it functions to provide instruction to its students. Teachers are restricted in what they are able to contribute to curriculum development by the ways their jobs are constituted—particularly by the expectation that they must spend virtually all of their working hours tending groups of thirty students and presenting a curriculum consisting of up to five basic subject areas that is not of their own making. (Some will point out that many teachers are not capable of doing even this much well but, ironically, the textbook-based system that makes it possible for the least competent teachers to function at all also keeps the better educated and more capable teachers from participating as full professionals.)

Administrators and policymakers who are pushed to be

accountable all too often resort to the use of standardized achievement tests to try to demonstrate that their school programs are providing the desired results in student development and learning rather than supporting the use of a wider range of assessment approaches. Textbooks and the curriculum they represent fit in very well with the use of standardized achievement tests as criterion measures. By producing textbook programs, commercial publishers have, in effect, taken up the slack left by a lack of assertive, creative professional curriculum leadership at the local level.

Textbooks and Curriculum in the Future

In this final section we make some suggestions for a future course of action that we believe will have a positive impact on schooling and teacher professionalism. Our emphasis is on the overall curriculum and curriculum building, but we think that textbooks still have an important part to play, at least for the near future. Most of the suggestions are not new, having been advocated by a number of individuals, professional organizations, and/or teacher education institutions over the past five or six decades, but all have yet to be taken really seriously enough to be vigorously implemented.

1. *Ever-increasing emphasis should be put on curriculum development and implementation at the local level.* Local educators can, of course, get help and guidance from outside sources, but the curriculum they devise should be a local curriculum and the local courses of study they devise should become the main guides that teachers refer to when planning units and lessons, selecting teaching approaches and instructional materials (including textbooks), and devising means for assessing student progress in light of local goals and objectives.

In some cases, this will mean that already developed local courses of study in the basic subject areas actually become the instruments that guide instruction. In other cases, it will mean that local teachers and administrators will have to get together to develop the curriculum that best fits the needs of their students and the educational aspirations of their communities. One way to begin implementation is to see what aspects of the local curriculum may already be covered by the textbooks currently in use and then developing additional materials, resources, and teaching strategies to fill in what is missing from the textbooks.

2. *Teachers should work to become the main professional educators who are responsible for developing and implementing the curriculum and*

assessing its effects on student learning and development. Although it cannot be accomplished in a short time simply by willing it through administrative fiat, our goal should be to bring all teachers up to operating at Herrick's Level I, that is, as professionals who, given the educational goals of the community, select the concepts and skills to be taught in the various subject areas, determine the teaching approaches best suited to their students, work with students and others in the school and the community in planning appropriate learning experiences, and play a key role in evaluating student progress.[2] As they achieved this goal, teachers would become the main devisers of the school curriculum and guides to instruction, but they would no longer be the exclusive administrators of it. Instead, they would train and coach others—older children, instructional aides, other adults to participate and they would coordinate the work of all the educational agencies of the community so that, together, they would work optimally to promote the optimal growth and development of children.

Accomplishment of this goal means that the teacher's instructional role will have to receive more emphasis while the custodial/administrative role is decreased. Instead of continuing to be captive to the textbook and groups of thirty students all day long, teachers will have to have time during the school day to plan, to confer with colleagues, to prepare learning resources, and generally to promote their own growth as professionals. Albert Shanker asks us to imagine,

as Seymour Sarason invites us, a school in which the "egg crate" structure has been abolished, in which it is illegal to deliver instruction in the lockstep, factory mode to which we are habituated, and new arrangements permitting flexible class size and customized education become possible. Imagine, too, a school in which there are lots of adults performing valuable and necessary responsibilities, but the title of teacher is restricted to individuals who meet the requirements of the role.[3]

Achieving this goal will take time and it will require fundamental changes in the ways in which teachers are educated, both preservice and in-service. The main stress in teacher education—both preservice and in-service—must be on producing teachers who are experts in the main areas of human knowledge, how that knowledge develops in young people, and how best to facilitate that development using resources available in both the school and the wider community. As the Holmes group suggests, all teachers should have a good liberal education, and most will want to build special expertise in one or two subjects that can be shared with colleagues as well as students.[4] Teachers with less experience or less appropriate training should be able to receive in-service help from more experienced and more capable colleagues under some combination of teaching team organization, mentor teacher guidance, and enrollment in advanced courses.

3. *The curriculum of the future will require the use of a wide range of instructional resources.* In order to implement a flexible curriculum that is tailorable to the requirements of different local student populations and community settings, the "new professional" teacher must be able to select subject matter for day-to-day instruction from sources that are vastly more varied and extensive than that which can be contained in textbooks of 250 to 450 pages. This is where supplementary print material, film and video resources, field trips and laboratory facilities, and libraries can assume much more importance. In particular, this is an area where the emerging electronic technologies can make an enormous contribution with on-demand computer-assisted instruction, electronic databases accessed over networks, and computer-based assistance to teachers in planning instruction and background information.

Two technological developments look particularly promising as supports to local curriculum development and teacher professionalism. The first is "desk-top" publishing via word processors and laser printers that should make it easy for teachers to share with their colleagues and others the teaching units, background materials, student booklets, student-generated materials, and other instructional materials they have developed. For example, treatises on aspects of local history—some written by students—could be printed and made available for use by other classes in the future, as well as teacher-made resource units and articles reporting on recent developments in the natural sciences or in the world.

The other promising development involves computer networks and their potential for facilitating the sharing of a wide range of materials between schools as well as between schools and other sources of information such as libraries, archives, and other information repositories. Materials obtained via computer network— whether lesson plans, historical accounts, census data, student assessment approaches, or whatever—can be accessed essentially on demand and printed and distributed locally for use by students and teachers.

4. *The professional organizations to which teachers and other*

instructional leaders belong should provide major support for both local curriculum development and the development of the professional teacher. These organizations can set new standards for professional training and practice, help to develop and facilitate access to instructional resources, provide in-service staff development services, and push for the restructuring of the school as an institution. The subject area-oriented organizations can help teachers and policymakers identify what knowledge from the disciplines that underlie the school subjects contributes most to student development in understanding and functioning in the world in which they live. These organizations can also help teachers build understanding of the various knowledge areas and produce resource materials for use by both teachers and students in the schools. Above all, the main thrust of the professional support activities of these organizations must be on the enhancement and enablement of the teacher as the key educational agent.

5. *Revised educational policies and different roles for administrators will be necessary.* As the parts teachers play in the development of instructional programs grow, the roles of school administrators and policymakers will necessarily diminish. At the building level, teachers should share administrative decisions that must be carried out in support of instruction—for example, the grouping of students, allocation of teacher and support staff time, selection of instructional resources, and coordination with other community agencies—much the way that college professors rotate in and out of the position of departmental chair. Each school faculty might designate a "headmaster" from amongst its ranks (one who teaches part-time) and give the remainder of the job now filled by a principal over to a good school secretary and other support staff to provide logistical support for the teachers, much as hospital administrators provide for their medical staffs. In addition, district central offices will have to be reconstituted so that they respond to school building staff needs by providing logistical and fiscal support rather than by issuing directives.

6. *Continuing role of the textbook.* For the foreseeable future, the textbook will continue to play an important role in school instructional programs. Certainly, present multigrade textbooks will be used as they are now to maintain school programs, both in districts where no curriculum reform is initiated and as transition resources in districts where new programs are being developed but have not yet been fully implemented. Textbook programs can also serve as "training wheels," as it were, for beginning teachers in the teaching of

subject areas in which they are not yet able to operate as full professionals.

But we would hope that new roles for the textbook would be found in the curriculum of the future, for surely the nationally marketed textbook is still a potentially valuable instructional tool that can continue to serve as one among a number of specialized instructional resources. The large and small commercial publishers, with the array of resources they command, can render valuable service by producing books and booklet series that contain (a) content that is truly national (or at least, "nonlocal") such as covering aspects of history and geography, mathematics, and science; (b) background and inquiry-oriented guides for students (and teachers) on the "ways of knowing" of the academic disciplines that underlie the basic school subjects; and (c) "handbooks" for use by students as resources in support of developing their understanding and skill in areas such as writing and problem solving.

20/20 Foresight: Looking Back Sixty Years from Now

When we look back on the American educational scene after another sixty years, what will we see? Textbooks and the institutional structures that support it have dominated American education for many decades and appear to be so firmly entrenched that it might take a revolution to bring about significant changes. At a number of times during this century, new approaches to the curriculum and alternative technologies have emerged to challenge the textbook's dominance, so far unsuccessfully. Given this past experience, it is entirely possible that nationally marketed textbook programs will continue to be the main structurers of many local curricula, and that the potential contributions of the emerging computer and related electronic technologies have to make to school programs will be minimal. Thus, it would not be too surprising if sixty years hence, when we look back on the same scene that has been the subject of this Yearbook, the nationally marketed printed textbook had maintained its position as a dominant educational force in a society otherwise preoccupied with computer chips, digitized images, and whatever follows from these.

However, at least one significant change in the elementary-secondary textbook's status has taken place recently that may make the next sixty years look very different. The textbook has emerged from being a virtually invisible element in studies of school programs and teaching to become a prime object for research and criticism. If we couple this change with other factors such as the keen dissatisfaction with the present status of our school programs, the recent surge of interest in the upgrading of the teaching profession, the continuous ballooning of scholarly research that makes textbook passages both oversimplified and quickly obsolete, and developments in computer technology together with a new generation of young people who will be much more comfortable with that technology than most of their elders, there is a strong possibility that revolutionary changes in the American educational landscape are in the offing.

FOOTNOTES

1. Sloan R. Wayland, "Structural Aspects of Education as Sources of Stability and Change," *Proceedings of a Faculty Seminar on Educational Theory* (New York: Horace Mann Lincoln Institute of School Experimentation, Teachers College, Columbia University, 1961), pp. 106-129.

2. Virgil E. Herrick, "The Concept of Curriculum Design," in *Toward Improved Curriculum Theory*, ed. Virgil E. Herrick and Ralph W. Tyler, Supplementary Educational Monographs, No. 71 (Chicago: University of Chicago Press, 1950), pp. 37-50.

3. Albert Shanker, "Tomorrow's Teachers," *Teachers College Record* 88 (Spring 1987): 423-429.

4. For recommendations on teacher education, see *Tomorrow's Teachers: A Report of the Holmes Group* (East Lansing, MI: The Holmes Group, 1986). For a report on his work on teacher knowledge, see Lee S. Shulman, "Those Who Understand: Knowledge Growth in Teaching," *Educational Researcher* 15 (February 1986): 4-14.

Name Index

233

Subject Index

Adoption states: list of, 176n; variations in policies among, 162-63

Alternative instructional materials, in schools: importance of design in software for, 211; needed changes in teacher training and research related to, 212-13; needed models for use of, 212; prerequisites for effective use of, 213-14

American Association of Publishers, 98, 109, 120, 136

American Association of School Administrators, 130

American Educational Research Association, 56

American Federation of Teachers, 142

American Library Association, 33

A Nation at Risk, 89, 130, 137, 165

Association for Supervision and Curriculum Development, 34

Audio-visual materials, in schools: attitudes of teachers and students toward, 198-99; constraints on teachers' use of, 210; general availability of, 196; importance of design qualities in, 200-1; use of, 196-98; visual literacy in relation to, 200

Back to basics movement, influence of, on textbooks, 49

Basal readers: attention to vocabulary development and readability in, 25; cost of development and marketing of, 92-93; emphasis in, on phonics, 27; example of specificity of directions in, 185-87; studies of, 49-50; tension between technique and substance reflected by, 25-26

Biological Science Curriculum Study (BSCS), 46, 48, 151, 155

Book Manufacturing Institute, 120

California State Board of Education, 155

Center for Study of Reading, University of Illinois, 122

Change, in education: new views of process of, 211; recent studies of, 210

Checklists, use of, in evaluation of textbooks, 168

Citizens for Excellence in Education, 139, 140

Civil Rights Act, 129

Civil Rights movement, 43

Cognitive technologies, example of, as alternative to textbooks, 215-217

Commission on Economy of Time in Education, 34

Commission on Life Adjustment Education, 35

Commission on the Reorganization of Secondary Education, 34, 35

Commission reports, effects of, on textbooks, 34-35

Committee of Fifteen, 34, 35

Committee of Ten, 34, 35

Computers in schools: access to, 204; future of, 208-9; instructional capabilities of, 205; possibility of student control, in use of, 206; rapid spread of, 202-3; use of, 203-4

Consensus (regarding textbooks): difficulty of obtaining, for high-quality textbooks, 147; evidence of, in the market place, 147-48

Controversies regarding textbooks, effects of, on relationship between administration and teachers, 141-42

Council for Basic Education, 137

Council for Economic Education, 138

Council of Chief State School Officers, 130, 136

Court decisions, affirmation by, of school board responsibility for curriculum and instruction, 128

Cultural literacy, conflicting demands for materials pertaining to, 87

Curriculum: efforts to obtain consensus on content of, 87-88; importance of wide range of resources for, 229; lack of national mechanism for control of, 8; lack of leadership for, in schools, 19; new roles for textbooks in, 10-11; textbook publishers as makers of, 10-11; textbooks as embodiment of, 5-7; suggestions for future of, 227-31

Curriculum development: anticipated different role for administrators in, 230;

238

INFORMATION ABOUT MEMBERSHIP IN THE SOCIETY

Membership in the National Society for the Study of Education is open to all who desire to receive its publications.

There are two categories of membership, Regular and Comprehensive. The Regular Membership (annual dues in 1990, $25) entitles the member to receive both volumes of the yearbook. The Comprehensive Membership (annual dues in 1990, $45) entitles the member to receive the two-volume yearbook and the two current volumes in the Series on Contemporary Educational Issues. For their first year of membership, full-time graduate students pay reduced dues in 1990 as follows: Regular, $20; Comprehensive, $40.

Membership in the Society is for the calendar year. Dues are payable on or before January 1 of each year.

New members are required to pay an entrance fee of $1, in addition to annual dues for the year in which they join.

Members of the Society include professors, researchers, graduate students, and administrators in colleges and universities; teachers, supervisors, curriculum specialists, and administrators in elementary and secondary schools; and a considerable number of persons not formally connected with educational institutions.

All members participate in the nomination and election of the six-member Board of Directors, which is responsible for managing the affairs of the Society, including the authorization of volumes to appear in the yearbook series. All members whose dues are paid for the current year are eligible for election to the Board of Directors.

Each year the Society arranges for meetings to be held in conjunction with the annual conferences of one or more of the major national educational organizations. All members are urged to attend these sessions. Members are also encouraged to submit proposals for future yearbooks or for volumes in the series on Contemporary Educational Issues.

Further information about the Society may be secured by writing to the Secretary-Treasurer, NSSE, 5835 Kimbark Avenue, Chicago, IL 60637.

RECENT PUBLICATIONS OF THE NATIONAL
SOCIETY FOR THE STUDY OF EDUCATION

1. The Yearbooks

Eighty-ninth Yearbook (1990)

Part 1. *Textbooks and Schooling in the United States.* David L. Elliott and Arthur Woodward, editors. Cloth.

Part 2. *Educational Leadership and Changing Contexts of Families, Communities, and Schools.* Brad Mitchell and Luvern L. Cunningham, editors. Cloth.

Eighty-eighth Yearbook (1989)

Part 1. *From Socrates to Software: The Teacher as Text and the Text as Teacher.* Philip W. Jackson and Sophie Haroutunian-Gordon, editors. Cloth.

Part 2. *Schooling and Disability.* Douglas Biklen, Dianne Ferguson, and Alison Ford, editors. Cloth.

Eighty-seventh Yearbook (1988)

Part 1. *Critical Issues in Curriculum.* Laurel N. Tanner, editor. Cloth.

Part 2. *Cultural Literacy and the Idea of General Education.* Ian Westbury and Alan C. Purves, editors. Cloth.

Eighty-sixth Yearbook (1987)

Part 1. *The Ecology of School Renewal.* John I. Goodlad, editor. Cloth.

Part 2. *Society as Educator in an Age of Transition.* Kenneth D. Benne and Steven Tozer, editors. Cloth.

Eighty-fifth Yearbook (1986)

Part 1. *Microcomputers and Education.* Jack A. Culbertson and Luvern L. Cunningham, editors. Cloth.

Part 2. *The Teaching of Writing.* Anthony R. Petrosky and David Bartholomae, editors. Paper.

Eighty-fourth Yearbook (1985)

Part 1. *Education in School and Nonschool Settings.* Mario D. Fantini and Robert Sinclair, editors. Cloth.

Part 2. *Learning and Teaching the Ways of Knowing.* Elliot Eisner, editor. Paper.

Eighty-third Yearbook (1984)

Part 1. *Becoming Readers in a Complex Society.* Alan C. Purves and Olive S. Niles, editors. Cloth.

Part 2. *The Humanities in Precollegiate Education.* Benjamin Ladner, editor. Paper.

Eighty-second Yearbook (1983)
> Part 1. *Individual Differences and the Common Curriculum.* Gary D Fenstermacher and John I. Goodlad, editors. Paper.
> Part 2. *Staff Development.* Gary Griffin, editor. Paper.

Eighty-first Yearbook (1982)
> Part 1. *Policy Making in Education.* Ann Lieberman and Milbrey W. McLaughlin, editors. Cloth.
> Part 2. *Education and Work.* Harry F. Silberman, editor. Cloth.

Eightieth Yearbook (1981)
> Part 1. *Philosophy and Education.* Jonas P. Soltis, editor. Cloth.
> Part 2. *The Social Studies.* Howard D. Mehlinger and O. L. Davis, Jr., editors. Cloth.

Seventy-ninth Yearbook (1980)
> Part 1. *Toward Adolescence: The Middle School Years.* Mauritz Johnson, editor. Cloth.
> Part 2. *Learning a Second Language.* Frank M. Grittner, editor. Cloth.

Seventy-eighth Yearbook (1979)
> Part 1. *The Gifted and the Talented: Their Education and Development.* A. Harry Passow, editor. Paper.
> Part 2. *Classroom Management.* Daniel L. Duke, editor. Paper.

Seventy-seventh Yearbook (1978)
> Part 1. *The Courts and Education.* Clifford B. Hooker, editor. Cloth.

Seventy-sixth Yearbook (1977)
> Part 1. *The Teaching of English.* James R. Squire, editor. Cloth.

The above titles in the Society's Yearbook series may be ordered from the University of Chicago Press, Book Order Department, 11030 Langley Ave., Chicago, IL 60628. For a list of earlier titles in the yearbook series still available, write to the Secretary, NSSE, 5835 Kimbark Ave., Chicago, IL 60637.

2. The Series on Contemporary Educational Issues

The following volumes in the Society's Series on Contemporary Educational Issues may be ordered from the McCutchan Publishing Corporation, P.O. Box 774, Berkeley, CA 94702.

Boyd, William Lowe, and Walberg, Herbert J., editors. *Choice in Education: Potential and Problems.* 1990.

Case, Charles W., and Matthes, William A., editors. *Colleges of Education: Perspectives on Their Future.* 1985.

Eisner, Elliot, and Vallance, Elizabeth, editors. *Conflicting Conceptions of Curriculum.* 1974.

Erickson, Donald A., and Reller, Theodore L., editors. *The Principal in Metropolitan Schools.* 1979.

Farley, Frank H., and Gordon, Neal J., editors. *Psychology and Education: The State of the Union.* 1981.

Fennema, Elizabeth, and Ayer, M. Jane, editors. *Women and Education: Equity or Equality.* 1984.

Griffiths, Daniel E., Stout, Robert T., and Forsyth, Patrick, editors. *Leaders for America's Schools: The Report and Papers of the National Commission on Excellence in Educational Administration.* 1988.

Jackson, Philip W., editor. *Contributing to Educational Change: Perspectives on Research and Practice.* 1988.

Lane, John J., and Walberg, Herbert J., editors. *Effective School Leadership: Policy and Process.* 1987.

Levine, Daniel U., and Havighurst, Robert J., editors. *The Future of Big City Schools: Desegregation Policies and Magnet Alternatives.* 1977.

Lindquist, Mary M., editor. *Selected Issues in Mathematics Education.* 1981.

Murphy, Joseph, editor. *The Educational Reform Movement of the 1980s: Perspectives and Cases.* 1990.

Nucci, Larry P., editor. *Moral Development and Character Education.* 1989.

Peterson, Penelope L., and Walberg, Herbert J., editors. *Research on Teaching: Concepts, Findings, and Implications.* 1979.

Pflaum-Connor, Susanna, editor. *Aspects of Reading Education.* 1978.

Purves, Alan, and Levine, Daniel U., editors. *Educational Policy and International Assessment: Implications of the IEA Assessment of Achievement.* 1975.

Sinclair, Robert L., and Ghory, Ward. *Reaching Marginal Students: A Prime Concern for School Renewal.* 1987.

Spodek, Bernard, and Walberg, Herbert J., editors. *Early Childhood Education: Issues and Insights.* 1977.

Talmage, Harriet, editor. *Systems of Individualized Education.* 1975.

Tomlinson, Tommy M., and Walberg, Herbert J., editors. *Academic Work and Educational Excellence: Raising Student Productivity.* 1986.

Tyler, Ralph W., editor. *From Youth to Constructive Adult Life: The Role of the Public School.* 1978.

Tyler, Ralph W., and Wolf, Richard M., editors. *Crucial Issues in Testing.* 1974.

Walberg, Herbert J., editor. *Educational Environments and Effects: Evaluation, Policy, and Productivity.* 1979.

Walberg, Herbert J., editor. *Improving Educational Standards and Productivity: The Research Basis for Policy.* 1982.

Wang, Margaret C., and Walberg, Herbert J., editors. *Adapting Instruction to Student Differences.* 1985.

Warren, Donald R., editor. *History, Education, and Public Policy: Recovering the American Educational Past.* 1978.

DATE DUE
